W126

MIDWINTER, E.

Red roses crest
the caps

03832430

D1145937

# Red Roses Crest the Caps

Ancient and modern Lancashire: the successful 1880 side and their 1988 counterparts.

ERIC MIDWINTER

# Red Roses Crest the Caps
## The Story of Lancashire County Cricket Club

It is little I repair to the matches of the Southron folk,
Though my own red roses there may blow:
It is little I repair to the matches of the Southron folk,
Though the red roses crest the caps, I know.

Francis Thompson  'AT LORD'S'  (1907)

The Kingswood Press

03832430

The Kingswood Press
an imprint of Methuen London

Michelin House, 81 Fulham Road, London SW3 6RB

Printed and bound in Great Britain
by Richard Clay Ltd, Bungay

*Acknowledgements*

All illustrations have been provided by the Lancashire C.C.C. Library, and grateful thanks are due to the librarian, The Revd Malcolm Lorimer for his generous assistance in this regard. The statistical section is fully based on the Lancashire C.C.C Yearbooks, and has been checked and updated to 1988 by the librarian, to whom, again, many thanks are due. Robert Warburton, Assistant Secretary, Lancashire C.C.C read and checked the text for inaccuracies, and I would like to express my warm appreciation to him.

# Contents

# Introduction

Writing a history of a county cricket club such as Lancashire is like being a war correspondent in the Hundred Years War. One can peer through the fog to a half-shrouded start, but the plot is ill-defined and the pattern impossible to comprehend, not least as an even less certain future continually beckons.

Lancashire has endured for 125 undulating years, and, to declare an interest, I was born a short railway ride from Old Trafford and I have been a conscious supporter for two-fifths of its history. One hopes that it is still possible to quieten the beating heart and apply a little objectivity. In a more secular age, cricket and, more especially, football teams have filled a gap in the emotional, possibly the spiritual life, of human kind. At the very least, they offer cultivated diversion to those who follow them with varying degrees of passion.

This history adopts that standpoint. It knows little or nothing of strife in the dressing room midst the reek of linseed oil or wrangles in the committee sanctum. It deliberately stays front of house and avoids the backstage commotion. This is the view from the partisan audience, recognising that county cricket is an art form for spectators. This includes not only the relatively few actual watchers but the thousands more who follow Lancashire's progress through the press and radio: 'How's Lanky doing?' is the question often posed on bus or train of the traveller with a *Manchester Evening News*, whose back page will reveal the worst. And, by virtue of this relationship, Lancashire became a social institution, at once reflecting and flavouring the culture to which it was attached.

As with any entertainment, one looks for excellence. This study majors on the great teams and the great players of Lancashire's history. In 1904, a year in which Lancashire won the Championship, Ella Wheeler Willcox and D'Auvergne Bernard wrote their oft-quoted monologue, 'Laugh and the world laughs with you', which includes the lines:

> Feast, and your halls are crowded,
> Fast, and they'll pass you by;
> Succeed and give, and they'll let you live,
> But fail – and they'll let you die.

It is a phenomenon well known to sports clubs, and this book tends, like the Levite, to pass by on the other side at the not inconsiderable moments when Lancashire are in trauma and agony. The nearest to a discernible pattern is to argue that Lancashire have produced five or six accomplished sides, one or two of them of exceptional refinement, and, in natural concert with these, some 50 or so fascinating and brilliant performers. The deeds of both are described here, and Lancashire's tale becomes a classic parabola. Its history witnessed a steady and at times impressive growth to a halfway point, in the years between the two world wars, when the club enjoyed its most notable and sustained triumphs. Since then, and although there have been occasional minor upward curves, the major graph has curled downwards. The rise and fall of these elevens, and their members, constitutes the nearest to a plot.

Tribute must be paid to other historians of Lancashire, and, in particular, the sound and stimulating work done by two famous Manchester-based journalists. A. W. Ledbrooke's *Lancashire County Cricket 1864–1953*, published in 1954, and John Kay's *Lancashire*, published in 1972, proved to be a secure base for further operations, while John Marshall's *Old Trafford*, published in 1971, was also a most useful helpmate. Lancashire's own admirable series of yearbooks were, of course, an indispensable source, and other authors and commentators are mentioned and acknowledged in the text.

This, then, is an attempt to observe Lancashire county cricket primarily as an entertainment, as a pleasurable component in the field of collective leisure. It is, naturally, not all wine and roses. St Thomas Aquinas, in his Aristotelian fashion, taught that man must apprehend the misery of hell to taste fully the joy of heaven. This theological tenet holds good for dedicated Lancashire fans, relishing the rarer tastes of paradise the more avidly because of their more regular diet of soggy failure, at least in the post-war years. One must not flinch entirely from these woes, and due explanation is offered for them: but the emphasis remains on Lancashire teams and players that have royally entertained.

# 1. Rowley's Years

*Red Rose in Bud*

Lancashire County Cricket Club was established at the Queen's Hotel, Manchester on 12 January 1864. Not many yards away there were soup kitchens and other dreary signs of general distress. The American Civil War raged, and its impact in England was most severely felt in and near Manchester. With the Confederate states, who supplied nine-tenths of the raw cotton to the textile area around Manchester, successfully blockaded by the Union navy, many mills had been forced to close. Whole communities were thrown on poor relief, and the workhouse, built on the hypothesis that idleness was the sole cause of unemployment, could not cope with this massive shutdown. Coming hard on a phase of abundant growth and investment, it was perhaps the first grim warning that the new industrial economics were at the hazard of world events.

There ensued the Great Cotton Famine, with starvation rife, and with an estimated £10 million lost in wages and profits over the 1861–65 period. In Manchester and the surrounding cotton townships there was a consequent epidemic of typhus, known in this incarnation as Famine Fever, and soon this was capped by an outbreak of cholera. The boards of guardians, in control of the poor law, spent £2 million in succour of the sick and hungry, while gigantic relief appeals, most notably one under the chairmanship of Lord Sefton, netted as much again. It was to be some time after the end of hostilities in 1865 before the Lancashire cotton trade was back to normal.

Yet thirty-four gentlemen gathered themselves, in the very midst of this unprecedented disaster, and started a famous cricket club. The middle-class are long practised in the craft of remaining blinkered to the desperate plight of the lower orders, and this may be a part explanation of their aplomb. Nonetheless, this startling phenomenon of structural underemployment adversely affected employers as well as employees, while the ravages of typhus and typhoid did not always discriminate between master and servant, as, three years previously, the Prince Consort had discovered to his fatal cost.

Nor must it be thought that a county cricket team was devised as a distraction for an aimless and potentially restless workforce, in the fashion that mills and factories were to promote brass bands and football teams. The cricket club then was a bourgeois habit, designed for the gentry, and only later to become a source of innocent merriment for the urban workers. There might be some estate or even village teams that included a talented groom or farmhand, and eventually the game would unfold its wings and embrace a wider fraternity. But the cricket club was a club in the formal sense of a subscribing membership, such as one would find at the Manchester Athenaeum, where Charles Dickens presided over a soirée in 1843, or any of the splendid London clubs. County clubs have never diverted from that constitutional formula, unlike, for instance, Football League clubs which are more strictly commercial companies, with shareholders and directors.

Thus the Lancashire club, like its compeers on the county scene, began and remained a subscription-based institution, simply because it arose from the actions of members of existing cricket clubs. The gentlemen who braved the outward manifestations of famine and infection to assemble in the Queen's Hotel were, in fact, the representatives of twelve existing clubs. Some just sent one or two. J. Smith, of Accrington, J. Yates and S. G. Greenwood, of Blackburn, E. Whittaker and E. Hobson, of Ashton-under-Lyne and J. Swailes of Oldham came from districts bitterly beset by unemployment and illness. Some came from further afield. D. Long, H. Royle, W. Horner and a Higgins whose initials have been erased by the ravages of time, arrived from the Liverpool club, with H. M. Tenent, from the Northern club on the outskirts of Liverpool, Alec Eccles from nearby Huyton, and T. Wall of Warrington.

Not unexpectedly, the Manchester clubs dominated the scene. Western C. C. and Broughton C. C. provided four delegates each: R. K. Birley, J. Becton, R. Entwistle and H. Ashton from the former, and J. Whittington, J. B. Payne, R. Crawshaw and the

Revd F. W. Wright from the latter. Longsight sent J. W. Allison and E. J. Bousfield. The Manchester club itself fielded a full eleven: S. H. Swire, Frank Glover, H. W. Barber, the brothers E. B. and A. B. Rowley, D. Bleakley, T. Fothergill, Captain Ashton, A. Birley, E. Challender and J. Holt jun. It must be noted that it was, therefore, a Manchester meeting for Manchester men, with a few invited from nearby townships and Manchester's large neighbour, Liverpool, but with no representation from the north and north-west of the county.

This was not surprising. South Lancashire, with its two chief cities and its textile belt, had a huge population, and, of course, the clubs represented were those that played one another and whose members knew one another. Transport north and south was not so easy as east and west, and, although cricket was played elsewhere in the county (Preston was a notable absence from the Queen's Hotel meeting), Manchester was its main setting. The point has to be urged, however, that this was the case, and that, for instance, there was no general rallying of the shire, its county headquarters still at Lancaster, to the cause. Lancashire Cricket Club was, in the event, the creature of Manchester and its environs, and so it has continued. The meeting at the Queen's Hotel was not a very long nor controversial one. Mr Horner, of Liverpool, was voted to the chair, and 'the resolution to form a county club was adopted'. That, until June when the first fixture was organised, was that.

One needs to reflect a little on the previous history of club cricket in the area in order to understand how this brief, stirring and successful meeting came to take place. The earliest flickerings of cricket in Lancashire have been dated in 1781, and the Manchester club had been in existence since at least 1818, when Jonathan Rowlandson was elected its president. Games were played at the Crescent, Salford, just across the Manchester boundary, then later at the Moss Lane playing fields near Chorlton Road, Hulme, at that time a prosperous and select township. A pleasantly named Cricket Street was to recognise that fact. Games were sometimes made up of 'sides', that is, of teams made up of club members, a convention that was to last a long while in footballing and cricketing circles and is still, of course, extant in tennis and golf clubs. Other local clubs would have formed some of the opposition. For example, a team from the Manchester Garrison, then manned by the Coldstream Guards and the Queen's Bays, participated in a match drawn because – luckless Mancunian omen – of rain. One soldier was explicitly dismissed for 'foot before wicket', but, more significantly, each side was joined by a professional, Carter and French, both of Liverpool, for the Garrison and Manchester respectively. The use of the professional, born in the country-house and patron's XIs of the eighteenth century, was much earlier to be found in cricket than in football. Thomas Waymark, usually regarded as the father of cricket professionals, was groom to the Duke of Richmond. Soon there were also independent players, like Carter and French, who normally plied their trade in concert with another, such as tanner or blacksmith, which might conveniently be abandoned for an afternoon's cricket.

This professional bandwagon began to roll swiftly. William Clarke established the All-England XI in 1846, and this pre-Packer 'exhibition' team toured the country, usually playing twenty-two locals and winning handsomely. In 1847 the All-England XI visited Manchester, and their display was distinguished by a score of 64 by George Parr, his 'fleetness of foot and assurance of eye' being remarked on this occasion. Eventually there were half a dozen or so professional circuses, one of which was organised by W. G. Grace to his considerable profit. As late as 1873, for instance, Grace's XI included fixtures at the Broughton club and on Alexandra Park, Manchester.

The touring sides offered a glimpse of the genuine cricketing article to the remotest districts, and served to spread a knowledge of and enthusiasm about cricket. The experience was evidently required. In 1842 the Manchester club had been flattered to receive an invitation to play the MCC at Lord's. Here was Manchester, the most thriving town perhaps in the kingdom, four years after its businesslike incorporation as a borough, called to give an account of its cricketing prowess at headquarters. The outcome was a pitiable humiliation. Manchester were dismissed for a calamitous 59, and the MCC responded with a cultured 220. Manchester 'gave up the match', and forfeited a second innings, so disastrous was their showing. It was as much the fashion of the defeat as the actual score which caused distress. Roundarm bowling, legalised since 1828, was not practised by the Mancunians, and their 'very deficient' underarm bowling 'afforded the Marylebone gentlemen much amusement in hitting it away'.

The Manchester gentlemen slunk home northwards, and began

to modernise their methods. They widened the circle of their fixtures. As well as Broughton, there were games with Liverpool, Sheffield and Shrewsbury. In 1844 a representative Yorkshire side provided the opposition. Names begin to emerge. There were 'the great family of Rowleys, seven in number', and Joseph Makinson, 'one of the finest players of his time', and others, such as the Revd F. W. Wright.

Next, better premises were sought, and, in 1847, the Manchester club moved a mile and a half from Moss Lane to the site of the Royal Botanical Gardens and later the White City greyhound stadium. In 1849 and again in 1851 there were fixtures with the Yorkshire county XI, and then, in September 1857, there was a notable victory over the strong Surrey county team. The match was played at the Western cricket club ground at Eccles, and Manchester employed three professionals for the occasion. They were John Wisden and Lillywhite, both to earn fame through their cricketing and annuals, and Fred Davies of Nottingham. It was, however, one of the Rowley brothers, Alec, who took the laurels, for his bowling was decisive in an exciting three-run victory, Surrey's only loss during a tour of ten games. It was matches like this which whetted the appeitites of Manchester's young tyros and made them yearn for the larger stage.

Manchester were forced in this same year to move again. The Art Treasures Exhibition for 1857 was held in Manchester, and the cricket ground and its surrounds were required. There was dismay and acid opposition to this among the Manchester membership, most of whom found cricket of more interest than Victorian art treasures. Nonetheless, the matter was settled amicably, and the club moved a few yards to the south along the Chester Road from Manchester, and settled for all time on the famous Old Trafford Ground.

It had been used by 'miscellaneous groups' for cricket, but now it was formally developed for that purpose. The cost of the lease was about £1000, a remarkable real estate investment. There were eight acres, and a pavilion was erected on the north, that is, the city side. It had a dining room and a wine cellar, and a residential basement for Thomas Hunt, now the club's Yorkshire-born professional, whose widow, incidentally, was the recipient of Lancashire's first-ever benefit. Some matches were played at Rusholm while the ground was prepared, but, by June, all was ready for the opening match against Liverpool. Liverpool did not manage a hundred in either innings, and Manchester celebrated their inaugural game at Old Trafford with a 31-run victory.

Playing standards and material standards both improved. The temporary fencing was replaced by effective boarding, a very positive sign of Manchester's determination to earn respect as an esteemed club. A new pavilion, at a cost of £900, was built, and Surrey, invited to mark its opening, were again defeated. At this time E. Whittaker, who was also an Ashton member, was secretary, and he must deserve special mention for ensuring these improvements, by no means inexpensive, occurred. During this period traffic could approach the ground from Chester Road and Warwick Road, but the nearest station was Old Trafford, some little way away, and arrival by rail involved a stroll along a narrow footpath. Later Warwick Road Station would be opened, giving direct rail access to the ground.

It was doubtless the activities of the existing counties, in particular, Surrey and Yorkshire, that led the gentlemen of Manchester and some neighbouring clubs to aspire to that condition. In 1864 there was just a handful of counties, Sussex, Nottinghamshire and Kent among them, but, considering the early origins of county matches in the eighteenth century, county cricket was a limp and tame affair, rather overshadowed by the 'Exhibition' elevens. Interestingly, it was immediately after a game at Broughton against the All-England XI that the leading Manchester cricketers decided to invite others to join them over the winter at the Queen's Hotel.

Thus the new status they sought was not of enormous moment. In essence, it was the proper ambition of developing and unfolding talents to compete at a slightly higher level by a pooling of personnel. As Fred Reynolds, a great Lancashire stalwart, put it in his memoir of the county's early doings, 'the amateur talent of the county had for some time been recognised as of a very high order'. The discussion at the Queen's Hotel touched on 'the possibilities and desirability of spreading a thorough knowledge and appreciation of the game throughout Lancashire', and, according to the *Blackburn Standard*, it was hoped 'to introduce other good cricket into every part of Lancashire'. It was proposed, perhaps after the pattern of the touring sides, to play not only in Manchester but in Preston, Liverpool, Blackburn and elsewhere, with the object of developing a wider interest. An annual subscription of a guinea was resolved, and the hope expressed that some of the money would be devoted to ground improvements at Old Trafford, accepted as the headquarters of the new Club. It is salutary to recall that a guinea might have been the weekly wage of many employed by those founder members while, during the Cotton Famine, thousands of families were forced to manage on three shillings a week.

There was what A. N. Hornby called 'a plentitude of support', and the name of S. H. Swire was emerging from the pack as, again using Hornby's phrases, 'an excellent organiser' and 'a resourceful diplomat'. He had become a member in 1858, nominated by Mark Phillips, who was to become Lancashire's first president, and seconded by T. T. Bellhouse, well known for his cricketing prowess locally. He was soon 'in the thick of it throughout', becoming secretary of the Manchester club in 1862 and picking up the reins from E. Whittaker. He was to the fore in mounting the Queen's Hotel inaugural meeting and in forcing the pace towards the establishment of a county club.

Nothing illustrates more lucidly the extended club role of county activity than Lancashire's opening forays. They played eight games in 1864, none of them against another county.

Lancashire's first-ever game was against Birkenhead Park Club and Ground, and it was played at Warrington, halfway point between Manchester and Birkenhead, on 15 and 16 June 1864. The match was drawn, but with Lancashire poorly placed. The newborn county scored 169 in the first innings, and Birkenhead Park responded with 143. Then Lancashire were dismissed for a dismal 78, and, when stumps were drawn, Birkenhead Park were 90 for 1, requiring only 15 for victory.

It is appropriate to honour Lancashire's first chosen elect with a roll-call. E. B. Rowley was probably captain, and his brother, J. Rowley, also played. S. H. Swire and T. T. Bellhouse were included, along with J. Becton, W. Robinson, J. Fairclough, G. H. Grimshaw, B. J. Laurence, J. White and F. H. Gossage.

The return match at Birkenhead was likewise drawn. Lancashire scored 234 and Birkenhead Park just overhauled them with 235. Lancashire then batted through, being all out for 174 and leaving no time for their opponents to bat. Manchester enjoyed fixtures with Shrewsbury. Now the Gentlemen of Lancashire played two games with the Gentlemen of Shropshire, who were evidently attempting to emulate the Mancunians by broadening the base of their game. Lancashire defeated them heavily at Liverpool by an innings and 23 runs, the Salopians collapsing twice for 128 and 101, while Lancashire compiled 352, with H. W. Barber, one of the Queen's Hotel fraternity, scoring 81. This was Lancashire's first-ever win. It was immediately followed by their first loss, for at Shrewsbury, in the return, they were dismissed for 96 and 140, and the Gentlemen of Shropshire (191 and 46 for 2) won by eight wickets.

The same pattern was repeated in the two games between the Gentlemen of Lancashire and the Gentlemen of Warwickshire. At Warwick the home side won by four wickets, while on Lancashire's first outing at Old Trafford, they were fortunate to win by nine wickets. The other two fixtures were with the Gentlemen of Yorkshire. Lancashire beat them by an innings and 22 at Broughton, and then there was an evenly matched draw at York.

The first season ended with three wins, two defeats and three draws, a commendable start. What is interesting is the use of the 'gentlemen' label, frequently deployed in that period, and, in fact, no less than 43 amateurs played in those eight games. In part, it was a matter of when busy commercial and professional men were free, and, in part, an effort to spread the interest. Almost all of them were from the Manchester club or its close neighbours. B. J. Lawrence, who played in the first game, and W. Horner, who chaired the Queen's Hotel meeting, were both from Liverpool. These matches were marked by another feature. Lancashire fielded professionals for the first time, and Hickton scored 80. Holgate, Nicholls, against Birkenhead Park, and Coward were also employed.

In the summer of 1865 Lancashire played their initial inter-county match. It was against Middlesex, who had also started life in 1864. This historic event took place over 20, 21 and 22 July at Old Trafford, and, providentially, Lancashire won by a healthy 62 runs. £25 was taken at the gate. Another memorial is required, a roster of Lancashire's first actual county eleven: R. Blackstock, F. J. Cooke, R. Iddison, J. F. Leese, J. Makinson, E. Whittaker, E. Bousfield, A. B. Rowley, S. H. Swire, W. Perry and F. Reynolds.

The scores were: Lancashire 243 (J. Makinson 45) and 178 (A. B. Rowley 60); Middlesex 243 (R. D. Walker 84) and 116. Apart from the oddity of the tied first innings, the match was remarkable for V. E. Walker's achievement in taking all ten Lancashire wickets in the second innings. From the Lancashire viewpoint the crucial feature was the hard labour of their two professionals, Roger Iddison and Fred Reynolds. They took 14 of the 17 wickets falling to bowlers. Lancashire then lost the return match at Islington by ten wickets, managing only 112 and 130 against the 226 and 17 for 0 of Middlesex.

Lancashire played only two other games that season, losing to the Gentlemen of Shropshire at Liverpool, and drawing a game ruined by rain at Broughton with the Gentlemen of Yorkshire. Thus the pattern of the next few years was laid down, with a small number of county games interspersed with as small a number of minor fixtures. In 1866 home and what were then known as 'out' games were played with Middlesex and Surrey, who were visitors to the Wavertree ground in Liverpool. In 1867 the Yorkshire county XI were played for the first time, as recognised officially. This was on 20, 21, 22 June at Whalley, near Blackburn and Lancashire lost. They also lost two other games with Yorkshire that season.

Some respect was saved, however, when the Gentlemen of Lancashire swamped their Yorkist counterparts at Old Trafford. E. B. Rowley made 219 and F. Whittaker 146 out of a massive total of 586, rare today and then one of the highest totals for any class of cricket.

On 23, 24 and 25 May 1867, the two great 'Exhibition' elevens clashed in aid of the Cricketers' Fund. The All-England XI and the United All-England XI were the teams. Because of disputes among northern professionals, the MCC stopped patronising the fund and endeavoured to launch the Marylebone Professionals' Fund. However, what is significant is that Old Trafford was now regarded as a suitable venue for such a fund-raising match.

Finances were not too stable. 'An annual deficit', as Hornby puts it, 'was customary', usually in the region of £100 a year for county matches. It was little wonder that a proposal in 1868 to allow free admission to such matches was refused, although, of course, administrative overheads were – and are – higher with a paying audience. A year or so later, and at a cost of £160, a small wooden 'public' pavilion was added to accommodate a small number of non-members, while, in a manner customary in county cricket for many years, A. B. Rowley improved the formal pavilion at his own expense.

The seasons wound on. Just four or five county matches were played, with not even Yorkshire consistent opponents. Surrey were usually played, home and away, while other opposition included, on occasion, Hampshire, Kent and Derbyshire. By and large, the county did reasonably well, with Surrey often on the receiving end of a beating, but *Wisden*, in 1870, warned 'the county of commerce' that their efforts would be vain 'unless the Lancashire gentlemen reform their fielding'. Since 1864, the year of Lancashire's establishment, a champion county had been declared but Lancashire had not yet made a great mark in the competition.

It is the nature of early history that these seasons should furnish a log of interesting curios. There were the first centuries. In 1866 Roger Iddison scored 106 against Surrey at the Oval, and the following year, in the most impressive debut ever made for the county, James Ricketts scored 195 not out, also against Surrey at the Oval. He was the first Lancashire player to carry his bat in a county match. Unluckily, his ten-year career never lived up to that potent promise, a not unfamiliar tale of Lancashire hopefuls. The Revd Frank Wynward Wright became the first amateur to score a century, with 120 not out against Sussex at Old Trafford, in 1869, and thus the first Lancashire centurion on the home ground. Born in Oxfordshire but educated at Rossall, he played little more cricket, being occupied with his scholastic duties in Eastbourne. He had attended the inaugural meet in 1864.

William Hickton, who later represented the Players and who played about six years for Lancashire, became the first Lancashire bowler to capture all ten wickets in an innings. In their second innings at Old Trafford in 1870 he dismissed Hampshire at a personal cost of 46 runs, although the academicians dispute the first-class status of this match.

More dolefully, it must be recorded that, in 1871, in their own débutant county game, Derbyshire shocked Lancashire by dismissing them for 25, still the record low score by the county. However, that was an unusual occurrence, and, in general, the Lancashire side was improving. A. N. Hornby, having made his début in 1867 at Whalley in the first-ever game with Yorkshire, now regularly topped the averages, although the captain, E. B. Rowley, continued to make notable contributions. Roger Iddison, James Ricketts, Cornelius Coward, William Hickton and Fred Reynolds were the leading professionals, and Iddison and Coward added much agility to the fielding. Fred Reynolds became Lancashire's first cricketing beneficiary in 1870, although, unfortunately, Surrey were beaten early in the second day, and a single-wicket game was hurriedly contrived to eke out the time. The amount he earned is not known.

Peculiarly in an age when amateurs were scarcely considered as bowlers, Arthur Appleby was often Lancashire's premier attacker. Born at Enfield, near Accrington, this tall, left-arm fast bowler, often pitching just short of a length and cutting in from the off, had some fine analyses. These included 8 for 68 against Surrey in 1869 and 7 for 37 against Hampshire in 1870. In 1871 he became the first Lancashire player to take 50 first-class wickets in a season, with 52 at an average of 17. He was perhaps the first Lancashire player to make a mark for the Gentlemen against the Players. Apart from some useful bowling, he scored 102 for the Gentlemen in 1872 at Lord's. He also toured Canada and the United States with R. A. Fitzgerald's team in 1872 – the first overseas tour by an MCC party.

Arthur Appleby was one of several Lancashire stalwarts who were keen to support the Lancashire League that was just emerging. It was the beginning of an uneasy relationship between the county and the leagues that was to persist into the present era. On the one side, the leagues were to provide a wholesome nursery for the county; on the other side, they were to offer a tempting and, in some degrees, less exacting billet for many potential first-class cricketers. What is certain is that the early success of league cricket helped cause the end of itinerant county cricket around Lancashire.

By 1871 the position was lucidly clear. Old Trafford was the headquarters, and the Manchester club undertook to pay all the expenses of county matches, then at a cost of about £120 a summer, provided that all home matches were played at Old Trafford. The Manchester club subscription was raised to two guineas, and the Lancashire fee was reduced to no more than 5/- from the original guinea, although, around 1870, it had already been reduced to 10/-. Very significantly, the selection of the Lancashire team became a function of the Manchester club.

What now transpired was that Manchester employed them to play for the county. In 1872, for example, Manchester played an extremely long fixture list of 32 matches, that is, a couple a week, and they lost only one. On most of these occasions, Manchester virtually fielded the county side. Incidentally, their match with Birkenhead Park that season was played with four instead of three wickets, just to add yet another curiosity to the record.

In essence, Manchester played a regular set of a score of fixtures against top-ranking clubs, interspersed with half a dozen games, under the label of Lancashire, against other counties. That concentration of Manchester influence, and players and ground, which had been at the hub of the county club's creation, was now total. Lancashire and Manchester were wellnigh identical.

## The Importance of Manchester

Manchester was, according to the historian, Asa Briggs, 'the shock city of the age'. For some years in mid-century it was the most prominent provincial town in Britain and, in some respects, bid fair to challenge the supremacy of London. It quickly became the capital of the thriving North-Western region, perhaps of the North as a whole, and, with so many other developments occurring there, it is no surprise to remark the rise of a successful cricket club.

Population was the initial key. The 40,000 of 1780 had become a massive 350,000 by the time Lancashire's county cricket was established. That ninefold expansion was founded on the cotton trade. There were over 200 cotton and silk mills in the parish of Manchester itself, but, beyond that, the town served as warehouse and trading post for the textile region and also developed appropriate manufacturing industries. Charles Macintosh began his famous business in rainy Manchester in 1824. The best banking facilities outside London were found there, and its Royal Exchange, rebuilt for the third time just after the birth of Lancashire cricket, had the largest room in the world then devoted to commerce, very necessary for its well-over 3000 members.

Everything was happening at once. Created a borough in 1838, Manchester became a city only a few years later in 1853, and its first bishop, James Prince Lee, appointed in 1847, was to supervise the building of no less than 110 new churches in his diocese. The assize courts were opened in 1864, Lancashire's first year of cricketing activity, while, two years earlier, the first wholesale co-operative society was launched and ensured Manchester became the national headquarters of the co-operative movement. Modern roads, water and sewage systems, a modern police force and prison, and a modern fire brigade were other products of this maelstrom of energy.

There were cultural and recreational elements. Manchester was the first provincial town to take advantage of the 1850 Free Libraries Act, and the first city to lay out three municipal parks. Owen's College was soon to be the first constituent college of the new northern university. Queen Victoria visited Manchester in 1851, the year, incidentally, the term 'Victorian' was first coined. She wrote in her diary of 'the orderly and good behaviour of the people' who were 'painfully unhealthy looking'. It was the year of the Great Exhibition, and the Prince Consort was to the fore in persuading Manchester to house a provincial sequel. This was in 1857, and was the very exhibition that drove the Manchester club off its then location and on to the Old Trafford site. Prince Albert persuaded the Manchester authorities to concentrate on the arts and to eschew a general exhibition, and the Arts Treasures Exhibition at the Botanical Gardens was Britain's first-ever display of pictures from private collections. The Queen herself, her husband and the Prince of Wales were among the 1,300,000 visitors, and John Ruskin was one among several celebrated lecturers. The music was provided by an exhibition chorus and orchestra, overseen by Charles Hallé. Their services were retained, and the long-running Hallé concerts began in 1858.

Eventually they were to be performed in the Free Trade Hall, the third version of which, in Venetian style, was opened in 1856. Built on the site of the 1819 Peterloo Massacre, when the military had fatally clashed with a huge crowd demanding parliamentary reform, it was as much symbol as institution. The headquarters of the Anti-Corn Law League, it was the architectural manifestation of Manchesterism. There truly originated middle-class consciousness, the proposition that, in the phrase of John Davies, himself a prosperous Mancunian, 'man must be the architect of his own fame'. Benjamin Heywood added an essential nonconformist flavour to this anti-feudal notion of private enterprise: 'trade should be as free,' he proclaimed, 'as the winds of heaven.'

Thus the shopocracy of Manchester introduced an abrasively radical note into national politics, with men like Richard Cobden and John Bright its chief exponents. It was marked by a belief, little short of religious, in free trade, operating within the ambit of a local government efficient enough to keep clear the arena for commerce: hence the desire for an effective police or a passable road network.

By the same token, the new industrialism 'forced to the surface the problems of class', as Friedrich Engels, then resident in Manchester, was quick to observe. Two-thirds of the population was working class: there were 80,000 alone working directly in the cotton industry. As Engels and others described, the conditions in which most of them existed were viciously degrading, filthy, noisome and desperate beyond the power of modern imagination to visualise.

Chartism, the rallying cry of the workers' movement in early Victorian times, was, therefore, as much a ramification of Manchesterism as the Anti-Corn Law League. While *Chamber's Edinburgh Journal* might, in 1858, refer to Manchester as 'the very symbol of civilisation', Elizabeth Gaskell's novel of Manchester working-class life, *Mary Barton*, offered, according to one reviewer, an insight into 'the whole science of starving'. The perceptive Frenchman, Alexis de Tocqueville, wrote of Manchester in 1835 that there were 'homes of vice and poverty, which surround the huge palaces of industry and clasp them in their hideous folds . . . here civilisation works in miracles, and civilised man is turned back almost into a savage'.

Manchester, as it brought into being a great cricket club, was thus a curiously frightening city, the first large community split completely on grounds of industrial class, with abject poverty and distress on the one hand and with untold wealth on the other, with Alfred Waterhouse's mock-Gothic town hall slowly rising between 1868 and 1877 to bear witness to Manchester's solid worth. Charles Dickens wrote of Manchester that it was 'every whit as wonderful, as fearful, as unimaginable, as the oldest Salem or prophetic city'.

This was the ambience from which Manchester gentlemen sallied forth to try their cricketing fortunes against the MCC or other established and perhaps more aristocratic sides. This is why Manchester's humbling defeat at Lord's in 1842 stung so bitterly. Here was a proud race, but one without roots and traditions. The Lancashire amateurs were, by and large, a parvenu group, at once fiercely independent and maybe a trifle insecure.

Certainly by the time the county club had settled into its early and quite long-standing pattern of a few county matches, home and out, each season, some of the 'shockability' of Manchester was growing calmer. This probably, in indirect manner, affected its cricketing condition.

That is to say that trade began to seem, and be accepted as, respectable, and the stringent radical tones of the 1840s and 1850s grew more mellow. The centre of political and economic attention turned to Birmingham, the second, later and different model for industrial city-life. Manchester lapsed into conservatism. Two events especially betokened this slide away from reforming firebrand zealotry. One was the defeat of John Bright in 1857, when he ceased to be an MP for Manchester, a personal tragedy he blamed on ingratitude and snobbishness. Manchester gentry had 'cooled down to a genteel tone', so much so that – the second event – the Conservative leader, Benjamin Disraeli, found himself addressing the faithful in the Free Trade Hall in 1872: a modern-day equivalent might be Fidel Castro finding himself warmly welcomed at the Republican Party Convention.

All of this very much depressed the astute Richard Cobden. Instead of becoming more cultivated and enlightened, using commercial prosperity as the platform for an Athenian type of civilised progress, the successful Manchester tradesmen and commercial tycoons were, in Cobden's eyes, mimicking the effete lordlings of England. In a striking phrase, he claimed that Manchester businessmen were 'glorying in being the toadies of a clodpole aristocracy'.

With all due respect to county cricket, it did, perhaps even until the Second World War, lean heavily on the landed aristocracy to give it political prestige and economic support. One would have to say of cricket that, in tempo and credo, it tends to be conservative, rather than radical. Manchester, as it approached the last quarter of the century, fitted the pattern impeccably. Eruptions, volcanic in intensity, had thrown up 'the shock city of the 1840s'. It had the population, the prosperity and the facilities to play host to significant cultural amenities, a county cricket club among them. It was, however, in the late 1860s and the 1870s, when the city turned from its fiery revisionism and sought to be more conventional and gentlemanly, that the county club started and became consolidated.

A county cricket club was and remained the sovereign badge of a pastoral, traditional, all but non-intellectual heritage. There can be little doubt that the first gentlemen of the Lancashire club had made their brass in the ferment of industrialised Manchester, that their ambition and self-esteem alike were fired by success, and that they looked, among other cults, to county cricket to clad their bourgeois flesh in an aristocratic mantle. The Manchester man aspired to be the Lancashire gentleman.

*Toward the First Championship*

Throughout the 1870s these Lancashire amateurs, with the help of two or three 'professors', slowly improved the status of the county side. Although W. G. Grace praised Lancashire for retaining, like his native Gloucestershire, a large measure of amateurs, *Lillywhite's Annual* of 1871 was more critical. It pointed out that Lancashire cricketers were 'irregular in their support and their defection is at times disastrous. Probably more recourse to professionals will have a better effect'. Thus the fine endeavours of A. N. Hornby and Arthur Appleby were crucially supported by the recruitment of two legendary bowlers, Alec Watson and Richard Barlow, the latter, of course an equally legendary batsman. William McIntyre, a third professional, shared the bowling with them, while Ricketts, although never to approach the excitement of his début century, was a fourth. Later in the decade, the famous amateur all-rounder, A. G. Steel, began his beguiling career, along with 'the prince of wicket-keepers', Richard Pilling. They both played their first match against Sussex in 1877.

During those seasons, the County Championship was haphazard in design and ambivalent in outcome. It is interesting to note that *Wisden*'s list of county champions does not always tally with the complete records included in W. G. Grace's *Cricket*, published in 1891. The chief yardstick was that defiantly Victorian one of assessing by fewest losses, an exceedingly assured approach. For instance, in 1872, Notts, with two wins, five draws and no defeats are credited with the title, but W. G. Grace placed Surrey at the top of the list, with seven wins, two draws and three losses.

Allowing for these interpretative vagaries, Lancashire remained mostly in mid-table, ranging from third in 1870 and 1878 to seventh, with five losses, in 1876. It should, however, be remembered that few games were involved. Lancashire, strangely, no longer played Middlesex, and, indeed, had only two fixtures in 1870 and 1872, four in 1871, 1873 and 1875, and five in 1874. From 1876 to 1879, eight fixtures were arranged. Over these ten seasons Lancashire did in fact win 26 of the 53 Championship matches played, losing 20 and drawing only seven. Hornby was ordinarily top of the averages and the only batsman to appear in the national averages, with 34 in 1873 being his best year. The exception was 1875 when Barlow headed the national list with an average of 38.8.

Appleby grew less conspicuous, and the name of Alec Watson catches the eye. He took 48 wickets (average 9) in 1873, 51 in 1876, 96 in 1877 and 49 in 1878. However, A. G. Steel took 164 wickets in 1878, the first Lancashire player to take a hundred wickets in a season, although, to be sure, most of them were for teams other than Lancashire. McIntyre impressed with 89 wickets in Lancashire's matches in 1876.

There are several notable displays, by team and by individual, during this phase. In 1872 Lancashire beat Yorkshire and Derbyshire twice each. The professional bowlers, McIntyre, Barlow and Watson, took the 73 wickets that fell to bowlers in those four games, the other seven batsmen being run out. That opening partnership of myth and poem, Hornby and Barlow, was soon in full swing. Their unbroken 148, for instance, gave Lancashire a comfortable ten-wicket win over Yorkshire in 1875, and 'Dicky' Barlow was already building his reputation of being one of the most notorious stonewallers – the term now has an antique ring – in history. That was Lancashire's first-ever opening century-stand.

Hornby made his maiden century in 1870, 132 against Hampshire at Old Trafford, and he followed this with a couple more, 138 against Surrey in 1873 and a 100 against Gloucestershire in 1878, both at Old Trafford, and his first in the Championship. During the 'seventies he scored five other centuries, two of them in 1873 and 1877, for the Gentlemen versus the Players. There was some admirable bowling as well. McIntyre took 8 for 35 against Yorkshire in 1874 and 8 for 31 against Derbyshire in 1877. A. G. Steel took 9 Yorkshire wickets for 63 during his successful performances, and, briefly, the Cambridge University player, W. S. Patterson, shone. In 1875 he took nine wickets when Leicestershire paid their first visit to Old Trafford; in 1876 he hit a century in the university match at Lord's and was batting with G. F. Grace when the Players were beaten by one wicket in the so-called 'Glorious Match'; and then, in 1877, he took 24 wickets in his only two games. In all, this talented student played only seven games for the county.

Thus did 15 seasons fitfully pass, sometimes with county fixtures difficult to arrange and, as the results suggest, only a weakened side available for some 'foreign' matches. Nonetheless, something nearer a balanced attacking force was emergent. The beau ideal of the epoch was amateur batsmen combined with paid bowlers, and Lancashire were now near to this target. Since 1873 more attention had been given to qualification 'to prevent cricketers playing for more than one county per season', and Lancashire had joined the other counties in agreeing to this. Richard Iddison was one who had moved to and from Yorkshire over a brief span of years.

Now Lancashire offered a much more settled promise of security to their three key bowlers, Watson, Barlow and McIntyre, and this sensible deal slowly paid dividends. About the same time the veteran Fred Reynolds became the Pooh Bah, the Lord High Everything Else, of Old Trafford. He was made 'responsible for collecting subscriptions, managing the cricket department, keeping the ground in order, attending to the comfort of members and being present on the ground on all necessary occasions'. In essence, he became club coach and mentor of the Manchester side, which acted as Lancashire's training school. He received £60 a year and a rent-free cottage on the ground, where he also enjoyed the pigeon-shooting rights – although he once incurred the committee's ire by inviting his companions, 'not being members of the club', to add to the fusillade. As for the collection of subscriptions, he scorned what now would be called the mail-shot, preferring to wait upon members in their offices, where physical confrontation obviously counted for much by way of persuasion, and where libations of whisky were bestowed upon him by way of relaxation. He published his memoirs in the 1880s, and retired in 1908 on a £100 annual pension, having devoted 44 unstinting years to the Manchester and Lancashire clubs.

Eventually, in 1879, Lancashire shared the Championship jointly with Nottinghamshire, but, in many ways, it was the preceding summer of 1878 which saw Lancashire climb on to a higher plateau in terms of its institutional history. It was in that year that, apropros of Lancashire, the public appeal of cricket reached fruition, and that marks a significant stage in the club's story.

There had already been signs, especially at 'roses' matches. The Saturday of the 1876 Yorkshire fixture at Old Trafford was witnessed by a huge crowd, said to have been the largest seen at a county match. In July 1878, however, two consecutive home matches constructed a watershed in six days, and popular interest in county cricket was doubly guaranteed.

The first game was the first visit of Gloucestershire, complete with the 'all-resistless Graces'. It is the match immortalised in his older age by Francis Thompson, when, overwhelmed by the emotional recall of that encounter, he could not bear to watch his favourite play in London and turned, most happily for posterity, to penning cricket's finest idyllic poem, honouring 'my Hornby and my Barlow' who obliged with an opening stand of 108, while A. G. Steel took nine wickets in the match. W. G. Grace crowned the occasion with a not out fifty, which pulled his team back from the brink, the honourably drawn match ending with Gloucester 111 runs behind and five wickets in hand. In parenthesis, one might add that the author's namesake and distant ancestor, William Evans Midwinter, Gloucestershire's first professional and, to the joy of all sports quiz devotees, the only man to play for Australia versus England and vice versa, was also on view. He scored 22 and 25 in that low-scoring game, and bowled commendably against 'new-arisen Lancashire'.

However, the game was important not only for its distinction and for its lyrical undertones, low as well as high, but for its spectatorship. The ground was swamped, and the authorities taken completely by surprise. 28,000 attended on the three days, and on the Saturday – then the third day – there were 16,000 officially present. Nearly £800 was taken, although, on the Saturday, an estimated extra 2000 swarmed over the fences, as the hastily improvised turnstiles were of little avail. Turnstiles were a novelty. They had first been utilised in 1871, the year when, and there is no coincidence, bank holidays were introduced, and the notion of paying spectators flourished.

Farmers' wagons had hurriedly been drafted into service as temporary stands, but, with the dilapidated nature both of these and the rickety turnstiles, the arrangements proved disastrous. The game was several times held up, as spectators encroached on the playing area, in part under the pressure of the crowd, in part at protest against the feeble organisation. Some began to tear up sods of turf, which incensed the never mild-tempered Hornby. Remembering perhaps how his opponent, W. G. Grace, had dealt summarily in the past with truculent spectators, he rushed into the crowd, gave the transgressor a series of what were described as 'hard knocks' and delivered him unto a police constable.

This was a time when the Cup Final was watched by only 2000 or so people, and it is likely that the Gloucestershire gate was then a record provincial sports crowd, paying admission. These strange scenes were immediately followed by the first visit of an Australian team to Old Trafford. Two stands were specially erected, and, in spite of poor weather, the gates were almost as huge as for the Graces' visitation, and over £700 was taken. Charlie Bannerman entertained with his big hitting, Spofforth took 9 for 53, and Vernon Royle dazzled with his exhibition of cover-point fielding for Lancashire, in a rain-spoilt draw.

The Australians had already shattered the ego of the MCC with that famous rout by nine wickets in one day, 27 May. Although their batting was a little frail, their bowling, and that of F. S. Spofforth in particular, astonished a nation which scarce regarded amateurs as bowlers, while some of their field placing and throwing proved to be revolutionary. Equally revolutionary was Lancashire's 'unprecedented' doubling of the admission charge to a shilling.

Lancashire played twelve games in 1878, ten of them in the Championship, or eight for those annalists who allowed Derbyshire no place in the charmed circle. They won six, drew three and lost three, finishing third behind Middlesex and Gloucestershire (who won the return match against Lancashire at Bristol) in the table. Hornby scored over 500 runs, and Steel, as well as the three reliable professionals, took many wickets. 1879 beckoned.

1879 was an extremely wet season, highly favourable to bowlers, although, true to tell, it was not Lancashire's waged bowlers who starred that summer. Rather was it A. G. Steel's year. The 21-year-old contributed a model all-round performance. Following up his luxurious haul of 1878, he took 93 wickets, being one of only three amateurs, as opposed to eight professionals, in the national averages. He was also fourth in the batting averages, with 553 runs, an average of 27, and a top score, oddly, of 93. Hornby, with 606 runs, at an average of 30, was second to Grace. That list comprised seven amateurs and three professionals.

Lancashire, like Nottinghamshire, won three and lost one, the two sides drawing four and six respectively. They shared the Championship on the principle of fewest defeats, Lancashire losing only to Yorkshire. They beat Gloucestershire and Kent, and savaged Yorkshire in the return contest at Old Trafford. Defending a meagre sum of 180, Lancashire won by an innings. Steel, having taken 14 for 112 against them in 1878, now opened the bowling in both innings and routed the white rose enemy.

Today one would delight in the appearance of a leg-spinner such as A. G. Steel: one would be astounded to find him opening the attack. Lancashire's draws were with Gloucestershire, Kent and Nottinghamshire (twice).

Yorkshire had other reasons for complaint. They won seven, and drew three – but lost two. W. G. Grace, in his records, clearly places them at the top of the Championship table, with Lancashire third. He also rejects any mention of Derbyshire, whom Lancashire beat twice, giving them a further two wins in some annals. Barlow weighed in with a hat-trick against Derbyshire at Old Trafford, the first ever for Lancashire, although, that same summer, A. G. Steel performed the same feat in the varsity match at Lord's. All in all, it was still somewhat messy, but Lancashire's joint win stands definitively in *Wisden*, which cannot be gainsaid.

With that muted triumph, E. B. Rowley stepped down from the captaincy he had enjoyed certainly since 1866, and probably for most of the first two seasons of Lancashire life. For 14 or 16 summers he had commanded the gradually evolving unit, and it owed much to Edmund Butler Rowley. A sound fielder and vigorous batsman, he never achieved the high merit of a Steel or a Hornby, although, much earlier in 1862, he had represented the Gentlemen versus the Players. Now he was about forty years of age, and his task was done. It was one he had shared with his six brothers, of whom he was the fourth in line, and, like the Walkers of Middlesex or the Lyttletons of Worcestershire, it made of Lancashire something of a family business. Alexander Butler Rowley, a tall, free-ranging batsman was a better cricketer than Edmund, but his business life prevented him from playing much. He was an excellent administrator, giving great assistance to Sam Swire, the club secretary, especially in the formative years, and, after Mark Phillips had been president for one year, 1873, A. B. Butler was elected to the presidency from 1874 to 1880.

In 1880 A. N. Hornby commenced his lengthy tenure as captain, a period to be remarked for its fresh success and also for its controversial disagreements.

# 2. Hornby's Years

## *The Championships of 1881 and 1882*

The 1880s mark the emergence of Lancashire from its own medieval age into the brighter glare of early modern times. From the misty recesses of its first score of years as an active county there evolved a club and a side of some coherence. Even the team photographs begin to lose that air of a group of disparate personages, some lounging, some leaning, and adopt a more disciplined mode. This happened, to some extent, naturally, as arrangements became more sophisticated, not only at Old Trafford, but across the first-class game. It also happened because Albert Neilson Hornby, now aged 33, brought martial and inspirational leadership to the cause, unifying the team round him and developing its manifest strength. If Edmund Rowley was the Joseph of Lancashire cricket, dreaming dreams of probable deliverance and glory, Albert Hornby was its Moses.

Nor was the milk and honey slow in arriving. 1880 was a goodish year, if not as successful a one as 1879. Hornby himself had a fine season, scoring 200 more than the second-best batsman, W. Robinson. A sprightly hundred by him, when Lancashire followed on, proffered sufficient leeway for Surrey to be beaten by 60 runs. The bowling was not penetrative enough, and William McIntyre, everpresent for eight seasons, was now dropped after three games. Alec Watson's 79 wickets easily constituted the best haul.

Lancashire were twice beaten by Notts, the second time in an exciting low-scoring contest at Trent Bridge, Lancashire 72 and 46, Nottinghamshire 66 and 53 for 6. Nottinghamshire were undisputed champions, but, in the following summer, they were undermined by a 'schism', the then vogue term when professionals caused disruption with their quest for improved wages. It left something of a vacuum, and Lancashire responded with what *Wisden* termed 'a series of brilliant successes almost unparalleled in the history of county cricket'.

On the very first day of the season Lancashire thrust aside Derbyshire for 102 and sped, by the fall of the first wicket, to 157. Following that simple victory over Derbyshire, Nottinghamshire and Kent were beaten. There was then a refreshing interlude when the Aigburth ground at Liverpool was opened. Lancashire's opponents were Cambridge University, and they won with a day to spare, Lancashire's only loss in 1881. The Cambridge team included the three Studd brothers, G. B., who carried his bat for 106, J. E. K. and C.T., and three Lancashire amateurs, A. G. Steel, O. P. Lancashire and J. R. Napier. Steel took 6 for 22 and 5 for 69, and guided his university to a bounding seven-wicket victory over his county.

Back on the more profitable county trail, Lancashire notched up five more wins, over Surrey, Derbyshire, Yorkshire, Gloucestershire and Yorkshire again. Steel bowled Grace twice in the Gloucestershire match, their second innings reaching no more than 42. Then there were draws with Nottinghamshire and Surrey, both of them with Lancashire holding the advantage. Despite being all out for 76, Lancashire next trounced Surrey at the Oval. Surrey made only 36 in the second innings, Crossland demolishing them with 7 for 14, and ten wickets in the match, the first hint of the troubles that he was both to suffer and cause at the Oval. The return Gloucestershire match was drawn because of poor weather, again with Lancashire holding the whip hand, but, in the final game of the season, Kent, always vulnerable in the 1880s, managed only 38 and 61 in two miserable efforts. Nash took 12 for 47 in the match.

Six of the ten victories were by an innings, and all the draws would, with happier fortune, have been likewise converted: it was a remorselessly triumphant march, bringing, in reward, Lancashire's first unshared Championship. Hornby had led from the van. He scored 118 of the 157-stand in that opening match with Derbyshire, and, in fact, scored two centuries against them, his 188, not out, being the highest score of the season. He also made a hundred against Kent, and, with four more fifties and an average of 50, he scored twice as many as anyone else. In the last game, against Kent, he just scraped a couple of runs, and, with a bare 1002, became the first Lancashire player to total a thousand in the season for the county, a feat not to be emulated until 1893. With 1531 runs in all first-class matches, he topped the English averages, with even W. G. Grace's flame dimmed.

Apart from W. G. Grace and C. T. Studd, A. G. Steel was the only amateur to appear in both the national batting and bowling lists, with 834 runs, including a century for the MCC at Scarborough, and 125 wickets, second only in quantity to Peate, the Yorkshire bowler. Much of this was performed in support of Cambridge, but, in five games only, Steel scored 353 and took 41 wickets. As with most winning combinations, the bowling was deadly and collective: Steel's leg-breaks, Watson's off-breaks, the dual left-arms of Barlow and Nash, and the as yet immature pace of Crossland. Although Allen Hill, the Huddersfield round-arm bowler led the English averages, Nash, Watson, Barlow and Steel were second, third, fourth and sixth, a phenomenal measure of their combined assault and battery. The three professionals captured 200 wickets in first-class fixtures. Barlow's county average was 9, and, of course, he contributed manfully with the bat (591 runs) as did the Yorkshire-born professional, W. Robinson (407), Alec Watson (304) and the emergent Briggs, as yet of no account as a bowler (367). These four professionals were content to plod steadily on, pursuing their stolid trade, if normally overwhelmed by the dash of the skipper.

The same excellence graced the following summer, that of 1882, but the strong Nottinghamshire team was restored to its rightful potency, and challenged mightily. W. G. Grace awarded the title, in his opus on cricket, to both counties, although *Wisden* had at first given the title to their opponents. It was soon generally conceded that it was a tied Championship, and thus was recorded in subsequent annals. It now ranks as the third of Lancashire's titles, and this in four years.

Rather more matches were played, 20 over against the 15 of 1881, and Somerset briefly joined their senior brethren. Middlesex had played one match with Lancashire in 1881, following a lengthy absence of such fixtures, and there was a double billing. Derbyshire remained a slightly bewildered shire, with Grace, for instance, steadfastly refusing to acknowledge their senior status. Nottinghamshire also beat Lancashire in their only defeat of the season, and some felt that entitled them to the title, other things being equal. As it was, Lancashire won ten of their 14 county matches, again drawing three, while their solitary loss was the only one in 27 Championship games. They did, however, lose three other first-class matches, including one, narrowly and excitingly, to the touring Australians, and the other two, also at the beginning of the season, to MCC and Cambridge University.

Thereafter the bowlers, with Crossland now in warlike form, dealt contemptuously with weak opposition. Derbyshire were demolished twice, the second time managing 77 and 55; Somerset were routed for 29 and 51, with Nash taking 12 for 38 in the match, and Crossland 6 for 7 in the second innings; Kent were out for 71 and 139; Middlesex were beaten twice, the first at Lord's after a sparkling 131 from Hornby, and the second, at Old Trafford, to end the season with a string of seven wins. There were, along the way, draws with Surrey and Yorkshire, but both return fixtures were won, the Yorkshire match at Sheffield by 16 runs in a thrilling finish and with Barlow demonstrating he could play freely with a decisive 68. Gloucestershire were twice beaten. Barlow, in more typical mood, scored 9 out of the first 71 assembled, as Lancashire won at Old Trafford, while, down at Clifton, and after fine batting by Barlow and Hornby, the Grace brothers nearly prevailed. Lancashire were home by a mere 13 runs.

The two crucial matches were against Nottinghamshire. The Lancashire batting at Trent Bridge was woefully undone by Shaw and Flowers. Although the Lancashire bowling was competent, Nottinghamshire won by 37 runs. The return at Old Trafford was a draw. There was a soupçon of excitement when, with only half an hour left of play and with Lancashire 118 ahead, Nottinghamshire abruptly lost four wickets. Arthur Shrewsbury put an end to such nonsense. Nottinghamshire, having also lost once and that to Yorkshire in June, ended the year with a wellnigh identical record to Lancashire.

It had been a great year for Barlow. He had 1088 in all matches (795 for the county) and 90 wickets (67 for the county). When Lancashire were forced by the Australians to follow on, he soldiered through two chanceless days, carrying his bat for 66 in the face of Spofforth, Palmer, Giffen and Boyle. That was one of his most epic essays into strict defence. A. G. Steel, too, had a fruitful year, with 739 runs, but with many fewer wickets. Nash and Watson were once more among the wickets, taking over 120 between them in county matches, while W. Robinson proved once more to be a capable batsman. He scored centuries against Middlesex and Kent. His captain, A. N. Hornby, again scored heavily, his all-round total of 1383 (774 for Lancashire) being second only to Ulyett's 1542.

However, the surprise of the summer was the increased velocity of Crossland, who leapt to the head of the national averages with 105 wickets and an average of 9.7. Eighty-three of his victims were in county matches, and he seven times took five or more wickets in an innings. It was, in reality, his pace which chiefly sustained Lancashire's quest for the Championship, but, as he prospered, so did the shadow of controversy lengthen. Lancashire was to find itself the focus of unpleasant attention, and 1882 witnessed the beginnings of such argument.

Before describing and analysing that forthcoming row, it is proper to measure this triumphant Lancashire team against later Championship winners. It was certainly a powerful side of comprehensive talent. In Hornby and Barlow it enjoyed the impetus of a classic start, with professional obduracy in league with amateur brilliance. Robinson and, to a lesser degree, Watson were stalwart supporters, but with amateurs, Vernon Royle and Allan Steel, irregular in attendance and Briggs not yet in his prime, the middle order was a trifle unsettled, compared, say, with the Lancashire elevens of the inter-war years.

Once Crossland introduced high and accurate speed into the attack, the bowlers served splendidly in all departments, so much so that people said it mattered not who opened the bowling. Nash, Watson and Barlow, together with Steel, when available, meant Lancashire had five of the most proficient bowlers in England on hand. Most teams were struggling to secure a hundred against them, even on decent wickets. Later Lancashire elevens were to have a more celebrated singleton of a bowler – a McDonald or a Statham – but none was to field five of such joint consistency at a time.

In the third area, that of fielding, the Lancashire team of 1881–82 was famously adroit, and it has been claimed that they rank as one of the most formidable combines ever. Hornby himself, of course, was sharp and eager in each and every position, and, unlike some of the captains of his era, was a declared enemy of the slouch. He was a most watchful captain, off as well as on the field, and insisted on the strictest standards of demeanour and concentration. The Revd V. P. F. A. Royle was the nonpareil cover point, the Harvey or the Bland of his day, and he was accompanied on the offside by the youthful Briggs and the older Barlow, fine fielders both. Indeed, Briggs was, in his early years, played as much for his fielding, for 'a vague feeling that he looked like a cricketer'. Robinson was a safe outfielder, and his fellow professional, Watson, was as reliable at slip. Steel, also, fielded with the panache of the student athlete.

So competent a circle of fieldsmen would, nonetheless, have looked much less imposing had it not been for the wicket-keeper, Richard Pilling. With the unhurried and calm presence of the most efficient air traffic controller, he maintained cricket's equivalent of flight paths and other aerial communication at world-class level. He kept wicket in all Lancashire's 33 games over these two Championship seasons, and, apart from exemplary parsimony when it came to extras, he himself caught 56 and stumped 33, a roll-call of 89 dismissals. Richard Pilling was the first, great, English professional wicket-keeper.

A. N. Hornby brought a rattling blade, adept keenness in the field, and a martinet oversight to the captaincy; he added a fourth and final quarter to his escutcheon. He proved to be a well-informed and cunning leader, not only capable of building and moulding his colleagues into a superior outfit, but of assiduously sapping at the weak linkages of his opponents. It is true that, in days gone by, perhaps until the coming of one-day cricket, fielding was not consistently sound, so that Lancashire's all-round radiance in the field shone the more beacon-like. It is the more, then, to Hornby's credit that he learned the modern lesson early, tutored, as some others failed to be, by the radical improvement in Australian fielding from 1878 onwards. Under his guidance, Lancashire batted tidily and bowled convincingly, but, above all, they harried the opposition in the field mercilessly, hunting them down with superb catch, speedy pursuit and unerring throw.

'It was difficult,' wrote Grace, 'to find a weak spot in the eleven. In batting and bowling they could compare favourably with any county: but it was very much owing to their brilliant fielding that such good results awarded their efforts.' Thus spake Zarathustra: and this is, perhaps, an appropriate juncture to pause and reflect on the individual stature of the leading members of this excellent team.

## A. N. Hornby

Because of his tininess, his agility, a certain swarthiness and a barefaced fearlessness, Albert Neilson Hornby was nicknamed 'Monkey' as a schoolboy, a sobriquet which adhered for the rest of his life. He weighed less than six stone when he won his place in the Harrow XI of 1864, during a 20-year span when the Harrovian batting was powerful, too powerful, almost every year, for Eton.

A son of Blackburn, born in February 1847, he never grew to more than medium height and a normal weight of around eleven stone, but an abundant flow of electric energy was generated from within the sparse frame. He accompanied Grace to Canada in 1872, he was badly injured by Spofforth when the Australians famously vanquished MCC in 1878, he played in the only match against the Australian eleven during Lord Harris's tour of 1878–79, and he played in two home Tests. It was his duty and sorrow to captain England in the late summer of 1882, when, after a most close encounter, with one spectator dead of the anguish and another having gnawed bits from his umbrella handle, the Australians narrowly won, with Spofforth taking 14 for 90. Hornby, however, earned praise for his shrewd handling of the English bowling. For the Gentlemen, he was a notable contributor, twice reaching fine centuries, and scoring over a thousand runs for them. In all, he scored 17 centuries, ten of them for the county, and, in those seasons of fewer fixtures and rougher pitches, he passed a thousand runs twice.

Few players managed so long a career, for Albert Hornby was easily persuaded to don the pads and pick up the cudgels again, so that he appeared as late as 1899, giving a span of 32 years since his 1867 debut. By that time he was 52, and had played in 292 games, even more than his faithful adjutant, the redoubtable Barlow. During this lengthy and productive stretch, he amassed 10,649 runs for Lancashire, and just over 16,000 runs in all cricket, at an average of a little more than 24. A. N. Hornby was the first Lancashire player to accomplish this feat. Only Johnny Briggs of those whose careers were concentrated in the Victorian era emulated him. He often topped the Lancashire averages, and in 1881, his best year, he led the English averages.

Trimly moustached, close-cropped dark hair belligerently parted in the centre, his unmistakable, bareheaded figure was well known on Victorian cricket grounds. Perhaps a little too cavalier on occasion for his own progress, he repeatedly played forward and struck the ball at what W. G. Grace called 'a terrific pace', and he ran like the wind. Particularly with Richard Barlow playing the grumbling Sancho Panza to his Don Quixote, his terrier-like adventures between the wickets were legendary. He demoralised the opposition with his astonishing darts and scurries, and, oftentimes, he perplexed his comrades.

He was impetuous and as daring in the field, and, according to W. G. Grace, it was Hornby's turbulent rush after the ball into a packed crowd, resulting in injury to an elderly spectator, which led to the formal introduction of boundaries. In 1879, when trouble brewed over Billy Murdoch's run-out in Australia, and Lord Harris was struck, it was, predictably, Hornby who apprehended the chief offender. A. N. Hornby was never far distanced from the action. Nor was he content to rest when cricket was over. He was a runner, and, like Grace, in his younger days, a hurdler, and he was also a boxer. He played soccer on occasion for Blackburn Rovers, and he was a rugby international. Although almost 30 when first capped, he played nine times for England at rugby. Like several of his generation of middle-class amateurs, he was passionate about sport in all its forms.

His commitment was total. A devoted product of the public school system, he practised its tenets lifelong. W. G. Grace, never the most diligent of ablutionists, found Hornby's constant cold showers appalling: 'Ugh, Monkey, you make me shudder,' he snarled as Hornby indulged in yet another chilly douche. Like Grace, Hornby was, however, not above the odd tactic which might have been thought out of place on the playing fields of Harrow. Once, at Bristol, he shifted a fielder silently with Briggs in mid run-up. Grace, no stranger to the stratagem, cried 'I can can see what you're doing,' even as he prepared to play his stroke.

A. N. Hornby continued to influence Lancashire cricket for many years, after having consolidated it in the first place. So many counties had depended on an essential patron or leader: W. G.'s father, H. M. Grace, with Gloucestershire, the Revd G. L. Langdon with Sussex, I. D. Walker with Middlesex, and, most famously, Lord Hawke with Yorkshire and Lord Harris with Kent. Indeed, this personal factor was one of the distinguishing reasons why some counties prospered, and others floundered. Apart from his long captaincy, he was the county's president from

1894 to 1916, and during these 22 years he played the watchful autocrat. He died, aged 78, in 1925.

In the last analysis, Albert Neilson Hornby's prestige rests most largely on his powers as a captain. During his many years as skipper, Lancashire were fifth three times, and those were their worst seasons. Mostly, they were second or third, apart from the Championship years, and this was, needless to say, a fine level of consistency. He was a martinet, and hated to be crossed, or even counselled. When bowlers complained of tiredness, Hornby conjectured putting them on at both ends; when the youthful MacLaren complacently informed Hornby that he could field everywhere except point, that was precisely where he was positioned; A. E. Stoddart had the same experience when he proposed not being stationed in the long field; when Hornby suspected Arthur Paul and James Hallows had practised with insufficient devotion, he forced them to open. They put on 250, and it is not written whether A. N. Hornby watched with pain or pleasure.

In the substantive phase of his captaincy, Hornby guided Lancashire to 91 wins out of 162 played, an exceptional record. He was a clever and astute captain, a careful student of the game and its practitioners. He was, Grace tells us, 'almost idolised' by the Lancashire players, and it is sure they followed him with eager conviction. The key to his generalship was his adeptness as a trainer of units. He was one of the first cricket captains to think collectively and gather his players into a team. The parts fitted together, and they worked hard for each other, their fielding strength being an indicative token of that togetherness.

A. N. Hornby represented the second generation of Lancashire business prosperity, off to Harrow, and then funded by the family to play cricket for a lifetime. Although he did not find himself at Oxbridge, he was, obviously, accepted and respected by the aristos of the cricket establishment, a decisive illustration of industry's graduation up the social scale, and Lancashire's place in the social sun.

He was not, perish the thought, referred to as 'Monkey' by the respectful Lancashire staff, which he nurtured and disciplined with a mix of pride and ferocity. He wrote of them as 'men who, in all the varied departments of the game, represent its truest interests, and are as well conducted as they are clever. Indeed, I wish', he continued, 'to speak in the highest terms of professional cricketers generally, who engaged in a game of the most searching nature, and, by their respectfulness and respectability, make their profession one for which there is much admiration.'

No colonel praised his battalion in more fulsome or genuine words. This was A. N. Hornby, known to his cricketer-soldiers as 'The Boss', and, by quite a long way, the most successful captain Lancashire has known.


## Richard Barlow

In righteous prejudice, the *Manchester Guardian* criticised W. G. Grace for allocating more space in his book, *Cricket*, to the scarcely legendary exploits of HH Prince Christian Victor of Schleswig-Holstein than to the solid achievement of Richard Gorton Barlow. Grace did have a soft spot for the aristocratic lineage he himself lacked, while he did not have a soft spot for the Barlows of cricket. It was not just that one of Richard Barlow's four hat-tricks was against the Gentlemen in 1884, and Grace, along with John Shuter and W. W. Read, were the victims. It was because, in Grace's own curt sentence, 'he has the patience of Job and takes rank with the Scotton and L. Hall type of batsmen'. He scores ten, said Grace, while Mr Hornby makes a hundred.

Born 28 May 1850 at Barrow Bridge, Bolton, Barlow was spotted by William Hickton, the Lancashire professional, playing for XXII of Staveley (Derbyshire) versus Parr's exhibition eleven. His career began with a good and a bad omen. His very first ball, against Yorkshire at Sheffield, produced a wicket, and he was run out in his very first innings, by A. N. Hornby, for a duck. He continued to bowl his accurate slow-medium left-handers to order, ending with 736 wickets for Lancashire and many more in representative cricket. He continued to be run ragged, then run out by Hornby, and 'then he gives you', said Barlow with doleful pride, 'a sovereign'. In his score or so seasons with the club, 1871 to 1891, he scored nearly 8000 runs, but with only four centuries, at an average of 20, not to be sniffed at in those days. He scored another 591 runs in his 17 Tests and took 30-odd more wickets. He is one of very few to have opened both batting and bowling for his country, and in three tours of Australia he played in every single game.

The contrast with A. N. Hornby, as to tempo between the wickets as well as pace of scoring, has established a model of the darting amateur and the dour professional as opening pair. *Aficionados* of variety might imagine a music hall double act consisting of the lugubrious ruminations of Robb Wilton and the explosive pyrotechnics of Ken Dodd: that would give some flavour of the comparison, and, incidentally, both comedians had a Lancashire birth qualification.

It is, then, as a slow batter that Dicky Barlow came to prominence. It is curious that, in his era, batting managed to be both faster and slower than in later years. With notable exceptions, no one emulates Jessop's run-rate, while Barlow made the modern school of adhesive batsmen – your Baileys, your MacKays – look as if they had been maddened into passionate impulse by a diabolic goad.

Tallish, bearded, grave of countenance, his barrier was founded in the most frustrating of forward defences. He was, in a dying word, a stonewaller, and he drove bowlers berserk by that strict obduracy: 17 in 135 minutes against Yorkshire; 26 in 130 minutes against Kent, and so forth. Nottinghamshire suffered painfully. Once, at Liverool, he carried his bat in the first innings, 44 out of 93, and then was last out in the second, 49 out of 188. On another occasion against Nottinghamshire, he carried his bat for 34 in 225 minutes, and then, in an ultimate reduction of run-getting and also against Nottinghamshire, he spent 150 minutes being five not out at the conclusion of Lancashire's innings of 69. As he was 80 minutes getting off the mark, the remaining 50 minutes were, mathematically, seven times as exciting.

An age which knew of stonewalling also spoke of batsmen being 'castled' when bowled. These architectural allusions were very appropriate for Dicky Barlow. He carried his bat an astonishing 50 times, for Lancashire in 11 of these innings. After Ricketts's fine effort at the Oval in 1867, R. G. Barlow's name appears, in fact, eleven times consecutively on the Lancashire list of 35 carried-bats, C. Hallows being the next in number with six. Barlow hated to be castled. After William the Conqueror had constructed his dominating fortresses, he could have left a Richard Barlow in charge of a Tutbury or a Pontefract and proceeded about his other business, a Domesday survey of East Anglia here or a great council at Winchester there, reassured that it was in the securest of hands.

That degree of concentration, day in and day out, and not forgetting the fatigue of Australian trips, was remarkable. It betokened a man steeped in cricket to an extreme, mightily obsessed with possession of the wicket as the function of cricket, the professional approach all but reduced to absurdity. Nonetheless, the trick was often that, with an innings thus sheet-anchored, the carefree amateurs could make merry, and so it often proved. There does seem, however, some rough justice in the fact that, for someone who stopped the ball so often, Barlow is one of an uncommon band given out for hitting the ball twice – for the North versus the South, in 1878.

Like Grace, he was eager, when not batting, to be bowling, and two or three of his analyses – 5 for 3 against Kent in 1878, 6 for 3 against Derbyshire in 1881, 5 for 10 against Gloucestershire in 1884 – are truly astounding. When his playing days had to be grudgingly forsworn, he turned, not too successfully, to being coach and ground manager, in place of Fred Reynolds, for a year or two, and, more triumphantly, he became an umpire. Indeed, he umpired for 21 years, as long as he had been on Lancashire's books. During and after his playing career, he had a shop on Stretford Road, Manchester, a cricket ball's throw from the county ground, and, when the county were engaged in 'out' matches, its windows were festooned with telegrams updating the scores, a precursor of today's ticker-tape. The shop was, naturally, a magnet for the fans, who might, Barlow probably reasoned, buy an article or two, excited by the county's progress. They might, for instance, have bought from his shop a copy of a ballad composed in praise of the county side. He was not all solemnity. His interest in choral activity spread to him occasionally leading, his gravelly, deep-throated bass in the van, a spirited singalong in the professionals' hut, not entirely to the liking of the committee and members who thought such behaviour unseemly. It was there he solemnly chewed the lunch brought for him each day by his dutiful wife. His fascination for cricket was endless, and, for example, he anticipated the future with a newfangled wicket protector for use in bad weather. He wrote weightily on cricket, and, put simply, he submitted his life to the game entirely.

He took a benefit against Nottinghamshire in 1886 and raised £1000. There was a sizeable crowd, and Dicky Barlow knew his duty. He diligently subscribed to his dual reputation for getting runs and getting them slowly with a cicumspect half-century over 180 minutes. In retirement he lived in Lytham, where his home was awash with cricketana. Even the bathroom was full of mementoes and bric-à-brac. He died 31 July 1919, at the age of 69, one of very few cricketers to be celebrated in poetry of acknowledged excellence. Richard Barlow might seem a most prosaic man to find himself thus honoured, and yet, for a person to be so utterly possessed by a pastime as he was by cricket, is surely an issue of emotion and of psychology. The match which gave him most personal pride typifies his holistic approach. The wicket for the North's second innings at Trent Bridge in 1884 was so gruesome that Spofforth, leading the Australian attack, vowed his opponents would be out for less than 60. Richard Barlow batted four and a half hours for a chanceless century – and he also took 10 for 48 in the match.

## Richard Pilling

Richard Pilling stares out sadly from the sepia photographs. Lean and cadaverous of frame, somewhat emaciated of face and with deep-sunk eyes, his moustache a mournful, unlucky horseshoe, in his long white shirt, he puts one in mind of either Joe Keppel or Jack Wilson. Wilson, Keppel and Betty were the grotesque Egyptian sand-dance trio, possibly the most archetypal of all music hall acts, and Richard Pilling's photo conveys something of their ritual resignation.

How is that melancholy to be explained? In the first place, the longer exposure of late Victorian camera-work has left many cricketers transfixed for all time in sphinx-like earnestness. The Victorian photographer seldom caught the fleeting smile or spontaneous chuckle. In the second place, he was a sick man, who was ill off and on from 1883 and who broke down completely over the winter of 1889. The committee was concerned enough about his value to the side to attempt various cures, including an expensive trip to Australia, a rare tribute, in those times, to the regard in which he was held. He died, 28 March 1891, at Trafford Bar, no distance from Old Trafford itself, and he was honoured as one of *Wisden*'s cricketers of the year that same spring. He was only 35, and he died of consumption.

In the third place, the nineteenth-century wicket-keepers might be forgiven an expression of patient fortitude. They faced a variety of bowling, wider in scope than is found today, and a conspicuous amount of impoverished throwing, and they were faced with often unreliable pitches. They knew nothing of the inter-galactic protection adopted by their successors in the present generation, placing their faith in thin gloves and beggarly pads.

Richard Pilling was known as 'The Prince of Wicket-keepers', the pick of his generation, with only the Australian, J. M. Blackham, deemed to be close to him in skill. W. G. Grace had him for a Bedford man, but other records suggest Norfolk was his birthplace. Certainly he was not an indigenous Lancastrian, and, observed from far-distant Old Trafford, perhaps Bedfordshire and Norfolk do merge into a nebulous East Anglia. He was born in July 1855 and made his debut in 1877, against Sussex. He played in eight Tests against Australia, and toured the Antipodes twice.

Apart from the assorted leg-spin of A. G. Steel and the guile of Richard Barlow, Pilling had chiefly to contend with the enormous pace of Crossland, he of the suspect action. He was forced to wear special armour for that heroic task, and he stood up for Crossland, as he insisted on doing for every bowler. When it is recalled that, at long stop, Alec Watson 'was almost knocked over on one or two occasions', the courage of Richard Pilling is the more to be admired. In the immediate post-war years, Godfrey Evans earned much respect when he stood close to the wickets for Alec Bedser, but Crossland was nearer a Lindwall in velocity.

Valiance is one thing: effectiveness is another. There is no point in standing tight to the stumps if byes and dropped catches prevail. Richard Pilling was effective, and, of course, it meant the batsmen could not stray too far forward in the hope of converting Crossland's length to overpitch. W. G. Grace complimented Pilling on his 'quick, neat, and quiet style', and by general consent he was the doyen of stumpers, 'equally effective', as Grace also endorsed, on both sides of the wicket. On occasion, he batted with spirit, and his stand with Johnny Briggs of 173 against Surrey at Aigburth in 1885 remains Lancashire's tenth, and only surviving Victorian, wicket record.

Richard Pilling played 177 matches for Lancashire between 1877 and 1889. Over those 13 seasons, he stumped 153 and caught 333, a tally of 486, a score or so more than Engineer, who played in almost the same number of games, if very many behind the prestigious Duckworth, who kept for Lancashire over twice as many times. Pilling's average approaches three victims a match, superior to anything achieved by any other Lancashire wicket-keeper, and ensuring him of a place in the record of the grand custodians of cricket's history.

Like all included in that fine catalogue, it was more than catchings and stumpings. It was also the confidence that superb wicket-keeping inspires, engendered by seeing the chances rarely muffed and the throwing-in always taken. The swift and skilled wicket-keeper, such as Richard Pilling, makes ordinary fielding gain in stature, and all are agreed that, with his grievously premature departure, the Lancashire fielding looked all of a sudden ragged and unworthy.

Lancashire have enjoyed the sight of 54 of their stalwarts representing England, and, oddly, over a quarter of them have been opening bats. From Hornby to Fowler, it has been the county's speciality, and a number of other internationals have opened the batting for Lancashire, if not for England. One seeks far and wide for wicket-keepers. Apart from Duckworth and Farrimond, there are none, Pilling apart, to be found, although Engineer, of course, was a distinguished Indian and Rest of the World keeper. Truth to tell, Lancashire have frequently found wicket-keeping a puzzling berth to fill, and, over the eras, the records tell of too many all-buts behind the stumps.

It is interesting that Lancashire have been blessed with the services of only three distinctive wicket-keepers: but what a handsome and superlative threesome. Pilling, Duckworth and Engineer must rate among the best dozen known to world cricket. As A. N. Hornby, writing of Richard Pilling, asked, 'How many thousands, indeed, on both sides of the globe, witnessed poor Pilling's skill?'

## A. G. Steel

W. G. Grace was always very circumspect in detailing who was amateur and who was professional in his published batting and bowling lists, the clue being the preponderance of unpaid batsmen and of paid bowlers. Apart from himself, it was a rarity to find an amateur in both rosters, but, occasionally, as in 1880 and 1881, Allan Gibson Steel accomplished this feat. Merseyside has not been as fruitful with cricketers as with boxers or footballers, so here, too, was another rarity, for A. G. Steel was a Liverpudlian, born in the September of 1858.

Unluckily for Lancashire, his academic training and subsequent legal duties meant his county appearances were irregular. In all, he played only 47 matches for Lancashire, scoring just less than

2000 runs (average just less than 30) and taking 238 wickets at a cost of 13. He was one of a family of cricketers, but A. G. was far and away its leading light, even if the resultant illumination was of more benefit to Cambridge University and the Gentlemen.

It was said of him that he never bowled better than in his last year at Marlborough, and he arrived at Cambridge with a fullblown reputation. For once, the bubble did not burst, and, from being a freshman, he dominated what some argue is the strongest ever light blue team. Apart, in 1878, from thrashing Oxford, they also annihilated the Australians. In four varsity games, A. G Steel took 38 wickets, and also added 182 runs.

His success at Cambridge led to his immediate incorporation, aged only 19, within the ranks of the Gentlemen, then enjoying, courtesy of W. G. Grace, a purple patch, and, again, Steel was highly successful. He went on to play in 13 Test matches, mostly at home, but including four during the Hon. Ivo Bligh's tour of Australia. On that trip he scored over 500 runs and took 152 wickets, average just under 7, and he reached an undefeated 135 in the Sydney Test. He enjoyed the distinction of a home Test century, with, in 'unceremonious fashion', 148 at Lord's in 1884. In the same year, also at Lord's, he took another hundred off the Australians, this time for the MCC. On four occasions he captained England, in the three Tests of 1886, all of which England won, and as deputy for Grace in the first 1888 Test. Apart from Hornby's twice and MacLaren's score of times, he is the only Lancashire player to captain England against Australia. He took 29 wickets and scored 600 runs for England, and, after Johnny Briggs, he stands roughly equal with Ken Higgs, both with averages of a little under 21, as second in Lancashire's Test bowling annals (minimum 20 wickets).

He was of medium build, dark and aquiline of feature, sporting a ponderous moustache of a style associated with Old Bill in the First World War and RAF pilots in the Second World War, Jimmy Edwards emerging as a post-war 'handlebar' prototype. He was as near nerveless as a cricketer can be, and his cleancut hitting owed not a little to his unwillingness to be cramped by the convention of getting set. However, of his seven fine centuries, only one was for Lancashire.

Although judges place him in the élite of all-rounders, his bowling probably had the edge. His pace was judiciously chosen. He did not rely on flight, and was thus able to boost pace sufficiently to check the venturesome forward driver. Sometimes a delivery would be quite rapid. He was an intelligent and thoughtful round-arm bowler, concentrating on the ball just short of the half-volley and breaking both ways. He favoured the leg-break and, in dampish summers, was much feared. He has been termed, if only for the first years of his career, 'the most dreaded bowler in England', and, at a time when the slowish leg-break was not much utilised, its strangeness was an advantage. In seasons 1878–81 he took 474 wickets.

His confidence must have soared, as, from the age of 16, he found success so readily at hand. Of course, as the years passed, and as the irregularity of his first-class play continued, some of the smoothness of drive and accuracy of leg-break deteriorated. Although he played occasional matches for Lancashire until 1893, it must be said of A. G. Steel that his promise never had the full opportunity to reveal itself, and assessments of him are based on his prodigious activities as what, in *Nicholas Nickleby*, is described as 'the infant phenomenon'.

He is certainly Lancashire's chief amateur all-rounder, and, after MacLaren and Spooner and perhaps Hornby, the county's finest amateur batsman. Lancashire has possibly been unfortunate with its great amateurs, for Spooner was another to find consistent appearance difficult, and MacLaren was not always as regular as might have been wished. Contemporary with Allan Steel was the Revd V. P. F. A. Royle, Vernon Royle, the sweetest of cover points. Born 1854, and living until 1929, he made only 74 appearances for Lancashire, and these were spread over nearly 20 years, from his début in 1873 to 1891. So threatening was he at cover that Tom Emmett, the Yorkshire star, chided a foolhardy partner, seeking a run to Royle, reminding him that 'the policeman' was on duty there. Royle played once for England, in 1879.

Lancashire lacked a supply of gifted amateurs, who might teach in public school a couple of terms and be available in the summer, or, quite simply, who had sufficient private income to support them. After MacLaren and Spooner, and with the mercurial exception of Ken Cranston, himself a baleful instance of the rule of irregular or fleeting amateurs, Lancashire never again fielded a top-class unpaid player. They found amateurs to captain the county, some of them competent cricketers, some of them competent leaders, but, certainly by the First World War, the days of Lancashire's four highly talented amateurs was at an end.

In a sense, it was Lancashire's own choice. Hornby's revolution had been to create a club which entertained its membership, and drew in a supporting audience, rather than recruited its eleven from its membership. The principle of forgathering and developing a strong, relatively well-paid group of professionals had been adopted, and, increasingly, Lancashire were loath to do what some other counties did, that is, drop a sound 'pro' to find an occasional place for the vicar or schoolmaster on holiday. On the other hand, other counties appeared to discover richly accomplished amateurs right through to the silvery days of Peter May, David Sheppard, Colin Cowdrey and Ted Dexter. Such cricketing affluence bypassed Lancashire, and they were already fast on the way to becoming a primarily professional outfit.

As for A. G. Steel, his interest in the game remained – we find him objecting to changes in the lbw law in 1902 at the general meeting of the MCC and he was president of MCC in that year – and his place in Lancashire's story as an impressive young all-rounder of world repute is secure. He died in the summer of 1914, just before the Great War began.

### The Paid Bowlers: George Nash, John Crossland and Alec Watson

While 'the run-stealers flicker to and fro', the bowlers go about their laborious business, and, alongside Richard Barlow and A. G. Steel, Nash, Crossland and Watson completed perhaps Lancashire's most effectively widescale attack of all time. It was their misfortune to be severally associated with the throwing controversy of the age. George Nash was left-armed and slow, so that, while his elbow was claimed to be ineluctably bent at delivery, he was never so adversely condemned as John Crossland. John Crossland, a collier from Sutton-in-Ashfield in the county of Nottinghamshire, engendered terrifying pace, and his yorker was universally regarded with terror. Whatever the faults of his action, it was his sheer success which occasioned the fierce criticism. Alec Watson, by comparison, was hardly suspect at all, and this consistently sound right-arm spinner enjoyed a lengthy and honourable career.

All three were recruited from outside the county. George Nash was born in 1850 in Buckinghamshire, whence he returned to complete his career with decent and peaceful efficacy. He played for Lancashire from 1879 to 1885, and he died, aged only 53, in 1903. He was a meek and shy person, bringing a pleasing mildness to the image of professional cricket. The newspapers called him Jolly John Nash, after the chubby music hall performer of 'laughing' songs, 'Little Brown Jug' being one of his repertoire. It was not a sobriquet which spread fully to the terracing, perhaps because it was inapt for so inoffensive a man. He took 202 wickets for the county in his seven seasons, at the splendid average of 12. He took 8 for 14 against Somerset in 1882, while his best Championship figures were 8 for 79 against Surrey at the Oval.

John Crossland brought the overripeness of the mining argot to his cricketing duties. It was he who, on clean bowling a man of the cloth, howled with delight at 'downing his old pulpit', an epithet eked out with undeleted expletives. Despite, maybe because of, his colourful enthusiasm, he was made melancholy by the accusations hurled against him and found it hard to come to terms with being cast as the villain of the piece. For their part, the Lancashire authorities stood reasonably by him, and, as with almost all 'chucking' arguments, this one was ill-defined. He was undoubtedly strong of arm, and he once threw a cricket ball a hundred yards, standing still in a bathtub.

There was something of A. G. MacDonnell's legendary village blacksmith in his make-up. Roaring over the brow in primitive venom, the burly collier imposed a psychological bind on his opponents. He was also very accurate, and clean-bowled two-thirds of those victims. He played just eight seasons for Lancashire, and he took 245 wickets for the county, also like Nash at a cost of 12. His 7 for 14 at the Oval against Surrey was at once his best analysis and the initiation of the noisy case against him. Born in 1853, he also died in 1903, although he was even younger than George Nash.

Mancunians of a certain age wishful of buying and able to afford cricket and other sporting equipment were faced with a rival choice of Tyldesley and Holbrook or Alec Watson and Mitchell, a memory of an age when professional cricketers commanded a number of tributary crafts. Alexander Watson was born in Coatbridge, Lanarkshire, in 1846, and he turned out to be one of Scotland's most proficient cricketers. He was advised by A. Buchanan, while leading the Free Foresters in Scotland, to moderate his then quickish pace and to cultivate spin. After being professional for the Edinburgh Caledonian club, he found a paid engagement with the Rusholme Club in Manchester, and, having qualified by that relevant and active form of residence, he joined the Lancashire staff.

Small and slight in build, he bowled his off-breaks like an automaton, in unceasing, machine-like manner over many, many hours. He bowled without much flight, not too slowly and with low and sometimes shooting trajectory. His accuracy, in spite of the perkiness of his off-spin, was notable, and it continued many years. His rather Frenchified appearance, with minute goatee beard, florid moustache and wavy if receding hair, was well known on all cricket grounds.

Unlike the shortlived reigns of George Nash and John Crossland, Alec Watson sustained his career over 23 seasons, from 1871 to 1893. He played 283 matches for Lancashire, taking 1308 wickets (1383 in all matches) for an average of thirteen. He enjoyed some unusual days: 9 for 118 versus Derbyshire in 1874; 6 for 12 for the North against the Australians in 1886; 6 for 8 against MCC in the same year; and match figures of 9 for 13 versus Sussex in 1890. Yet it was not so much those glimmering days as the years of drudgery which mark out Alec Watson for reminiscence. He is fifth in the order of Lancashire wicket-takers, and, of those who have taken 500 or more wickets, he is very easily top of the all-Lancashire averages. From 1872 to 1889, he was only six times out of the top five in the national averages, and only three times out of the top ten. He was first in 1883 and 1886, and, coming second in 1887, he took a hundred first-class wickets, never a simple feat in those years of comparatively few qualifying games.

One of the most solidly meritorious of all Lancashire bowlers, Alec Watson not only plied away longer than Nash and Crossland, he outlived them considerably, dying in 1920, aged 76. He crossed the border early in the 1870s, just prior to the first migration south of the football 'professors' from Scotland. The notion of creating football as well as cricket teams for public entertainment was waxing.

As his sports business illustrated, the paid cricketers of that epoch might be groundsmen, coaches, bat and ball makers or, in the case of Wisden and John Lillywhite, almanac publishers. One of the least pleasing chores was bowling to subscribers, for this

could be laborious and irksome. These were known as the ground
bowlers. One anecdote tells of a Lancashire member who
demanded this privilege after six o'clock in the evening, and the
ground bowlers grumbled that the light had failed. The member
pompously insisted, and so the Lancashire bowlers emerged from
the hut they had hoped to vacate for a homeward journey and
processed to the nets. They marched, each carrying a lit candle,
not unlike that scene in *Snow White* when the dwarfs assemble
around the heroine's cortège. It was a somewhat direct hint, but,
compared with the crude and witless responses of some professional sportsmen today, it was not without a gentle humour, even
if it were viewed, in military parlance, as silent insubordination.

After McIntyre and alongside Barlow, it was the likes of Alec
Watson, together with men like George Nash and John Crossland,
who made the trade of professional cricket in Lancashire a
respectable one. But they were not cowed men, subservient
although they had to be to the whims of a not always knowledgeable authority. These were the men who set standards of skill, of
behaviour and of self-esteem for their many descendants. It was
very much in the tradition of the artisan upper crust of the
proletariat which, in other manufactures and trades, was developing over the industrialised areas of the country.

## The Throwing and Residential Controversies

By the exceptional criteria of 1881 and 1882, Lancashire underwent something of a lean spell until the end of the decade. 1883
started well enough, with a run of seven wins, although only four
were in the Championship. R. Taylor, a Rochdale amateur, and
Robinson accumulated 237 between them against Oxford University, but this (Lancashire's highest stand to date) and one or two
doughty innings from Hornby apart, the batting proved to be no
more than moderate. The county tumbled down the table, losing
five games in the Championship. 1884 was no better. Lancashire
were again fifth, with four losses in county games. Crossland,
Watson and Barlow all bowled well, the last-named taking 130
first-class wickets, but, apart from Steel, the batting once more
seemed tamed. The season was noted for the decently sentimental
abandonment of the Gloucestershire match at Old Trafford, on the
death of Mrs Grace. Hornby's decision to release the Grace

brothers to return to the home of the woman who had nurtured their cricketing skills was deeply appreciated by William and Edgar Grace. One would like to hope that such a proper respect might still be found in sport nowadays.

In 1885 Lancashire moved to third in the table, winning six and losing three of their 11 county matches. Barlow was steadiness itself at the head of the batting averages, but the happiest point of the year was Johnny Briggs's self-discovery as a bowler. So sudden and striking was this improvement that, with 79 wickets at a cost of about ten runs apiece, Briggs found himself at the top of the English averages. He was henceforth to be ranked as an all-rounder of world class. It must also be remarked that G. M. Kemp, later Lord Rochdale, scored Lancashire's first century against Yorkshire. Lancashire were third again in 1886, a summer highlighted by the début of Bennett Hudson, a Yorkshire-born professional, who made 98 against Sussex. A somewhat hysterical Hornby threw a county cap to him through the pavilion window, only for his eagerness to be disappointed, for Hudson played just five first-class games for the county. Lancashire won ten matches in 1887 to finish runners-up to Surrey in the first Championship to be decided on points, one for a victory and a half for a draw. Frank Sugg arrived via Yorkshire and Derbyshire to add solidity to the previously uncertain batting, while Watson and Briggs took over a hundred wickets each, the latter also weighing in with 800 runs to consolidate his repute as an all-rounder.

A year later, in 1888, Lancashire slipped to fifth, although Briggs now captured 187 wickets, topping the national averages, and scored nearly 900 runs. He was, however, something of a solitary star. Surrey inflicted upon Lancashire the first-ever one-day defeat in the history of the Championship, and this followed the nadir of the previous year when Yorkshire had scored a record 590 against the county. The high point of the summer was a remarkable victory over the Australians, chiefly engineered by the Revd J. N. Napier, playing one of his only two games for Lancashire. A vicar in Preston, he abandoned his flock long enough to make the top score of 33 in the Lancashire second innings, before taking 4 for 48 on a most fiery wicket. Briggs had 13 wickets in the match, and the Australians, requiring 90, were dismissed for 66. At A. G. Steel's suggestion, the score was printed on a silk scarf and presented to the joyful rector. Playing at Blackheath, W. G. Grace threw his cap in the air on hearing the good news.

Odd incidents, worthy of anecdote, but not cumulative in overall effect, had, then, dotted Lancashire's chequered tale through the 1880s. With four or five players of international status in the side, it was but a moderate display. There were external reasons, such as Nottinghamshire's enjoyment of a purple patch and a surging advance by Surrey, whilst the Lancashire batting remained normally inferior to its masterful bowling. However, one must be persuaded that the sting of 1881 and 1882 was drawn by acrid controversy.

Talented teams attract envious criticism as well as fulsome congratulation, and Lancashire was the target for two allied squeals of denigration. The first such fault-finding adverted to throwing. It must first be said that 'chucking' was by no means unknown among the amateurs of minor cricket. Bowling had slowly evolved from, literally, bowling, of the type now to be viewed in the parks and leisure centres of the land. First, the roundarm version had replaced underhand lobbing, and, as late as 1880, Frank Townsend, the Gloucestershire amateur, had taken 6 for 58 at Old Trafford with his underarm bowls. It was only in the 1860s that bowling with the arm above shoulder level had been legitimised, whereby the bowler was altogether liberated, and, indeed, observed to be the more puristic the closer the arm to the head.

Uniformity of propulsion was not yet apparent, and there were several men, bowling spontaneously and primitively, whose action was technically illegal, but whose motivation was not in question. That is, they bowled without intellectual analysis of their action or consciousness of unfairness. On the whole, the umpires kept mum, and the flaw continued unhindered. *Lillywhite's Companion* of 1880 protested against this lawlessness, and, in the first-class game, attention centred on Lancashire. Both Alec Watson and George Nash were under grave suspicion, but, as is usual in this issue, slower bowlers were not regarded as too troublesome. The real enmity was reserved for John Crossland, by 1882 the fastest bowler probably in England. He bowled straight, inclining toward a zippy yorker, and a huge proportion of his victims were clean-bowled, some testimony to the possibility that he did not pitch overly short.

Nevertheless, there is little doubt that his action was questionable and that, for a long while, he bowled – or threw – without check or inhibition. It first reached a climax at the Oval in 1882, when, as he bowled out ten of his 11 victims, ironic shouts of 'well thrown' arose from the partisan crowd. As previously hinted, the Oval spectators had already observed Crossland in volcanic flow, and found the sight infuriating. He found it hard to push his way through to the pavilion, assailed as he was by friend and foe.

1883 was worse. The demonstrations, as is their wont, escalated and spread. W. G. Grace silenced the Clifton crowd before taking a hundred off Crossland and his fellow bowlers, while noisy outbursts accompanied Crossland at Trent Bridge, Gravesend and the Oval. The Surrey match came near to abandonment, as, at the end of the home team's first innings, a row raged for half an hour.

The Australians had objected to the throwers in 1882, and Nottinghamshire dropped their fixtures with Lancashire from 1884 to 1886, because of 'grave doubts about the fairness of the bowling of two players'. Now Lord Harris, the aristocratic captain of Kent, decided to resolve the problem. After more overtures in *Lillywhite's Companion*, he proposed the 'absolutely satisfied' clause to be included in the umpires' instructions, and refused to play in the Old Trafford Test when Crossland was included in the squad. After Kent's defeat in 1885, Harris wrote at length to the Lancashire committee, in sorrow that they had not followed the lead of others counties in outlawing suspect bowlers. The return match at Tonbridge was allowed by Kent to go by default.

Lord Harris attempted to retain what he termed 'the most cordial character' of relations between the counties, and he expressly, and perhaps wrongly, exonerated Hornby from all blame. For its part, the Lancashire committee offered its beleaguered employees spirited backing, dispatching the correspondence to Lord's, reminding one and all that the bowlers had never been called for throwing, and that Crossland had been selected to play for the North versus the South at headquarters. The debate continued, and Crossland was subject to derogatory cries at Hove. Curiously, none of these dubious bowlers had been penalised by an umpire, and yet, some time later, the Lancashire amateur, G. E. Jowett was called for throwing at Liverpool in the Surrey match.

It is at this point that it seems, logically if not chronologically, the moment to introduce the second gripe mounted against Lancashire, and that was their use of professionals drafted in from outside the county. In a nutshell, Nottinghamshire had drawn the MCC's attention in 1883 to Crossland's residential qualification, suggesting that he lived in Nottinghamshire in the winter months. At first, MCC adjudged in Crossland's and Lancashire's favour, but, finding that he returned to the midland county in October 1884 for some five months, they reversed their decision and disqualified him. He played his last match against Cheshire at Stockport in June 1885 and George Nash, the other possible culprit, soon dropped out of the first-class game.

Whether Crossland was hounded the more for his doubtful action or his doubtful residential permit is a moot issue, but it serves to demonstrate how serious, and how confusing, a subject it was.

It became most acrimonious. Edmund Rowley, by no means an intemperate man, remarked that Nottinghamshire 'take up themselves the work of the umpires'. In one of cricket's more infamous exchanges, the two counties used the festive tide of 1883–84 for a heavyweight and decidedly uncharitable correspondence. Lancashire's Christmas card to Trent Bridge was in the form of cricketing rules as dictated by the Nottinghamshire Club. These involved Lancashire batsmen using broom handles, their bowlers being refused permission to bowl and no stumps being utilised, the umpires appointed being 'strictly Notts men', and Nottinghamshire refusing to finish the game should defeat loom.

Nottinghamshire replied with a rather more laconic and telling New Year missive, proposing 'the only rules necessary' for Lancashire players would be 'that they shall neither have been born in, nor reside in, Lancashire. Sutton-in-Ashfield men will have the preference'. Both Crossland and Briggs were natives of their specified township.

It was a vexed question. In the late 1860s some players had represented two and sometimes three counties during the season. Amateurs joined the most convenient club, while professionals, after the style of Victorian tradesmen, plied their craft wherever hiring was possible. Nottinghamshire had always taken the lead in the 'county-born' convention, and, eventually, in 1873 the MCC had confirmed the opinion of county representatives that cricketers, amateur or professional, should play for only one county during the same season, and that either birth or residence, as affirmed by two years presence, could act as the qualification. It is interesting that, in 1881, Lord Harris vainly tried to have the residential term decreased to one year.

Now Lancashire were perhaps the worst offenders or the most enterprising in this regard, depending on one's predilection. Commencing with William McIntyre, the fast bowler recruited in the 1870s, Lancashire had, in H. S. Altham's phrase, 'embarked upon a deliberate policy of professional seduction'. Certainly, by the time of the first outright title in 1881, five paid players were not Lancastrians, and, in fact, Barlow was the sole Lancashire-born professional. '. . . but it must not be forgotten,' wrote Grace, 'that other counties would have been glad to have had them on similar conditions, and that it was owing to the committee of the county club and the excellent judgement of Mr Hornby that they had been originally selected and their powers developed.' That was fair comment from a man who, despite his own ambiguous financial position apropos cricket, came from a county almost entirely dependent on amateurs.

It will be seen that the main reason for curbing professional migration was an attempt to obtain some control over too cavalier a series of transits, rather than to underline the ethics of county birthright. There was, of course, some scope for Nottinghamshire and Yorkshire to stand on the dignity of birthplace, for they both enjoyed an apparently endless flow of native-born cricketers. The trades of those two areas had been much later than Lancashire's in moving from small-scale to factory-based and from broken time to regular clock-working. The tradition of being available for a half-day or day here and there had nursed professional cricket in the broad acres and midland dales, and the heritage was a sound one. Other counties – Gloucestershire, Middlesex – saw themselves more as gentlemen's clubs, with a little hired help, usually bowlers, to assist with the chores.

Lancashire adopted a third tack. Its urban districts were well used to incomers. Business had attracted workers from all over the country and entrepreneurs from overseas. In particular, Manchester sought to reflect its influential situation in cultural manifestations, and the Lancashire committee, with Albert Hornby taking the lead, was anxious to develop a successful club, one capable of sustaining the pride of the new cottonopolis. The membership could find the money and a worthy team would draw a paying audience. Lancashire businessmen had an unbeatable economy: they yearned for a winning cricket team. They went about it the best way they knew how, by recruiting talent and then shrewdly deploying it. Soon others would copy.

One admits to a little ambivalence. One enjoys complaisantly the doings of one's fellow county-men, basking luxuriously in their reflections of provincial character. Equally, one rejoices in the association with success, whosoever provides it. That trait is very noticeable in football, where nationalities forgather to represent a suburb of London or a sector of Birmingham or Manchester.

This arises, in part, from the dual role played by each county, on the one hand a private subscriber club, and on the other hand an attempt to rally public support around local colours. Lancashire's approach was neither better nor worse than Nottinghamshire's or Gloucestershire's: it was different.

A key reason for the difference was the continued expansion of Manchester, and, indeed, its neighbouring towns. By the late 1880s Manchester's population had touched half a million, some of it due to the gradual consolidation of the surrounding townships after 1885 and which continued for a quarter of a century. Familiar place-names – Crumpsall, Chorlton-cum-Hardy, Moss Side, Didsbury and so on – were incorporated within the booming city.

Following the great municipal innovations and reforms of mid-century came the beginnings of modern transport. The 1870 Tramways Act introduced what Richard Hoggart called 'the gondolas of the people', the stately tram-cars to convey workers and employers alike in unhurried style. Train services continued to extend and improve, so that, by the last years of the century, Manchester and its environs were fully mobilised.

Manchester and the cotton towns fared prosperously in most of these years; living conditions were improved; and working hours were shorter – by now most workers were down to a 55-hour week, with Saturday half-day and a wakes week. It was the onset of the golden era of collective leisure, with many willing and able to forgather in groups and crowds for their entertainment.

The department stores and a score of music halls opened and thrived, while Belle Vue pleasure and zoological gardens in West Gorton, founded in 1836, soon became the Crystal Palace of the North. Blackpool was a Victorian invention, its famous tower erected in 1895. People went out to enjoy themselves. By the early twentieth century there would be 500 brass band performances a year in Manchester, attracting two and a half million spectators. There were the parks, like Phillips Park or Queen's Park, established in 1846. There were the horse races at Kersal Moor and Castle Irwell. There was cycling – the Manchester Wheelers began in 1883 – and there was the Agecroft Rowing Club. Manchester City, née West Gorton FC, started life in 1880, and Manchester United née Newton Heath Loco, about 1878.

In 1887 a special building was constructed for the Royal Jubilee Exhibition, 'a wonderful example of the spirit, energy and organising power of Manchester at that time'. Approaching five million went and marvelled at the exhibits of artistry and industry on display. A year later Manchester became a county borough, under the terms of the seminal local government statute of that year, and in 1893 its first Lord Mayor was elected. The *Manchester Guardian* had outstripped its local rivals, and, as newspaper readership extended radically in the last two decades of the century, its national prominence grew. And, of course, a lively aspect of the press boom was the coverage of cricket and other sports.

A. N. Hornby, writing in Prince Ranjitsinhji's *The Jubilee Book of Cricket*, summed up the progress made, the county club keeping vigorous time with the bustling cottonopolis:

The committee are mainly composed of men who in the past liberally aided it practically and financially, and from the time, some 25 years back, when an annual deficit was customary, the club has been worked forward to a position of affluence. It is a matter of such dimensions now that it is more of a huge business.

Hornby recorded some of the figures of this 'huge business'. There were 2800 members and 650 lady subscribers; whereas, at the commencement of his career, there had been two, there were now 23 professionals; as well as a doubling of county fixtures, the Manchester club now played 80 matches, four times as many as ten years previously; and over 200,000 passed the turnstiles. In 1894, Hornby reported, over £9000 was expended on a splendid new pavilion. 1894: that was the year Queen Victoria opened the Manchester Ship Canal and secured a further boost and dimension to the Mancunian economy, making possible, for instance, the success of the vast Trafford Park engineering complex, just across the way from Old Trafford. The club, said Hornby, had never been 'in a more healthy and flourishing position'.

Albert Hornby persisted in his keen-edged leadership of the

county for a couple more years, before sharing the honour with S.
M. Crosfield for two more seasons. Picking up the tale in 1889,
Lancashire won ten matches in the Championship, and shared a
triple title. These included the single defeats of Middlesex, and of
Gloucestershire, and spirited doubles over Surrey, Yorkshire
and Kent. There were three losses, to Nottinghamshire, Middlesex and Gloucestershire, and a drawn game with the powerful
Nottinghamshire combine. The title was shared with that
Nottinghamshire eleven and with a resurgent Surrey team, and, in
truth, with only eight really counting in the league, three winnners
was not too satisfactory.

It was, however, an extremely good year for the bowlers. Three
followed Attewell, the Nottinghamshire bowler, in the national
averages: Briggs, 140 wickets, average 11; Arthur Mold, showing
first promise as a fast bowler, 102, also at 11, and the consistent
Watson, 90 at 12 – and this in the season when the four-ball over
changed to five. Albert Ward, with 822 runs, came to public note
for the first time, but the batting, with Barlow injured, was only
moderate. Some of this was blamed on an Old Trafford pitch
which showed signs of disintegration, and Walker, the Trent
Bridge groundsman, was summoned to give a second opinion.

In 1890 and in 1891, Lancashire were runners up to Surrey,
hereabouts enjoying a spell rather akin to their form of the 1950s.
The illness and death of Pilling, the injury and sickness of Briggs
(although, in 1890, he took 86 county wickets, 158 in all matches
and topped the rather erratic batting) the dearth of Barlow's form
and A. N. Hornby's mounting years all created a burden. Fifteen
games were lost over those two seasons. There were memorable
days. Archie MacLaren made his début, while captain of Harrow,
at Brighton. Going in with the score 23 for 3, he made an
irreproachable 108 in just over two hours. In the same season,
Watson and Briggs scattered Sussex for 34 and 24, their match
figures, respectively, 9 for 13 and 10 for 41, while, in the next
summer, the pace of Mold brought him a haul of 129 wickets.

Lancashire lost another ten games in the next two seasons, 1892
and 1893, ending fourth and second. Throughout Hornby's
impressive reign, Lancashire never really played poorly. His
control was such that, even with luck or form running against
them, they rarely sunk low in the table. However, Hornby himself
managed to play eight times in those last two somewhat confused
years. With Barlow gone, a little too early for some tastes,

perhaps including his own, Briggs and Mold tolerated a huge onus, occasionally bowling unchanged throughout the day or the innings. In 1892, for instance, they shot out Somerset for 88 and 58, their match figures being Mold, 8 for 40, Briggs, 12 for 83.

Lancashire hearts were possibly more warmed in the early 1890s by several victories over Yorkshire. In one such contest, Albert Ward scored 180, then the highest individual score in a 'roses' match, before Briggs took 8 for 113. Watson and Briggs then bowled out Yorkshire a second time, for a convincing innings victory. Briggs also took 8 for 19 at Headingley in 1893, the scene of another Lancastrian win. The double was completed back at Old Trafford in an exciting match played before a crowd of 28,000. Lancashire made only 64 and 50. Yorkshire had scraped 58 in their first innings, and, relative to the abysmal scores assembled, made an ominously good start in their second. They were 24 without loss, and then, of a sudden, 47 all out, and Lancashire were home by nine runs. It was a storybook finish, with Ward catching Yorkshire's redoubtable Ulyett on the pavilion rails, cries of incompetent umpiring, and, predictably, Briggs taking 11 for 60 in the match.

Nonetheless, and compared with the halcyon days of the early 1880s, it was a little disappointing. Despite the remarkable feats of Johnny Briggs, Frank Sugg, Albert Ward and Arthur Mold, the chemistry was not quite right. The county even went so far, in the summer of 1893, as advertising for bowlers, and, smarting under the trenchant criticism of the seeming geographic ineptitude of the Lancashire committee, 'young ones, and Lancashire born preferred' was added to the bill.

Lancashire now turned with renewed hope to 1894. S. M. Crosfield, who was a solicitor, found that he could not often captain the side, as he had, along with Hornby, for two years. Hornby's gradient of retirement now saw him installed as Lancashire's president, and, intrepidly, he sought the appointment of his fellow-Harrovian, the young MacLaren, for the post. He was but 22 years old. Thus, in the year that the new pavilion, the basic construct of today's eminent edifice, was built. A. N. Hornby became president, and Queen Victoria opened the Manchester Ship Canal, Lancashire's most magnetic character assumed the reins of captaincy.

# 3. MacLaren's Years

## 424 at Taunton

Archie MacLaren, original and recurrent inspiration of the Cardus muse, began nervously as captain. There was a messy transition, as S. M. Crosfield, A. N. Hornby and a third amateur, A. T. Kemble, shared the leadership over nine games, before MacLaren took over an inchoate team. He had successfully skippered Lancashire once the previous season, but Lancashire were hereabouts losing match after match. His first two outings as skipper were losses to Nottinghamshire, by an innings, and to Kent. They were parlous days.

Now the youngest captain in county cricket began to reveal some of his dominant quality: the next two games were won, and, in fact, only one more county match was lost that season. Lancashire ended a commendable fourth in the table, chiefly because of the burden laid on Mold and Briggs. They bowled over 1500 overs and took approximately 240 wickets between them. Briggs had a disappointing benefit, arising from Lord Hawke's objection to a wicket that had been covered to guarantee play. Yorkshire won on a fresh and fiercesome strip, but Johnny Briggs enjoyed the modest vengeance of bowling the noble and intractable lord for a duck. He also bowled W. G. Grace four times in that season, while Mold took 13 wickets, including a hat-trick and, later, three in four balls in Somerset's one-day rout.

Archie MacLaren enjoyed a huge success with A. E. Stoddart's team in Australia over the subsequent winter, but, arriving home late after a detour via Japan, he missed the opening match, and failed in the next two. He then took himself off to be a preparatory schoolmaster in Harrow, leaving S. M. Tindall to captain a side of varying fortunes. It was, therefore, mid-July, just after the Eton and Harrow match, that MacLaren rejoined Lancashire at Taunton, where Tyler almost bowled him first ball of the match.

That was Somerset's nearest chance until MacLaren was over 250. A man who had played no first-class or much other kind of cricket for over a month now proceeded to consolidate his growing reputation. It was, as the newspapers said in their headlines, 'phenomenal scoring'.

Albert Ward, who had also done well with Stoddart's team in Australia, first of all added 141 with Archie MacLaren, and then A. G. Paul joined him in a partnership of 363 in a little over three hours. Paul's share was 177. It was Lancashire's first partnership of 300, and remains third in order of the county's stands. It was only 35 short of the then world-record partnership. At close of play Lancashire were 555 for three, and averaging a hundred an hour. It was not until 1910 that a captain was free to declare any time on the second day, although it is unlikely MacLaren would have missed the opportunity to overtake Grace's record of 344 and become the first player in first-class history to reach 400. At 792 he was eventually caught in the deep, having given just two harsh chances, for 424. It took him only 470 minutes, and included one six, that is, out of the ground, and 64 boundary fours, the second-most boundaries in an innings ever. Lancashire were all out for 801, and won by an innings and 452 runs. It was Lancashire's highest ever total, and, at that juncture, the highest first-class total recorded.

No one need pretend that Somerset's bowling was more than adequate, and Essex had scored 692 against it in the previous game. Nonetheless, their opening attack consisted of S. M. J. Woods, the Australian Test player and Somerset's captain, and E. J. Tyler, soon to be capped for England, and they ended the season with five wins to persuade one and all that they were genuine first-class material. There had certainly been quadruple centuries in minor cricket – for instance, Grace, with exactly 400 (because of a scorer's late adjustment in one version) in 1875 against XXII of Grimsby and A. E. Stoddart, MacLaren's friend, equally amazingly with 485 in a club game. But Archie MacLaren's 424 remains the highest first-class score in England, or by an Englishman anywhere, way out in front of Hutton's 364 in 1938.

Three times between the wars Ponsford, twice and Bradman passed MacLaren's figure, although MacLaren was a trifle grumpy over Tasmania being counted as first-class quality in 1923. Three times more since the war has the 400-mark been reached on the Indian subcontinent. All six of these emulations were completed on bone-hard wickets, while MacLaren, of course, was playing in a normal county match on an ordinary late Victorian pitch. And then in 1988 the precocious Zimbabwean, Graeme Hick, against poor Somerset at Taunton, scored a dazzling 405 not out – with finer bowling and fielding if on a pleasanter pitch with shorter boundaries.

It has rightly been said that, in the eight days of 1876 when he scored two triple centuries and over 800 runs in all, W. G. Grace redefined the concept of first-class cricket. Now his 'great favourite', Archie MacLaren, endorsed that revision. With three centuries in the last week of the season, he led Lancashire to second place, just behind Surrey, and himself to first place, above Grace, in the English averages. His county sum was 1162, average 58. Ward, with 1486 runs, and Mold, with 192 wickets, were his doughtiest allies. Crowds flocked to see them. 25,000 watched one day of the Yorkshire match and 20,000 turned up for the first day of the Kent match.

Yet, despite these achievements, the limelight justifiably remains on those first two days at Taunton. The skill, energy, determination and concentration required to score 400 runs, constantly avoiding the tiniest of slips that so conclusively terminate an ambitious innings, is extraordinary. Like the first 147-break at snooker or the first four-minute mile, it needs additional physical and mental stamina to break through the threshold ahead of the others. Quantitatively, it remains – the magnificent Hick, nearly a century later, apart – the best individual batting performance ever in the County Championship; indeed, there have only been some 30 scores of 300 or more in all the county matches. No bowler has taken 20 wickets in any match, let alone a County Championship match, although 14 have taken 17 wickets, and umpteen ten in an innings, most notably Hedley Verity's 10 for 10 against Notts in 1932. Archie MacLaren has some claim, then, to the finest personal performance in the saga of county cricket, and, away from the statistics, the doing of it commanded the kind of respect and stimulation that attends a theatrical creation by a great actor, the Hamlet of Olivier, the Lear of Wolfit. And, a judiciously sobering footnote, Somerset bowled 28 five-ball overs an hour, an heroic effort which shames the dilatory rates of the modern dispensation.

*The 1897 Championship and Afterwards*

For the fifth time in seven summers, Lancashire were runners-up in the Championship in 1896, a tribute to the magnificent bowling of Briggs (145 wickets) and Mold (137 wickets) and a thousand runs apiece from Frank Sugg and the dependable Albert Ward. With so strongly balanced a side, it was all but inevitable that the first prize would be gained, and 1897 proved to be one of Lancashire's greatest seasons. MacLaren relinquished the captaincy early on to the elder statesman, Hornby, for a couple of years, and, in fact, his teaching and other commitments made him an irregular until the turn of the century. On the credit side, however, they found two bowlers to support Briggs and Mold. It is difficult to exaggerate Lancashire's dependence on this pair. For example, when they took 97 and 144 county wickets respectively in 1894, the third best performer took only nine wickets. A. Hallam and Willis Cuttell, a Yorkshireman, qualified through residence in and playing for Nelson, lent them well-earned succour.

With A. N. Hornby insisting on the sort of preparation and practice that had perhaps been insufficient over the last two or three years, Lancashire made an ideal start. They beat Derbyshire, Hampshire, Leicestershire, Middlesex and Derbyshire again, all in good order, with only a draw with Nottinghamshire to deny them early maximum points. The Kent match, which was Frank Sugg's benefit, was, like others of that ilk, ruined by rain, and then the strong Surrey side defeated Lancashire. In mid-season, there was a flurry of wins and draws, the former over Somerset, Gloucestershire and Essex, the latter with Warwickshire, in both matches, Sussex and Yorkshire. Other teams, notably, Nottinghamshire and, surprisingly, Essex were in contention, and Surrey were preparing for a fine, late run. Nonetheless, and with Archie MacLaren returned in superlative trim – 596 in a handful of matches, including 244 in 300 minutes and his second double hundred in two years against Kent at Canterbury – the title was to be Lancashire's.

They won eight of their last 11 games, losing two to Essex and Surrey, who completed the double over them, and drawing with Middlesex. They beat Nottinghamshire in the last match, Cuttell taking 12 wickets, and Surrey, losing and drawing their last two games, had to be satisfied with the spot Lancashire had so often recently occupied. In one spell Briggs took 36 wickets in three games.

Apart from MacLaren's late summer surge, the batting was consistently impressive. For the first time, four batsmen – John Tyldesley, newly consolidated in the team, G. R. Baker, Frank Sugg and Albert Ward – passed a thousand runs. The 50-year-old Hornby was still capable of useful scores as well. The bowling quartet was even more telling, their joint penetrative endeavours producing no less than 445 wickets. Mold had 88 wickets, Hallam 90, Willis Cuttell 112 and Johnny Briggs 155. The range from Mold's dynamic pace to Briggs's intricate spin was sweeping enough to discomfort almost all teams, and Briggs's average in county games was 16.5. The wicket-keeping during these seasons was done by the competent C. Smith whose career record of 411 victims puts him in the big five of red rose stumpers, his Yorkshire birthright notwithstanding, although Lees Radcliffe, tidy and uneffacing, kept for most of 1897 owing to Smith being, as the journalists then ferociously termed it, 'maimed'.

Perhaps because of the vigour of Hornby's renewed generalship, perhaps because of the unremitting nature of the Lancashire attack, the fielding rallied and excited critical attention. MacLaren and Tyldesley brought fresh grace and strength to that department, the young amateur already judged to be, at international level, possibly the pick of English fielders. The fielding had not quite the comprehension and panache of Hornby's earlier champions, but it was measurably improved on the last few seasons, and, like many a title, much depended on it. The wicket-keeping, after Pilling, was inevitably less striking, assessed, that is, by his standard of perfection, but it was as good as any in England. The bowling was probably as purposeful as the 1881 attack, except that A. G. Steel added the piquancy of the leg-break as a fifth bowler, whilst the batting was overall more definite in aim and endurance.

One is now poised at the doorway to the golden age of batting, in some views, of all cricket, and 1895, in particular, MacLaren's 424 at Taunton, is often seen as the point of entry. It was also the season when Lancashire, and other counties, played over 20 county matches for the first time, for the Championship was now a larger and more organised affair. In 1897 Lancashire played 26 county matches, twice as many as when they took the title in 1881. To that extent, winning it necessitated a firmer and more lasting resolve, and there is little doubt that, by 1897, the title was that much more a precious prize. Incidentally, Lancashire also entertained, and defeated, the visiting Philadelphians in 1897, and Lancashire spectators had a rare chance of seeing the American J. B. King, one of the greatest fast bowlers in history.

Old Trafford was now well appointed and, both by members and fans, well attended. Since 1880 the Lancashire county and the Manchester club had stood in formal as well as organic union, and there was plenty of cricket for a sizeable professional staff, the seniors usually in receipt of £2 a week in the summer, and match pay, with a winter retainer of twenty-five shillings. It was decent money for a working man in the 1890s. Lacrosse was sometimes played at Old Trafford in the winter, while there were also occasional tennis championships. The committee still met at the Queen's Hotel, where the species had originated, or at a small office near the Royal Exchange. The link with cotton was by no means tenuous, and, until as late as 1937, an administrative office was centrally retained by Lancashire in Barton Arcade in the middle of Manchester. Then, after intermittent haggling over the lease and rejected offers of purchase, Lancashire bought the ground outright in 1898 for £24,000, a reasonable investment, one might today cautiously estimate. The crucial negotiator was James MacLaren, honorary treasurer from 1881 to 1900, and father of Archie. And Fred Reynolds was still in statu as assistant secretary, his wages now at £200 per annum.

As for the other counties, the famed 'octarchy' now faced rivalry from others, although, truth to tell, the 'octarchy' continued to fare uncommonly well. Derbyshire had flitted on and off the first-class stage, but became conclusively a member of the élite in 1895, while Somerset had replaced Derbyshire in 1891 and remained constant. 1895, the year of MacLaren's 424 at Taunton, was the season when the mould was broken. As well as Derbyshire, Warwickshire, Essex, Hampshire and Leicestershire were ushered into the first-class arena. Worcestershire in 1899, Northamptonshire in 1905 and, the only post-1918 entrants, Glamorgan in 1921, completed today's changeless 17. The number of county matches had increased from maybe a couple of dozen in the 1870s to about 150 by the end of the century. It had not been until 1886 that there had been a real distinction drawn between first- and second-class counties, which had led to some of the confusion about positions in the tables, and the points system offically dates from 1890, after a more informal set-up since 1888. Cricket had considered, and eschewed, football's innovations. In 1873 a primitive attempt to copy the FA knock-out cup failed, with Lancashire opining that cricket had no need, such was its popularity, for such a gimmick and fearing that gambling, the bane of pre-Victorian cricket, might return. The County Cricket Council, self-constituted in 1887, next proposed a promotion and relegation scheme like the Football League's. This was much opposed, especially by the lesser counties, and, indeed, the Council quickly collapsed, with full rights surrendered to the MCC in 1894.

The 1888 County Cricket Act had made minor changes to shire boundaries, and, more particularly, it had altered the metropolitan landscape, forming the London County Council, which, under Grace's captaincy, operated a county eleven for a handful of seasons from 1899. The northern and midland counties were not much changed; rather were their functions and administrations modernised. Thus there was a spankingly new endorsement for the county concept, just prior to the MCC taking over complete responsibility, albeit, from 1903, with a county advisory board. All this rationalisation took place as the amateur revival came to fruition. These were the palmy summers of C. B. Fry, Ranjitsinhji and G. L. Jessop. In 1900 there were only two professionals in the top 20 of the batting averages.

Arguably, Lancashire had the best of both worlds in MacLaren and Tyldesley. It was a double act that bettered the Hornby and Barlow one, and, at the same time, suited the mood of the era. Archie MacLaren was among the best three or four amateurs of that most gifted generation, while John Tyldesley was barely matched by a fellow professional when at his peak. Ward continued in regular productivity, but the other stalwarts, Baker and Sugg, were to finish in a season or so. It was, however, the bowling that caused anxiety, and the 54-year old Alec Watson was asked to stand by in case of emergency for the Surrey match at the Oval in 1898. Mold's knee bothered him, Briggs seemed stale, Hallam suffered illness and James Hallows was crippled with a strain.

Lancashire slumped to a disappointing sixth in a damp 1898, winning only nine. MacLaren did not play much, but he shared in a stand against Kent of 155 with Tyldesley, who scored 1918, average 39, in all games. Willis Cuttell, the Sheffield expatriate, distinguished himself by becoming the first Lancashire player to perform the double. All first-class matches considered, he just eased himself into that distinction with 114 wickets and 1003 runs. On the debit side, Tom Hayward, Surrey's equivalent of Johnny Tyldesley, blasted an undefeated 315 out of a total of 634. This is the highest total scored against Lancashire, and no other county has scored over 600 in an innings, although the Rest of England were 603 for 8 in the champion's match at the Oval in 1928. Hayward's individual contribution remains the only triple century administered against Lancashire. The committee was right to worry about the bowling.

Like Sarah Bernhardt, Albert Hornby retired again, the captaincy shared between MacLaren and the Oxford University player, G. R. Bardwell. Lancashire crawled up to fourth. Mold took a hundred wickets, and Tyldesley once more dominated with 1868 runs, average 42. Against the Australian tourists he scored 56 out of 102 and 42 out of 81, as Lancashire went down heavily. In the second innings, the next-best humanoid contribution was six, although extras managed 16.

As the century turned, the Lancashire committee strove to secure more completely the services of Archie MacLaren by appointing him assistant secretary for three years. His clerical duties were nil – Fred Reynolds still negotiated the administrative jobs of such a post – and his coaching was no more than involved him in the captaincy. It was rumoured that his salary was £40 a week. As, like several other amateurs, he also undertook journalist work – in his case, reports on Lancashire matches for the *Daily Express*, often with deadlines only met with the aid of other players – his financial position was a good deal firmer. Earlier, Lancashire had paid him generous expenses to tour Australia, and, later, MacLaren organised a tour to Australia at some profit to himself. In the years before the First World War he was also employed by a wine merchant, with the condition that his cricket playing would not be affected. Later he became private secretary to his close friend, Prince Ranjitsinhji. MacLaren managed to embrace every stratagem for being in receipt of money for playing cricket without losing his amateur status.

Like Grace and some other amateurs, MacLaren was caught on the horns of a Victorian dilemma. His father had managed to send only three of his several sons, including Archibald, to Harrow, and university was not economically possible. Yet his social standing was such that there was no fashion in which he could have been employed as a professional. For many such as MacLaren the term 'gentlemen' was more appropriate than 'amateurs', in the sense that it referred to social caste rather than lack of remuneration. The urban class-distinction of a commercial centre like Manchester was every bit as rigid as in the older rural economies. Like the parson and the ploughman on the village-green side, MacLaren and Tyldesley, wellnigh equal in prowess and spirit and conjoined by deep mutual respect, were yet parted by an uncrossable gulf. It was the same cleft which divided the members in the pavilion from the paying customers on the terraces. The purer establishment was no more happy with the accommodation made by MacLaren than it had been with the similar one made by Grace, and it has been suggested that, in part, it led to MacLaren's forfeiture of the England captaincy in 1903. But, for all the dark stain of hypocrisy, Archie MacLaren remained the businessman, while John Tyldesley was the tradesman.

Nonetheless, it suited Lancashire, a club wishful of finding favour with both its subscribing members and its spectators, and for eight years, with MacLaren at the helm, uncluttered by too many distractions, the county basked in success. It was a triumph of quality rather than prizes. Nottinghamshire in the formative years and latterly Surrey had offered the keenest rivalry, and now Yorkshire, winning six titles from the opening of the new century to the First World War, frequently confounded Lancashire's resplendent essays.

Lancashire were, in these years, runners-up twice and always in the top six, including their impressive championship of 1904. It was a phase of stirring individual deeds, like Briggs's 10 for 55 in 29 overs against Worcestershire in 1900 at Old Trafford, a feat only paralleled twice in the county's story; like the bowling of the tempestuous Brearley, who took 17 for 137 against Somerset in 1905, a feat only paralleled once. L. O. S. Poidevin, an Australian studying medicine at Manchester University, scored five centuries in 1905, and the all-round play of James Hallows, the bowling of another Australian qualified by residence, A. Kermode, the batting of the amateur, H. G. Garnett, and the arrival of Jack Sharp all lent assistance to the cause. Ward continued his quietly competent run-gathering a while longer, and, despite occasional poor patches and absences, MacLaren was always an enviable and predominant figure.

J. T. Tyldesley was in his pomp. In 1901 he added 408 other first-class runs to his 2633 for Lancashire to become the only Lancastrian with three thousand in a season. His average was 56, and, in 1904, 1906, 1907 and 1910, he passed the 2000-mark. It was accomplished with rare despatch and colour. These were days of huge scores. In 1905 Lancashire raced to 627 against Nottingham, with 250 from Tyldesley, and in 1906 they scored 531 against Kent, with 295, not out, from Tyldesley. As token of the high scoring, Kent lost by ten wickets although they totalled 584.

Reginald Spooner made his debut in 1899 and was, by the mid-1900s, a fluent batsman, if, unluckily for Lancashire and, indeed, England, he was perforce an irregular one, owing to his military duties. In 1906 he scored a hundred before lunch against Somerset, continuing to 240 in almost even time. Perhaps the occasion most to be savoured by observers of cricket's regality was at Aigburth in 1903. It was the dampest and chilliest summer since the Championship began, and the match against Gloucestershire was played in dismal, dank surrounds, with heavy rain foreshortening play substantially. Yet, in 210 glorious minutes, MacLaren and Spooner thundered away until 368 runs had been accumulated. It remains Lancashire's first-wicket record, and the second-highest stand for the county. MacLaren was out first for 204, Spooner following shortly afterwards with 168. MacLaren, then 32 and Spooner, then 22, represented overlapping generations: it must have been like watching Henry IV and Prince Hal combined in harmonious purpose.

## The Immediate Pre-War Years

It was not all, needless to say, plain and pacific sailing. Walter Brearley, MacLaren's bosom pal and not unlike him in disposition, was a creature of moods and absences, taking umbrage at slights and disappearing for spells. Sydney Barnes began and ended his nodding acquaintance with Lancashire. He played 46 matches over the 1899–1903 seasons, taking 225 wickets before returning to the leagues where he felt most comfortable and could dictate his own financial and sporting terms. Hallam, after much illness, went to Nottinghamshire in 1900, the reverse of most of the Old Trafford and Trent Bridge traffic. Briggs, having had the temerity to replace Rhodes in the England team at Leeds and take 3 for 53, was, that very evening, stricken so with a seizure that he had to be confined in a mental home. He recovered sufficiently to take 120 wickets in 1900, but relapsed and, sorrowfully, died in 1902. The left-handed James Hallows, uncle to Charlie Hallows, died in 1910, again only 37, and he did not play beyond 1907. Willis Cuttell went to be coach at Rugby School.

Bowlers fell like ninepins. Another dramatic case was that of Arthur Mold. His action had always been a little suspect, but there emerged an Australian umpire, Phillips, who had no truck with the respectfully closed eyes of some of his fellow arbitrators. He called Ernest Jones, the Australian fast bowler, Tyler of Somerset and the august personage of C. B. Fry, as well as Mold. No-balled at Trent Bridge in 1900, he was left out of his own benefit match against Yorkshire, taking some consolation from gathering in Lancashire's first £2000 haul. The county captains listed several bowlers who should, they agreed, not be used, but the Lancashire committee denied their authority, and played Mold in 1901. It should be added that MacLaren had been the only vote in favour of Mold among the county skippers. Jim Phillips no-balled him 18 times in the Somerset match at Old Trafford, an intrepid act which led to police protection being sought for him. Apparently under instructions from the grey eminence of Hornby to persist with him, MacLaren permitted Mold a longish bowl. It is true many players believed his action to be fair, and, in avant-garde mode, cine-photography was deployed in evidence on his behalf. Muttering the diffident and not unjustified complaint that someone might have told him he was throwing in 1889, A. W. Mold vanished from the game.

There were other diplomatic incidents, several of which revolved around the high-handed Archibald MacLaren. He resigned the captaincy because of his wife's health in 1902: Alec Eccles was appointed captain: Mrs MacLaren made a miraculous recovery, and MacLaren sought and obtained the post again. In 1901 the Old Trafford pitch was a hazardous one, the consequence of pebbles, the residue of a poorly sieved dressing. George Hirst removed Lancashire for 44 with some short-pitched bowling, an incredibly low score for that age and that batting line-up. C. J. Kortright, one of the deadliest of fast bowlers in the game, knocked out Tyldesley, who, in characteristic vein, returned shakily and then proceeded to hammer his Essex assailant. MacLaren cast a handful of the pebbles before an astonished committee when next it met. Repairs were made but, eventually, in 1908 Sam Apted, the Surrey groundsman, was called in to deliver a second opinion, as the wicket was still considered inferior.

In 1905 there was conflict at Brighton, where MacLaren insisted on batting beyond lunch on the second day, a decision so offensive to Fry that he commanded his men to bowl as in the game of bowls until the close came at 601 for 8. Nor did MacLaren enforce the follow-on, preferring to compile a further 302 for 6. He could be a most eccentric general, and a tactless one, too: he utilised his £800 testimonial fund to buy a car, the easier to manage the journey from Knutsford where his family had taken up residence, and this was much frowned upon by many of the subscribers. The motor car was still regarded as a frivolous and unnecessary adjunct to social life.

Having resigned or contemplated resigning on two or three occasions, MacLaren finally bowed out in 1907, marking the event with one of his most colourful aberrations. It was at Lord's, a place where Archie MacLaren was never at ease, due to his series of brushes with the authorities. After heavy rains and a minor pitch invasion by spectators, he claimed the pitch had been 'deliberately torn up by the public' and refused to resume the Lancashire innings, an action that led to widespread and rightful condemnation of him, for, of course, the umpires were the sole judges of the fitness of the wicket.

Although MacLaren continued to play on occasion for Lancashire until 1914, the captaincy passed for the remainder of the pre-war period to A. H. Hornby, heir of the still influential A. N. and known, predictably enough, as 'young monkey'. He could scarcely be expected to match his princely antecedent, and, although a determined leader and fearless cricketer, Lancashire fell away. Apart from being second in 1909, these were relatively lean years. Seventh in 1908 was, to date, Lancashire's worst position: they were eighth in 1913, and, ultimate offence, eleventh in 1914. Hornby, as impetuously partial to hunting as to cricket, was unsympathetic and brusque with the professionals, especially in the initial seasons of his rule, and never quite created a side to challenge collectively for the title.

These matters are relative to previous heady seasons, and, here and there, exciting cricket was played and enjoyed. Harry Dean, with his slow-medium left-arm swerve, bowled well, his so-called 'in-curve' gaining him 179 wickets in 1911, as well as at least a hundred victims in every season 1907 to 1913 inclusive. He was easily the most penetrating bowler of the immediate post-MacLaren years, and his 17 for 91 at Aigburth against Yorkshire in 1913 stands as one of only two occasions Lancashire players have taken 17 wickets in a county match. He was something of a MacLaren discovery.

Lol Cook, the off-spinner, contributed both accurate length and anguished appeals. Jack Sharp, Billy Huddleston, J. S. Heap, Spooner and Brearley on occasion, as well, ineluctably, as John Tyldesley, also did well. Ernest Tyldesley, Harry Makepeace and, in the 1914 season foreclosed by war, Cecil Parkin, made welcome starts to fine careers, but it was often more patches of brilliance than co-ordinated assault. Reggie Spooner scored 2300 runs in the sunny months of 1911. This included 200 not out, against Yorkshire (Lancashire's highest in the 'roses' matches), and 186 against Hampshire when Lancashire scored 676 in 6½ hours. Their victory, by an innings and 455, is the county's most convincing in its history. And, in the previous season, Lancashire had defeated Somerset by an innings and 248 runs. J. T. Tyldesley (158) and Alfred Hartley (234, a career best) contributed largely to a total of 558 for 6. There was also a piquant week in the June of 1913 when the brothers Tyldesley hit centuries together both against Leicester and Surrey, while, in the wetness of 1912, the Australians were beaten by 24 runs, and, in 1913, for the pleasure of George V, a third roses match was played at Aigburth during the King's Merseyside visit.

However, the most historic moment of A. H. Hornby's none too picturesque reign occurred in 1910. Lancashire had managed but 162 in response to Nottingham's 376 at Old Trafford, but the follow-on was not enforced, Lancashire were thus left something over five hours to score exactly 400 for victory. This they achieved. J. T. Tyldesley (91) and that most consistent cricketer, Jack Sharp (102), added 191 in 2½ hours, before Hornby, wondrously cured of a crippling limp, scored an unbeaten 55. He was, to quote from his *alter ludus*, in at the death, with just two minutes to spare. It was the first time a Championship side had hit more than 400 runs to win a game. As if not quite believing what they had attained, Lancashire then broke their own record, with 404 for 5 to defeat Hampshire down at Southampton. Sharp, Makepeace, Hartley and William Tyldesley made the majority of the runs and it took only 300 minutes.

Aside from chequered cricket, there were bubbles and squeaks of trouble off the field. Fred Reynolds, the Everyman of Lancashire cricket, severed his 48 years of connection with the club in 1908: he died in 1915. His replacement for the £200-per-annum post attracted over 300 applicants, among them military gentlemen and music hall entertainers. Richard Barlow replaced Reynolds as ground manager and coach, and, in turn, Albert Ward succeeded him in 1910. He was sacked in 1912, but, a year later, Arthur Paul, partner to MacLaren in Somerset's trouncing at Taunton in 1895, was appointed coach. It was all somewhat unsettling, and some of it was down to flustered economics.

Lancashire ran into serious financial troubles during these years, with, that familiar if unpopular equation, crowds down and expenses up. The members' subscription and the spectators' sixpenny entrance had been unchanged for close on 50 years, but a shilling charge, when the Australians toured in 1912, alarmed by the paucity of the gate. True, results were not inspired, but they were not catastrophic, although the increased absence of Mac-Laren must have been a factor. Nor was the cricket dull or lacking in colour. The leagues, with crowds frequently of four or five thousand, assuredly exerted a counter tug to the pleasures of Old Trafford, particularly as travel was negligible and the affair was disposed of during the Saturday half-day and early evening.

The cultural countdown to the First World War may also have had an effect. Other counties were struggling, too. The gold on cricket's shield became tarnished, and the age of Fry and Ranjitsinhji and Jessop, as well as of MacLaren, was drawing to an end before the outbreak of war. Edwardian confidence was sapped. The sinking of the *Titanic* in 1912 has become a useful timer for that gradual collapse of assurance, and there were other signs of instability. In sport, cricket, essentially the pastoral game, backward-looking and intent on its heritage, lost much ground to association football. Until the end of the century, double the number of people watched first-class cricket as football. But football, fast and quickly done with, became the national sport: in 1901 the Crystal Palace Cup Final attracted the first paying crowd of 100,000 encountered anywhere in the modern sporting world. Manchester United and Manchester City, and other nearby league clubs, became famous, and, although obviously they played in the winter, it was more a question of mood. Somehow football looked to the future and commanded an unrestricted allegiance.

The Lancashire committee, one must presume, stayed not to ponder such deep issues. Several tactics were tried to halt the spillage of funds, a withdrawal from the Minor Counties competition and insured gates among them. Over the winter of 1913–14 a committee scheme to reduce both the number of fixtures and the players' pay, bonuses and allowances was, to his credit, challenged by A. H. Hornby, their captain, although, to be sure, the president, his father, was his ally. One distressing item, very common in labouring conditions at the time, was the attempt to deny pay to those unable to play 'for any reason including injury'. The debate raged over into the Lancashire newspapers. Portentous leading articles were drafted and published. This early and severe endeavour to use the Geddes' axe had the effect of removing dead wood. The ground was clear for financial reforms, the introduction of season tickets and permits to invite friends into the pavilion, and so forth. In the short term, and as is so often the solution in county cricket, the minor crisis stirred worthy citizens to reach for their wallets. Lord Derby led the way, soothing with the balm of diplomacy and the lubrication of sovereigns.

Nothing more demonstrated the shakiness of confidence than the variety of changes proposed for cricket during these last pre-war years. The days of starting games were unsettled and first-innings points were introduced in 1911, with five for a win and three for a first-innings lead. In 1909–10 Lancashire convinced the other counties that the points system could be simpler, and that, instead of the percentge of points to matches hitherto utilised, victories should become a deciding factor. In some ways, it was a half-hearted return to the past, and Lancashire were hoist by their own petard. During a rainy season, they won 14 and drew ten, finishing fourth under their novel scheme, whereas the older dispensation would have made them second. One should not be unfair. The move aimed at the encouragement of more positive cricket, and, from one angle, Lancashire were to be congratulated for fresh ideas. Nonetheless, the tinkering of anxiety, rather than the full-blooded revision of genuine certainty, seldom pays.

So it was that Lancashire faced the 1914–18 war having suffered the worst reverses in its playing history, although, belatedly, some of its administrative posers had been solved. As they turned to that most grievous of conflicts, many Lancastrians must have consoled themselves with the remembrance of 1904, one of the greatest summers thus far in the county's saga, the inestimable peak of MacLaren's county career, and a dish saved to luxuriate over near the end of this pre-1914 chapter.

*The 1904 Championship*

The weather and Lancashire's cricket were alike glorious in 1904. The county was unbeaten; in fact, they processed from the early August of 1903 to the July of 1905 without a loss. They won 16, and Kent, with ten wins, were next in line, and were third, pipped out of second place by Yorkshire. Lancashire drew the remaining ten matches; they drew with the visiting South Africans, and they drew, over four memorable days, with the Rest of England at the end of the season. It was a breathtaking series of engagements.

Spooner and Garnett raced to 137 in 80 minutes at the start of the first game against Leicestershire, and, somehow, that was the talisman or portent for the year. Cuttell's bowling reduced Leicestershire, and, in the next game, Brearley's 12 wickets undermined Worcestershire, during which game Spooner, this time with Tyldesley, cracked 80 sparkling runs in three-quarters of an hour. There was a draw with Yorkshire at Whitsuntide, and then Kent were simply shrugged aside. They were all out for 42 and lost by an innings, Hallows and Cuttell proving the most dangerous bowlers.

James Hallows (9 for 71, match figures) and Willis Cuttell (10 for 51) joined lethal forces in the next match, and this time Surrey were the vanquished, managing only 82 and 56 in each innings. Then John Tyldesley showed his fierce mettle, with 210 in just over three hours, and down went luckless Somerset at Bath by ten wickets. Gloucestershire were swept aside by an innings – Hallows 9 for 37 – but Warwickshire proved unusually defiant, enforcing the follow-on. This time Cuttell exhibited fine batting prowess, and saved the match with a century. At Old Trafford, only a hundred from C. B. Fry and 50 from Ranji gave Sussex a draw, after their attack had been demolished comprehensively by Spooner and MacLaren. They both scored centuries before lunch, and added 223 in just over two hours for the declaration.

Down at Tonbridge, Kent were defeated, with Tyldesley's 82 the prime feature; then on to the Oval, where Surrey were beaten by 72 runs and Huddleston took 7 for 72. Lancashire, back home, completed the double over Somerset, with a massive innings of 580. MacLaren had 151 in 135 minutes, Tyldesley 103, Jack Sharp had 104 not out, and Willis Cuttell 101, four centurions in the innings. The Nottinghamshire fixture at Trent Bridge was drawn, but it provided a scene of unrelenting butchery. MacLaren (166) and Tyldesley (225) demonstrated the force of their dualism at its most destructive. Their shattering stand of 324 is still Lancashire's fourth-wicket record, despite the fact that A. O. Jones bowled 29 overs to that dynamic pair down the leg-side without one fieldsman on the off-side.

Alexander Kermode, of New South Wales and qualifying in June, now made his chief and most telling intercession into Lancashire's affairs. His nine wickets, and 196 from Tyldesley, was enough to floor Worcestershire; Brearley and he next shared 15 wickets as Derbyshire fell, at home, Lancashire scoring 172 in two hours to complete the victory; and, on to Old Trafford, where Kermode's 12 wickets skittled Middlesex, so that Lancashire, with centuries from Tyldesley, inevitably, and Hallows, won by eight wickets.

Essex were the following visitors to the county's headquarters, and they were given short shrift. Spooner and Tyldesley combined for 166 in a little over an hour and a half, with Sharp and A. H. Hornby taking a further 177 off a reeling attack. Walter Brearley's match figures of 14 for 151 finished this latest attempt to knock the cock from the midden. Gloucestershire were welcomed to Aigburth, and this time Hallows donned the mantle, with a match take of 12 for 90. His impressive form was sustained at Old Trafford in the game against Worcestershire. He had 11 for 144 and it was another win.

Then there were six frustrating draws. George Hirst took his benefit at Leeds against Lancashire in a tremendous clash, during which Tyldesley batted almost through the second innings for 108, not out, to salvage the match. Lancashire travelled south for a short south-eastern tour, and, at Brighton, their progress was arrested by the genius of Ranji. His 90 and 207 prevented Lancashire from winning. Poidevin, in reply, scored 153. At Leyton, Spooner's 215 allowed Lancashire to close at 505 for 6, but Essex responded, on an ideal pitch, with 559 for 9. A little demoralised and anxious, Lancashire fell apart at Lord's and had to follow on. However, the batsmen rallied and saved the day. Lancashire returned northwards, only to draw with Nottinghamshire at Old Trafford, Poidevin's exact hundred, not out, being the domestic highlight. At Liverpool, lowly Leicestershire also scrambled a draw.

The final match was at Old Trafford against Derbyshire. An innings of 104 by Tyldesley set up a solid Lancashire victory, and the season, after that set of dispiriting draws and without

Brearley and Hallows through the high days of later August, ended on a pleasing note. What is worthy of remark is that, despite that comparative hitch in the imperial parade, Lancashire were barely challenged for the title. Winning 15 out of 19 games had put them out of sight in a runaway triumph.

It was as near as county cricket has ever come to blitzkreig. Taking supreme advantage of a dry summer and the scorched earth of the country's cricket grounds, their panzer-like assaults were as frightening in pace as in weight. They scored plenty of runs. Tyldesley (2335, average nearly 67, just for Lancashire) Spooner (1699, average 47) MacLaren (1014, average 31, and after an indifferent start) found run-getting a simple task. James Hallows also topped the thousand-mark, and, with 107 wickets, became one of only three Lancastrians ever to perform the cricketer's double. L. O. S. Poidevin was not far behind with 800 or so runs, and Jack Sharp made a couple of valuable centuries. John Tyldesley scored no less than eight centuries, Reggie Spooner five, and Archie MacLaren and James Hallows three apiece.

But it was not the quantity of runs that counted as much as the speed of the slaughter. The old metaphor of a steamroller for crushing opposition could not be more inapt. Lancashire scored their runs at an average of something over 80 an hour, and, on several occasions, they scored a hundred an hour. Apart from the practical issue of providing sufficient time for the bowling out of the opposition, it is, as generals from Attila the Hun to Rommel appreciated, the pathetic bewilderment bred among one's enemies that is literally half the battle.

Surprise is an ally of speed in military circles. Lancashire had not been expected, not even by their nearest and dearest, to do well in 1904, but their bowlers found the energy and aptitude to perform above that doleful anticipation. Apart from James Hallows's 108 wickets, Cuttell took 105, with Brearley and Kermode providing incisive support at crucial moments. The fielding was supportive, but inclined to patchiness. MacLaren himself, a brilliant fielder, was subject to rheumatism, and Tyldesley was now over 30. Spooner remained supreme in the covers, and most of the work was solid, but there was not the inhibiting corral of Hornby's field, and the wicket-keeping was competent, but no more. MacLaren was not the captain Hornby was. His more fizzy temperament was inimical to the lengthy,

**1** MacLaren's victorious 1904 champions
**2** 'My Hornby and my Barlow long ago'

a) A. N. Hornby                    b) Barlow

**3** Archie MacLaren

**4** Richard Pilling

**5** Johnny Tyldesley

**6** Johnny Briggs

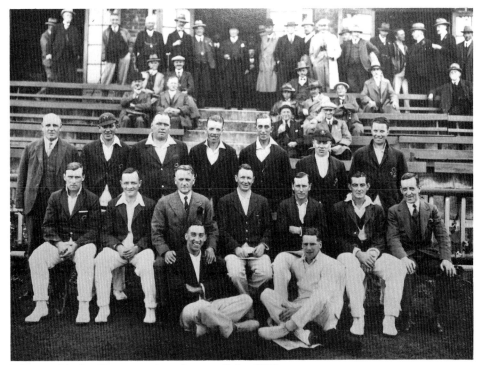

**7** Lancashire's all-conquering eleven of the 1920s

**8** Cec Parkin

**9** George Duckworth

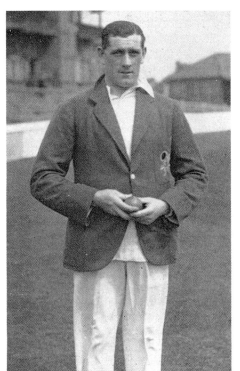

**10** Ernest Tyldesley, Frank Watson, Charlie Hallows, Richard Tyldesley and Harry Makepeace (*Manchester Guardian*)

often commonplace round of the county circuit, and, adroit tactician that he was, he never quite matched Albert Hornby's gift for co-ordination. Nonetheless, in 1904, he buckled down to that peripatetic drudgery, and, perhaps because of this, there was an answering response from the bowlers.

If, in bowling, fielding and captaincy, MacLaren's team dropped a few points against Hornby's eleven of 1881, no one would disagree that the batting was superior, and, certainly in style and tempo, has never been bettered at Old Trafford. A batting order led by MacLaren, Spooner and Tyldesley in their prime is as difficult to match as it was to contain. Imagine that trio let loose on Sunday afternoon for 40 overs, on a flat, covered wicket, with bowlers restricted as to run-up and over-quotient, with field-placing limited, and with a 75-yard boundary not only for fours but for sixes: the ground normally had to be cleared for six in their era. It is a feverish vision, somehow at once both torrid and chilling.

1904 was, as we have seen, something of a purple patch, and Lancashire were at a low ebb when, part-way through the 1914 season, the gruesome chaos of the Great War toppled the ordered calm of first-class cricket, as it did so many features of the old world. A Lancashire member would have to be quite ancient now to recall, as a child, the batting of MacLaren, the top-hatted and frock-coated membership, and even the more senior professionals taking their turn on the roller. The memories are dimmed, and this is possibly the relevant checkpoint to try and revive them with vignettes of Lancashire's Edwardian heroes.

### Archie MacLaren

Archibald Campbell MacLaren was and is, alpha and omega, Lancashire's greatest cricketer. He was born to the diadem, schooled from infancy to be, and believe in himself to be, a great cricketer. His preparatory school, Elstree, was awash with cricketing teachers, Vernon Royle among them, whilst Harrow, despite some setbacks, saw him develop a youthful mastery and precocious assurance.

He was a child of cotton. His father was a cotton merchant and mercantile agent, and Archie MacLaren was born in 1871 and initially lived in Whalley Range, then a township a little way south-east of the city, and, like some of those outlying estates, with its own private roads and gates. Although he made manifest a most aristocratic mien, he was not, then, of noble birth or breeding, and, like his hero and older friend, W. G. Grace, this sometimes left him a little sensitive to the élite of Oxbridge and Debrett, and, conversely, it to him.

Because he played cricket in the grand manner and relished the grand occasions, it followed that his international exploits often surpassed his more domestic enterprises. Some cricketers – Godfrey Evans and Alec Bedser, for example, since the Second World War – almost appear to find Test cricket easier than county cricket, so stimulated are they by the significance of the event. MacLaren played 35 times for England, a remarkable record in those years of fewer Tests, and only Washbrook, just, with 37, and, of course, Statham have more caps. All these matches were against Australia, and it is superfluous to add that no Lancashire player, and very few others, come at all near to that proud haul. He captained England 22 times, the most of any skipper against Australia; he scored 1931 runs for England, at an average of 34; and he compiled five Test centuries. He was also, needless to say, a boon to the Gentlemen, and, in 1903, with 168 not out, he joined with Ranjitsinhji and C. B. Fry in the most extraordinary batting. The Gentlemen declared at 500 for 2, and Fry and MacLaren added 309 in under three hours.

To underline this balance of national and local success, MacLaren also seemed to bat more brilliantly in Australia than back home. There is no parallel to the affection in which he held the Sydney ground. In 1897–98, his scores at Sydney were 142 and 100 (the first time a hundred in each innings had been achieved outside England), 109 and 50 not out, 61 and 140, and 65. In 1901–2, when MacLaren was captain, he continued his relay of successes with 145 and 73, 116, 167 and 92. No wonder Australian judges assessed him the best visitor from English shores they had witnessed, for that represents an average of almost 115 over 12 innings on one ground.

The truth of the contention may be observed statistically. Of 12 Lancashire players whose first-class careers were spent wholly with the county and who have over 15,000 runs, most scored a high proportion for the county and relatively few, as might be predicted, for England, the Players or other representative teams. MacLaren is unique in that 29% of his 22,237 runs were *not* scored for Lancashire. Half the others only have a proportion of

3.5% or less for other sides. Albert Ward, 13.4%, Ernest Tyldesley, 13.4%, his brother John, 15.7%, and Cyril Washbrook, 18%, are the only four with any sizeable slice of their first-class tally from non-Lancashire fixtures. These figures pertinently demonstrate not so much the amount of cricket MacLaren played outside Lancashire's ranks, but how well he did in English and other colours. Seventeen of his 47 centuries, over a third, were scored for other than Lancashire teams, and 12 of these were completed in Australia. By comparison, Washbrook's 76 hundreds include only 18 not for Lancashire, less than a quarter, nine of them overseas.

In justice, therefore, his story is England's more so than Lancashire's. That said, he averaged over 33 for the county in 307 matches, and he scored 15,722 runs for them – and he scored four centuries against Yorkshire, as well as his triumph of 424 in 1895. He made major contributions in two fine title-chasing campaigns. Yet his story often veers away from Old Trafford, even unto the end, when he assembled a Falstaff's army of cricketers at Eastbourne in 1921, when MacLaren himself was almost 50, and inflicted on Warwick Armstrong's Australians the only defeat of their trip. Out for 43 in the first innings, they managed to set their opponents 196, and ran out winners by 29 runs.

Archie MacLaren was a knowledgeable captain, ahead of his time in the tactical deployment of fielders and in the subtlety of psychological pressure. He manifestly lacked the virtue looked for by Napoleon in his generals, for MacLaren was a luckless captain, seemingly beset from Harrow to Eastbourne with lost tosses, unfriendly weather and crucial injuries. He has been called a joyless captain, and he certainly took a military view of his official duties. At county level, he was probably not so well respected as Hornby had been, in part because he lacked something of Hornby's innate, if stiff, courtesy. As an elderly Lancashire professional embarked on some leather-hunting toward the boundary fence, MacLaren shouted to Spooner, 'He looks like a spavined cab-horse.' It might, at a distance, raise a guffaw for reactive and improvised metaphor, but, for the struggling 'pro' and his comrades, it would sullenly lower morale. Incidentally, and on the subject of fielding, MacLaren was the peerless slip, deft and secure, of his generation, and perhaps the best slip-fielder prior to 1914.

As a batsman, he was a genuine artist, and, as important, a genuine entertainer. His combination of classical style and explosive energy place him in the rarest of top flights: in terms of spectating, there has probably been no more thrilling batsman to watch. In the contemporary descriptions of him, the impression formed is that he played each and every shot with the same spacious *élan*. The aeronautics of his address and attack were regarded with awe. Archie MacLaren began with the most elaborate back-lift the game has maybe known. It was not the hesitant vacillation of the modern batsman who prefers not to ground his bat as the bowler approaches. It was a full, confident backward swing, only momentarily checked in flight, for MacLaren, self-evidently, had already assessed line, length and pace, and the shot was determined. With the classic, left-shouldered stance, the curve of the bat flew down and through the shot fluently. Playing forward, the left leg was elevated almost in exaggeration, so that, for the second, MacLaren resembled the lunging fencer or the martial arts expert. Finally, there was the free-flowing follow-through, the trajectory of the bat completing the 360 degrees of the circle, and perhaps another arc of the circumference as well. It is said that Michelangelo could draw a wellnigh perfect circle freehand. Archie MacLaren did much the same with his bat.

It bears comparison with the golf drives of Arnold Palmer or Jack Nicklaus, and for one simple reason. The combination of eye, muscle, judgement and confidence meant that the cricket ball was tantamount to stationary as MacLaren connected. It was assurance to the level of arrogance. MacLaren disapproved of fast bowlers without deep fields, and when, in a representative match, the Yorkshireman, Ted Wainwright, lobbed one up for him to get fifty, MacLaren kicked it scornfully away. It is, however, wrong to classify MacLaren purely as a destroyer – a Jessop, a Botham – among batsmen. While still at Harrow, he learned, by dint of experience and grafting practice, the need to defend on pitches swampy or fierce. He became a fine bad-wicket player, his techniques adjusted to repel the most devilish of assaults. Tall and beautifully balanced, he played back in the most upright manner, never failing to play cleanly through the shot, frequently impelling away the ball through close-set fields. His 140 for England at Trent Bridge against Australia in 1905 is a telling illustration of this aspect of his science.

The nobility of his batting gave one and all an impression of the upper crust, but, in his day-by-day life, Archie MacLaren never complemented his blue-blooded cricket with casual success. A gambler, both narrowly apropos the racehorses, and, more widely, over a perplexing set of business and other projects, he never enjoyed quite the triumphs he was ambitious to attain. He was a strange mix of optimism and the reverse, in part through the inculcation of a firm stoicism. MacLaren is well known for having spirited Sydney Barnes out of the thin air of league cricket and transported him to devastating feats in Australia. This was in 1901–2, and MacLaren soon discovered, as did most, that the unsmiling Barnes was a righteously independent professional, not prepared to bow the knee or touch the forelock. The leaking tub in which they sailed was beset by storm and tempest in the Bay of Biscay, and a young amateur was beside himself with justified anxiety. The fearless and cool MacLaren comforted him with the speculative thought that, if they all drowned, that would mean Sydney Barnes would drown, too.

Michael Down, in his exceptionally readable biography of 'Archie', looks closely at the contradiction of his subject. Elegantly dressed and handsomely moustached, he could be genial and he could be disappointingly obtuse. His repute as a captain suffers from the selection of times when he persevered dogmatically with some stratagem in the face of decent sense. The wry conjugation – I am stubborn, you are obstinate, he is pigheaded – constantly applied to MacLaren. Michael Down is, as biographers are pleasantly prone, well disposed to A. C. MacLaren, just as, we are told, the victims come to love their torturers. He sees him, eventually, as an attractive Achilles with feet, and perhaps a few other parts, of clay. John Arlott is not so forgiving, astutely noting that MacLaren's every virtue overflowed into vice, his singleness of purpose, for instance, into intolerant rigidity. Over against this, Neville Cardus, for whom MacLaren lit the Olympian flame, considered him the noblest Roman of them all.

Possibly the balance lies in their public and private attitudes. Neville Cardus borrowed from the theatre to compare MacLaren with Brutus, and therein lies the truth of it. Like other actors and other sportsmen, MacLaren was wonderful to behold on his stage, but perhaps, at times, was petty-minded behind the scenes in private. It was, no doubt, preferable to enjoy him at a distance.

MacLaren was not unlike the grandiose actor-manager of his day. One might recall Sir Henry Irving, who died in 1905, and who was magnetic and pioneering and romantic in his stage persona, if given to a certain inelasticity of manner. Archie MacLaren bestrode cricket's stage, a captain-manager for much of his career, the genuine richness of his batting curtaining a fairly ordinary morality behind. Like the great actor-managers, he rose to occasions, batting out of his skin the larger the crowds or the more glittering the occasion. Like the great actor-managers, he was given to emotional foibles and preposterous tantrums. Like the great actor-managers, he was admired for the superabundance of his talent and personality.

Archie MacLaren was more Mark Antony, colossal in bearing yet weakened by flaws, than Brutus, inclined to a prissy, at times insufferable, goodness: Mark Antony, of whom Cleopatra said, 'His rear'd arm crested the world . . . but when he meant to quail and shake the orb, he was as rattling thunder.' The Somerset bowlers of 1895, *inter alia*, would have reckoned Cleopatra the E. W. Swanton of Alexandria. Archie MacLaren died of cancer in 1944.

### Reggie Spooner

One searches for synonyms for 'majestic' when Reggie Spooner's name is mentioned, and Peter Roget's assistance is keenly sought. His regal strokeplay made him monarch of all the cricket fields he surveyed, but, unfortunately for Lancashire, he was, like Richard I, a soldier-king. His martial duties took him to South Africa and Ireland when Lancashire supporters wished he might be locked in tourney in another war of the roses. Also like Richard Lionheart, he was fond of hunting, and a severe injury in pursuit of the fox incapacitated him one season. It is uncommon to hear of cricketers today omitted because of a hunting accident.

Although his career stretched from 1899, about the beginning of the Boer War, to 1921, just past the end of the Great War, he only played 170 matches for Lancashire. He only won ten caps, joining a rare set of golden oldies, C. B. Fry included, who never toured Australia. In fact, Spooner never toured anywhere.

It is, therefore, the more remarkable that, so fluent and charming was his batting, he earns a notable place in cricket's gallery. He scored just short of 10,000 runs for Lancashire, at an average of 37, to which he added just short of 500 runs for

England, at an average of 32. He scored 31 centuries, including one for England, in 1912 against South Africa, and four for Lancashire against Yorkshire. He had a highest score of 240, against Somerset, those longtime sufferers at Lancashire hands, in 1906. He also batted well opening for the Gentlemen.

He was born on 21 October 1880 and died on 2 October 1961, just a few days short of his eighty-first birthday. He was 18 when, in 1899, he scored 69 and 198 for Marlborough against Rugby at Lord's, and, opening on his début for Lancashire, once more at Lord's, he scored 44 and 83. Three years later, in the famous 1902 series with Australia, John Tyldesley and he added 127 in 80 minutes. He was not yet 22.

His striking rate for one who did not play regularly was impressive. He had a thousand runs for Lancashire in 1903, 1904, 1905 and 1906, while, in 1911, Jack Sharp and Spooner became the first Lancastrians after Johnny Tyldesley to score 2000 first-class runs in a summer. He participated in several glorious stands. He was involved in four opening stands of over 200, including two with MacLaren, and five others over 200, including four with Johnny Tyldesley. These must have been epic hours for the spectators. R. H. Spooner also adorned another great Lancashire tradition: he was a superb cover-point.

Neville Cardus wrote that Reginald Spooner 'put a bloom on the orthodox', and it was this higher colouring which hinted at kingliness. There was something purplish and imperious about his style, something which the puritanical, obsessed with a chaste tidiness, found a trifle florid. Like many graceful and flowing batsmen, he played the off-drive with an effortless beauty. Descriptions of his off-driving speak of the swiftness of his orbital swing and the sinuous dispatch of his wrists. Indeed, contemporary watchers repeatedly turn to his wrists, like critics to the forearm action of Steve Davis or the hands of Lester Piggott. That flashing downward surge of the bat and ultimate vibration of the wrists must have been like the stinging lash of the whip. The wrists were always the focus. Needless to say, the adjustment of his sharp vision allowed him the luxury of this brandishing approach, no less than it informed his lupine prowls through the covers. 'It was,' as the old Lancashire 'pro' told Neville Cardus, 'an education to bat with Mr Spooner.'

Reginald Spooner was wounded with the Lincolnshire Regiment in the First World War, and his son E. H. Spooner scored a century for Eton against the British Empire XI in the Second World War. In that first critical post-war year, 1945–46, R. H. Spooner, in the wake of A. N. Hornby, Vernon Royle and Miles Kenyon, served as Lancashire's president. His few games after the 1914–18 conflict were poignant reminders of a lost world. As late as the 1960s and after his death, the eyes of old men in the Old Trafford pavilion would glisten rheumily as they remembered R. H. Spooner.

## Johnny Tyldesley

By common consent, John Thomas Tyldesley is the county's most proficient native-born professional batsman, shrugging off any challenge from his brother, Ernest, or from Cyril Washbrook. Add amateurs and overseas players, and only MacLaren and Clive Lloyd approach him in these stakes for the title of Lancashire's greatest bat.

From John Arlott's classic selection of the best-ever hundred batsmen, J. T. Tyldesley is absent; nor is he mentioned, as are three or four Lancastrians, in the preface's shortlist of near-misses. It is a grievous omission. Nonetheless, to get 99 out of a hundred right is a brilliant *tour de force*. Even Homer nods.

It is the more surprising in that Tyldesley was no benign and pacific batsman that one might forget or ignore. He swashbuckled in the most piratical vein, and it was written of him that 'he was the very antithesis of the average modern professional'. In fact, just as the more dour amateurs were sometimes described as professional in approach, John Tyldesley's famous accolade was that he batted, in the golden age, like a gentleman. He played in 31 matches for England, and that included membership of the 1902 eleven, claimed by many to be England's finest. What is fascinating is that Tyldesley was the only professional batsman, taking a proud, gallant place alongside Archie MacLaren, F. S. Jackson, Gilbert Jessop, C. B. Fry and Ranjitsinhji. That is the measure of his audacious greatness.

He was born at Worsley on 23 November 1873, and he played 507 games for Lancashire, spanning the years 1895 to 1923, from his twenty-second to his fiftieth year. He scored just under 32,000 runs for the county, and just under 38,000 in all, a smidgeon behind his estimable brother. Cricket has known many fraternal duos, but no brotherhood, not even W. G. and E. M. Grace, can jointly boast of close on 80,000 first-class runs. With 86 centuries, an average of 40, and 1661 runs in Test cricket, his was a reign of merit as well as distinction. His highest score was an undefeated 295 against Kent in 1906, but, granted his explosive approach, it is his consistency and his bad-wicket play which must be extolled.

As to that first virtue, he scored 2000 runs in five seasons, including 3041 in 1901, and he passed the thousand-mark in 19 consecutive seasons, the First World War years, of course, excepted. If MacLaren daydreamed of Sydney, Tyldesley must have scanned the fixture list to find when next a trip to Birmingham was due. He scored centuries at Edgbaston in 1895, 1897 (one in each innings), 1899, 1901, 1902 (mercifully, for the Warwickshire bowlers, against Australia), 1903, 1906, 1907, 1908 and 1910. It is a formidable roster. Johnny Tyldesley could barely step on to the Warwickshire pitch and not score a hundred.

As to the second virtue, of mastery of the sticky dog, he was regarded as the chief negotiator of such horrors of his epoch. The history books speak, with caught breath, of his innings at Melbourne against a fierce Australian attack during the 1903–4 tour. The pitch was so dreadful that balls of decent length came on at the height of ankle or of throat. One of England's most revered coteries of batsmen was pathetically reduced to 103 all out. Tyldesley made 62 of them. Albert Relf was the only other to manage double figures, and it was one of those occasions when a half-century must be valued at four or six times its numerical worth. He top-scored with 97 in the first innings before the thunderstorms created a glue-pot.

It is a truism or assumption of cricket that it is an art form which reveals character. Johnny Tyldesley tried to disprove this single-handed. He was diffident and hushed to the point of withdrawal, with not the vaguest hint of extroversion in his make-up. If anything, he was of less than medium height, but of athletic, determined build. As sergeant-major to MacLaren's flamboyant colonelcy, his military moustache looks very authentic in the photographs of him as he stands, still and quick, left toe pointing at a 45-degree angle, relaxed but concentrating.

It was not that he was obsequious or unduly deferential. He never shirked from his responsibilities, and, for instance, he was always prepared to present a case on behalf of the professionals to the county committee, or, during the 1914–18 conflict, to help organise games in aid of the war effort. He was unfailingly polite, and, simply, reserved. In 1923 he took over as coach, at a salary of £300, from MacLaren, whose salary had been £550. For five or six seasons, he stood, respectful and greying, at a little distance from the nets, dispensing the wisdom of the ages in a whisper.

Yet, once he grasped a bat in his hands, the transformation was like unto George Formby seizing his ukulele, and becoming the insouciantly glittering star instead of the fatuous chump. His defence was as sound as a bell, and he played most shots with *élan*, but, with swiftness of foot as his base, it was the long arc from mid-off to gully where he enjoyed a vivid profligacy of run-making. Driving and cutting, he was murderous in his asaults. Slow bowlers feared him, and especially leg-spin bowlers. In a manner now sometimes seen, if not with the same accomplishment, in one-day cricket, he retired ever more impudently to the on-side, the more ferociously to strike with the spin, scattering whatever defensive fields had been uneasily sited on the off-side. No leg-spinner, not even the matchless Australian, W. W. Armstrong, sat cheerfully in the dressing room in anticipation of a session of bowling to John Tyldesley.

Either alien to his true character or only revealing of it in batting, J. T. Tyldesley was homicidal at the crease. Perhaps one must turn to the classic murderers of his era for comparison. Did not a contemporary of Tyldesley's, the mild-mannered Doctor Crippen, slaughter his wife with a bestial fury which has left him an abhorred creature of folklore? Johnny Tyldesley's unrepressed passions of batting had the same curious effect of the silent one turned manic for the nonce. Another macabre comparison might be the smiling, courteous Gurkha, equally prepared, at the right moment, to kill with consuming and unrelenting efficiency.

Johnny Tyldesley was, then, something of a paradox, the quietest of citizens, and the most murderous of batsmen. On 27 November 1930, a few days after his fifty-seventh birthday, he ate his breakfast, sat down on a chair to pull on his boots, preparatory to going to work, and died.

### Walter Brearley and Arthur Mold

Kenneth Grahame composed *The Wind in the Willows* in 1908, the season Walter Brearley took 154 wickets, his best summer of all, and he could well have been the model for Toad of Toad Hall's less malign traits. He was a strong and sturdy creature of ebullience and complacency. Self-opinionated, brashly convinced of his own ability, given to huge enthusiasms, forever falling into scrapes and indulging in unnecessary squabbles, Brearley was an amateur of an eccentricity no professional could have risked. A bosom comrade of Archie MacLaren and a member, albeit an immediately injured one, of the Eastbourne irregulars in 1921, he had much the same taste for dressing-room quarrels and miffed resignations. Going out to bat or to field, it was his practice to ignore the convention of the swing-gate, preferring to leap over the pavilion rail and bound into action. Indoors, he was just as likely to jump the billiard table, and, along with Archie MacLaren, he was famed as a bon viveur and raconteur.

To his credit, and here putting aside the mould of Toad, he was never lazy, vigorously throwing his energetic strength into the fray, and, on occasion, bowling from start of play to stumps. The amateur fast bowler was something of a rarity, for the repetitive effort involved was viewed as rather plebeian. Walter Brearley was scornful of so footling a notion. Tireless and optimistic to the point of conceit, he bowled quickly, with some late out-swing, off an eight-yard run, and his stamina permitted him to sustain brisk pace for hours. By the unexacting standards of the day, he watched his health with care, eschewing tobacco until close of play, if convinced, like many quick bowlers, of alcohol's value as a lubricant. He trained harder than most, and provided England as well as Lancashire with action of vim and liveliness.

Nothing more candidly displays his character, and reminds that angry incidents are not merely a manifestation of late twentieth-century Pakistan, as Brearley's spat with Jessop in 1905. Brearley's batting had, apparently, been laughed at by Gilbert Jessop, and, as he scored only 700 or so runs for Lancashire at an average of 6, the taunts may have been more undiplomatic than inaccurate. Brearley, good- or bad-tempered in motive, came alike to Jessop, and, in concert with J. H. Board, he slammed Brearley for 57 runs in four overs. Later, Brearley dismissed them both and a bitter victory was obtained, but Jessop criticised Brearley's beamers fiercely in the public prints and talked of never playing again at Old Trafford.

In between the rows, Walter Brearley, during the early seasons of the twentieth century, proved an economical and dangerous bowler. He took 690 county wickets, at a cost of under 19 each, including a hundred wickets a summer three times, and, a formidable record of penetration, 79 occasions when he took five or more wickets in an innings. Only a handful of Lancashire bowlers have improved on that last attainment. He also pleased everyone with 125 wickets in fourteen 'roses' matches. In all first-class cricket he took 844 wickets, including 48 in seven outings for the Gentlemen, and 17 more wickets in his four Test matches – he just managed to outdo that figure with 21 runs for England. He was particularly venomous against the Australians in 1905. His best analyses were 8 for 51 against Essex in 1904, and 8 for 61 against the same county in 1908, two good returns of 9 for 80 and 8 for 68 versus Yorkshire and Middlesex, respectively, in 1909, and eight wickets each against Somerset and Gloucestershire in 1911. His finest match analysis was 17 for 137 against Somerset in 1905, and, oddly, all this splendid bowling was perfomed on home grounds. That 17 wickets included four in four balls, and only Dean has matched that 17 in a Lancashire game.

Walter Brearley was born in March 1876, and he was 26 years old before embarking on his ten-year burst on to the first-class scene. He died in January 1937, well into his seventy-first year, and he received the accolade of a *Wisden* decoration in 1909. He was a parvenu. There was some family money and he came and went as he mostly pleased. His unconventional behaviour was not well received, and, sniffily, after the manner of Rattie, A. N. Hornby felt he was not a gentleman, for he lacked both the breeding and the schooling.

Walter Brearley followed in lineage from Arthur Mold as Lancashire's chief strike-bowler. Arthur Mold was born in Banbury, just inside Northamptonshire, in 1863, and, in fact, played for that county before joining Lancashire. He played for the county from 1889 to 1901, when his dubious action forced him out of the game. Where Brearley was born controversial, Mold had controversy thrust upon him. He died in 1921, not yet 60.

He packed a substantial amount of cricket into his baker's dozens-worth of seasons, playing in 260 matches and rarely missing a game. Seven times, six of them with Briggs, he bowled right through an innings, and, on 143 occasions, he took five wickets in an innings. In 53 games he took ten or more in the match, a

Lancashire record. Like Brearley, he bowled off a short, eight-pace run, generating much pace like the amateur through sheer shoulder and arm strength. He sometimes produced a rearing break-back. He reached the goal of a hundred wickets in seasons 1891 to 1896 and again in 1899, a high level of consistency. Indeed, in 1894 (207, average 12) and 1895 (213, average 16) he topped two hundred wickets in all first-class games. Only Cecil Parkin, twice, and McDonald were to follow this precedent among Lancashire bowlers. Mold 17 times took eight or more wickets in an innings, another Lancashire record. Among this golden bounty, his 9 for 41 at Huddersfield against Yorkshire (1890), his 9 for 29 at Tonbridge against Kent (1893) and, again versus Kent at Old Trafford, his 9 for 62 (1895) shine more brightly than the others. He had hat-tricks in 1894 against Somerset and, four wickets in four balls, against Nottinghamshire in 1895.

A significant fact emerges from this welter of impressive data. After Statham and Briggs, Arthur Mold, although not as famed as either of these or some others, contrived to be Lancashire's third-most successful bowler. He took 1543 wickets (1673 in all matches) at an average not much above 15. He appeared in but three Tests, taking seven wickets. Primarily, then, a stalwart county bowler, and whatever the kinks in his action, he brought conscientiousness as well as stamina to his chosen trade. His is a most distinguished contribution to the county's story.

## *Albert Ward* et alia

Albert Ward was the link between Richard Barlow and Harry Makepeace as Lancashire anchor-batsmen. Perhaps that remorseless threesome sit together on an astral plane, quietly debating the forward defensive prod, with the popular tune 'Heartbreaker' gently playing in the ethereal background. To be fair, Ward, who lived from 1865 to 1939, had a more enterprising range of shots than either ancestor or descendant, but, basically, his strategy, like theirs, was to offer rocklike defence. He carried his bat five times, once, for 45, against the 1893 Australians at Old Trafford, and, on another occasion, for 140, versus Gloucestershire, and in the same year.

He played for Lancashire from 1889 to 1904, but his main

seasons were compressed into the nine summers of 1893 to 1901, in each of which, like the acme of consistency, he registered a thousand runs. In all, he scored 15,392 runs for the county and nearly 18,000 in all cricket, and at an average of 30. This makes him one of the top score or so of Lancashire batsmen. He scored 29 centuries, the best of them his only double hundred, 219 for Stoddart's XI versus South Australia in Adelaide. One hundred and eighty-five against Kent at Gravesend in 1891 was his top Lancashire contribution, when MacLaren and he raised 215 for the third wicket. He was a partner in four other stands of 200 or more, allied once with Tyldesley as they reached 265 at Derby in 1901.

Albert Ward and J. T. Brown, of Yorkshire, joined in a similar stand of 210 at Melbourne in the fifth Test in 1895. While Brown hit out, Ward adopted his preferred defensive posture, and it won England the match. In the first Test he scored 75 and 117, his only England century, and, indeed, he showed great form on this tour. He won seven caps, scoring nearly 500 runs in Tests at the rewarding average of 38.

Albert Ward is not a figure of legend and reminiscence. Nonetheless, the data of his career over 330 games reveals that he was one of Lancashire's sturdiest batsmen. He was a most rational cricketer.

Lancashire enjoyed the services of other loyal professionals over the last decades before the First World War. George Baker, another dependable bat, played over 200 matches between 1887 and 1899, scoring 7000 or so runs with four centuries, before becoming coach at Harrow. A more attacking player, dynamic in his driving, was Frank Sugg, who earned a couple of caps early in his career in 1888. He played in 235 games and scored just short of 10,000 runs. His best seasons were 1896 to 1898 when he reached a thousand in each season. In that last year Ward and he put on 278 at Taunton, Sugg's share being 169. Two hundred and twenty at Bristol was the most productive of his 15 centuries.

It was more bowlers who took the eye as the Great War approached. Harry Dean was unlucky. His cricket with Lancashire began in 1906, and he filled the slot sadly left by Briggs. The war interrupted the smooth flow of his career, and he played only two or three seasons after the armistice. During that time, however, he took a hundred wickets in each of no less than eight seasons, 14 times he took eight or more in an innings, and four times did he take 14 or more in the two innings. At the end of the day, therefore, the faithful Dean stands sixth in the county list. He had 1267 victims for Lancashire (1301 in all games) at a cost of 18, and he was Lancashire's only bowler of note during the captaincy of Hornby junior. He played three Tests in the triangular tournament of 1912 and took 11 wickets. An astute left-armer, he had the knack of pushing the ball through quite quickly on dry days, while decelerating considerably and effectively when wickets were damp. Where he was unfortunate was that, as happens to many commendable cricketers, he ploughed the loneliest of furrows in a relatively unsuccessful team. He has never won the plaudits he deserved. Room should be found for a mention in dispatches for W. Huddleston, who bowled willingly in many games over the Edwardian period, and ended with 684 wickets, usually in dribs and drabs, except when, as a regular in the 1913 eleven, he took 113 wickets. In 1906 he took 9 for 36 against Nottinghamshire, and, happily, he lived long years to recall his hard if unheralded labours, dying in 1962 aged 91.

Jimmy Heap, who played about the same time as Harry Dean, was another spin bowler. He played over 200 games, only 40 or so less than Dean, and he took over 400 wickets. When conditions were spiteful, he could be extremely dangerous. His 9 for 43 against Northamptonshire in 1910 was one such time. His chief limitation was that, as they say in the North, he was a martyr to lumbago, and on some days could hardly stretch his back upright, let alone bowl accurate spin. Additionally, he had the makings of an all-rounder, for his 5000 runs, for an average of 19, brought succour to the later order. In 1914 he scored 132 not out, at Bournemouth against Hampshire.

It was the likes of Ward, Sugg, Baker, Dean, Huddleston and Heap who gave honest support to the glamorous thrust of MacLaren, Spooner and Tyldesley. As for Sydney Barnes, it is difficult to know whether to assess him as a Lancashire player or not. Self-evidently, by the act of playing, he must be the best bowler to have played for Lancashire. Despite his respect for Archie MacLaren, he never settled, and played only 46 games over five disjointed seasons for Lancashire. He took 225 wickets, at a cost each of 20, in these games, his finest day being at Leyton in 1903 when he took 8 for 37 against Essex. That was the one year – 131 – he reached a hundred wickets. By and large, his story is a much broader one than can be contained within the confines of a county history.

*Johnny Briggs*

Johnny Briggs has two unique claims as a Lancashire cricketer. One is that he has been their only all-rounder of acknowledged stature, and the other must await the valedictory paragraphs of this piece.

This biographical section was opened, properly, by Archie MacLaren, and, equally, it is right to close it on the high if poignant note of the tale of John Briggs. Like Crossland, he was born in Sutton-in-Ashfield, in Nottinghamshire. This was 3 October 1862, but he was playing as a professional in Lincolnshire, aged 14, before being spotted in a benefit match at Seaforth, near Liverpool, two years later by Richard Barlow and Alec Watson. Barlow took him under his wing and the young man, who also played some rugby league as a Widnes half-back, lived with the Barlows. Despite some early failure, Barlow's longheadedness soon paid off, and his protégé first as a superb cover-point, second as an attacking batsman, and third as a world-class spin-bowler, achieved international stardom.

His case for being regarded as Lancashire's premier all-rounder is straightforward. He is simply the only Lancashire player to have scored 10,000 runs and taken 1000 wickets for the county. He scored 10,707 (14,092 in all games) and took 1696 (2221) wickets. His batting average was 19 and his bowling average 15 – to which must be added the quiz-type fact that he is the only cricketer to have performed the hat-trick and scored a century in England v. Australia tests. He played almost 400 matches for Lancashire between 1879 and 1900. He scored ten centuries, including 121 for England at Melbourne on the 1884–85 trip. His best match figures were 14 for 122 versus Yorkshire at Old Trafford in 1891, although he twice took 15 wickets in non-county matches, one of them 15 for 28 at Cape Town in the South African Test. Fourteen of the 15 were bowled. Most satisfyingly, he became the second of only three Lancashire bowlers to take all ten, when he dismissed every Worcester player, for 55, in 1900 at Old Trafford, not long before his tragic ending. He 14 times took eight or more wickets in an innings, and he holds the Lancashire record – 161 – for the occasions in which five wickets have been taken in an innings. He took a hundred wickets in a season 12 times, and, until the advent of Statham, he stood proudly first on the roster of Lancashire bowlers. He won 33 England caps, a plentiful number for those days, and only MacLaren, Statham and Washbrook have more. He scored over 800 runs for England and took 118 wickets. He made six consecutive visits to Australia.

Although it is appropriate and necessary thus to list the facts and figures of his dramatically successful career, they must be regarded as no more than background information against which to reconstruct the character and meaning of this great cricketer.

For a score of years, at home and abroad, he batted, bowled and fielded with a harmonious mixture of shrewdness and enthusiasm, He had both the theoretical mind and the natural flair where often goodish cricketers lack something of one or the other, and, allied to this, was his own huge enjoyment of all these activities. Rarely did he despair and never did his keenness diminish. It might be said that he is Lancashire's best all-rounder because the competition is not brisk. That is true enough, for, apart from Barlow, Steel, Jack Sharp and one or two others, this has been a serious deficiency in Lancashire's saga. Nonetheless, and accepting that he was more of a bowler than a batsman, his is an enviable all-round record.

He was a circular little fellow. He was small and rotund and full of bounce, as jolly and rounded as a plum pudding. To the sphere of his body had been added the globe of a face, almost giving him the outline of a cartoon character or a Lucy Attwell drawing. His face was all simple lines, such as a child might draw. The moon-shaped face had an upward crescent for the smiling lips, surmounted by the downward arch of a thin, black moustache. The eyes were large, dark and luminous, plumped there like coals for a snowman's eyes.

With cap pulled down over his brow, he wasted no time, aggressive as a batsman, frequently to the point of foolhardiness, daring and venturesome in the field, to his own bowling as well as in the covers, and unquelled in buoyancy when bowling. Two joyful skips and a jump was all he required preparatory to his left-hand spinning. He had a tendency to round-arm, and never rose above slow-medium, so that his minute, if resolute, frame seldom tired. He was full of guile and gloried in his stealth, luring the innocent by artful variations of light and sufficient spin from leg to off. As he himself was known to remark, it was not what he did but what t'others thought he was doing that mattered.

Outside of cricket, he could put his mind to nothing, and, happy as a sandboy, there could be a waywardness in his approach to cricket itself which sometimes worried his mentors. However, once the action began, he was seized with the desire and the eagerness to give all he could, and, afterwards, he was a gleeful celebrant of any victory or share of the spoils.

He died in the January of 1902, only 39. He had been known as 'Boy' Briggs, partly because of his youthful prowess, partly because he was a Peter Pan figure who never grew up. He was given to pranks and jests, but mostly they were amusing and forever without malice. He was the first to laugh at himself, and no bowler has quite seen the joke of being punished as engagingly as Johnny Briggs. He was a childlike, almost a cherubic, sportsman, and, because of the generosity of his spirit, his quips and wheezes never irked, as sometimes they do with the precociously joky child. A cheerful friend and courteous colleague, he was, as Thomas Hardy wrote of Giles Winterbourne in *The Woodlanders*, 'one of nature's very gentlemen'.

And so to the second of his rare places in Lancashire annals. As sometimes happens on the theatrical stage or sporting arena, the essence of Johnny Briggs's personality conveyed itself to the audience. Some sort of telepathy or osmosis occurs, and the crowd picks up the emphasis of a disposition, although, in material effect, the clues of gesture and other acts seem to be sparse. The humanity and love of life of Briggs was recognised by all who watched him, and it would be a gross understatement to say he was very popular.

We are talking of the 1890s. We are talking of an Old Trafford inhabited by hard-hearted mill-owners in the pavilion, and horny-handed mill-workers on the popular side. It was not a locale for undue sentiment. Nevertheless, from all the accounts of his cricketing performance and its relation with the spectators, one slowly grasps that Johnny Briggs was held in the sort of profound affection, that, in fact, only an open-faced and open-hearted child might inspire.

Johnny Briggs was, then, the best-loved cricketer who has played for Lancashire, and his untimely and sorrowful death hurt and moved the county's vast following.

# 4. The Years of Triumph

## First World War and Its Aftermath

Along with the other counties, Lancashire sent a full complement of men to the war. Apart from John Tyldesley, who was too old and who helped organise some charity cricket, the entire staff enlisted, some never to return, as a plaque in the pavilion dolefully recorded. The losses included two amateurs, Harold Garnett and Alfred Hartley, whose cavalier strokeplay had lent middle-order support to the pre-war teams. Garnett, killed in 1917, scored 5599, and Alfred Hartley, killed in 1918, scored 5000 as well. The latter had notched 234 in 1910 against those old whipping-boys of Lancashire, Somerset. J. Nelson and E. L. Wright were both killed in the slaughter of 1918: they had not enjoyed substantial first eleven experience. Another loss was that of W. K. 'Billy' Tyldesley, also killed in 1918. A left-hand bat, with nearly 3000 runs and three centuries to his credit, he was one of the Westhoughton Tyldesleys. There were also Jimmy, a useful right-hand bowler who took over 300 wickets and who died aged only 34, and Harry who just played four games. Richard came later.

The Old Trafford pavilion was turned into a hospital for 80 military patients, and nearly 2000 wounded were tended there during the war. It was not closed as a hospital until February 1919. In 1916 kit was sent to the Ruhleben prisoner-of-war camp to enable a roses match to be played there. Subscriptions were well maintained, as the committee appealed for funds to keep the club afloat. The membership in 1914 was 1667, and it never fell below 1100 during the war. In 1916 the committee were able to fulfil their pre-war contractual obligations to the professionals, and, in general, to do what was possible to cater for their minimal needs.

As for some of the others, Cecil Parkin was a fuel organiser, and A. N. Hornby, never the one to throw up the chance of an administrative chore, was in charge of army remounts.

The slowness of demobilisation – Lol Cook was a long time arriving home – and the general dislocation caused Lancashire to propose two-day games for the 1919 season, and *Wisden* called it 'a sad blunder'. The cricketers, especially the captains, were ill-adjusted to the different attitude required, and, in terms of times of play and other features, it was a somewhat botched experiment, so much so that the device has never since been attempted. Lancashire drew 12 out of 24 played and ended fifth, a good win over Yorkshire ornamenting the season, with 14 wickets for Cecil Parkin and two high scores from Makepeace pleasing omens. Lancashire lost to the amateur Australian Imperial Forces eleven which stayed behind after the war for a first-class tour. Dicky Barlow umpired, just prior to his death in July.

For the next six years Lancashire performed competently and more. They were second in 1920, pipped at the post by Middlesex. The season included one fascinating example of the professional craft. Hampshire needed 66 to win at Liverpool, and Lol Cook and Harry Dean allowed the nightwatch batsman to linger for an hour, until the wicket took vicious spin, and Lancashire won by one run, a nice calculation. Lancashire never fell from the top five. In the sultry weather of 1921 the batting was strong, if the bowling was suspect; Charlie Hallows carried his bat a couple of times and topped the averages. The next year Lancashire shot from the starting-blocks with seven straight wins, only to lose five of the last thirteen. Parkin took 181 wickets at an average of 16. In 1923 he improved slightly on this with 186, and now Richard Tyldesley came into the reckoning with a hundred wickets. Ernest Tyldesley (2070 in 1922) and Harry Makepeace (2286 in 1923) emerged as the senior batsmen.

Lancashire continued this same solid display of efficiency in 1924 and 1925, losing only six Championship matches in these two years. George Duckworth and E. A. McDonald, the famous Australian, made their debuts in 1924, and, in 1925, as part of the £500 deal with that league club over McDonald's contract, Nelson became a venue for two county matches, and 10,000 rolled up to watch. Through the unalloyed dampness of 1924 Lancashire went unbeaten until mid-August, and critics argued that, had not Ernest Tyldesley's appendix halted him during a spell where he averaged 50, they might have been champions in 1925.

These last three seasons were crowned by phenomenal bowling. After Mold in 1894 and 1895, Lancashire bowlers have only thrice taken 200 first-class wickets in a season, and these were the years. Parkin (209 in 1923, and, at an average of 13, 200 in 1924) and McDonald (205 in 1925) were the celebrants. In those same three season, Richard Tyldesley, the perspiring leg-spinner, took 437 wickets, just for the county. Frank Watson had consolidated his place in the team, and, along with Hallows, Makepeace and Ernest Tyldesley, regularly scored his thousand runs. Most satisfactorily of all for the partisan was the beating of Yorkshire at Leeds for the first time since 1889, and with Yorkshire needing only 57. They succumbed to Parkin and Tyldesley on a rain-affected pitch for only 33.

These significant recruitments and developments to maturity of both batsmen and bowlers were careful and shrewd. It all pointed to an era of success. The frame of reference was sound. Since the war a fixed scale of payments had been agreed of £5 a match, £3 away and £1 home expenses, and a £1 winning bonus. A heavy expense had been agreed on the restoration of the ground and facilities, but, after poor attendances of only about 78,000 in 1919, spectatorship of a quarter of a million was welcomed in the mid-1920s. Profits were good – £3000 in 1921 – and, with men like the treasurer, Sir Edwin Stockton, encouraging its growth, member-ship was over 4800 in the sunny, dry summer of 1925. The membership fee was now two guineas, with admission to the pavilion side half a crown, and the popular side a shilling.

Myles Kenyon, a guiding influence for the county then and later, and, after him, Jack Sharp were the captains in these formative post-war years. Although he was a respected figure, M. N. Kenyon was no great shakes as a player, but Jack Sharp was a notable all-rounder. Like Harry Makepeace, he was a double international and had played on the right wing for Everton in two cup finals. Originally a native of Hereford, his first-class career began as long ago as 1899. He took over 400 wickets for Lancashire and scored 22,000 runs, standing sixth in the county's table of run-getters, as well as earning three caps in 1909 and scoring a century against Australia. In his later forties, his bulkiness and frequent illness told against him, and spectators were uncharitable enough to jibe at his sorry fielding. He resigned in favour – after much committee cogitation – of Major, later Colonel, Leonard Green, whose distinction it was to captain

Lancashire for three years, the three years in which they achieved their highest sustained level of attainment. He was 36 years old, with a good club record as a bat and, more importantly, a fine war record. A severe but just disciplinarian, and, as such, an exemplar of those dual military virtues, he commanded his troops with devotion to detail. He excelled in what would now be called man-management. A. N. Hornby would have appreciated the manner in which he cajoled professionals of varying temperament into a fighting unit. It is a tale well known to the makers of Hollywood movies – Yul Brynner and *The Magnificent Seven*, Lee Marvin and *The Dirty Dozen*, for example – but less evident in everyday reality. He scored over 3500 runs for Lancashire, including a century against Gloucestershire in 1923 before he was skipper, but he was, self-evidently, the worst cricketer in the team and probably understood less about cricket than any of his colleagues. But he understood something of character and enough of tactics to cope, and, by judicious leaning on the senior professionals, like a good company commander on his sergeant-majors, he fashioned great success.

It was a propitious time. The war left every family and every street bereaved, but a huge city like Manchester was able to shrug off some of the cares of warfare. In fact, with uniforms, bandages and other articles in big demand, the textile industry had fared well enough. Manchester was, outside London, the country's largest financial centre, the annual turnover of its Clearing House two billion pounds, twice that of Liverpool's. A million tons of freight through the Ship Canal made Manchester a thriving port, and, although raw cotton remained the staple and three dozen steam lines were involved with its import, the Ship Canal permitted Manchester the luxury of diversification. The Royal Exchange was built in 1921, by which time Manchester was already Britain's second oil port. In 1896 the Trafford Park industrial estate began business, the first and, for decades, the largest of its kind in Europe. Attracting firms like Ford and Westinghouse, the modern typology of the multinational company was established there. It was not far from Old Trafford. Any foolish fancies of sylvan charm were long past. Old Trafford was built around, in the township of Stretford, with residential and commercial edifices. It was surrounded by urban and industrial artefacts.

Luckily, there was little or no high-rise development, and Old

Trafford was an expensive and low-slung ground, so that, despite the drizzle, its reputation for light remained. From the pavilion balcony one may still espy the Derbyshire hills, when visible a sign of imminent rain, or, the local saw predictably runs, if invisible proof the rain has already arrived. Old Trafford also benefited, as it still does, from a refusal to pander to the more selfish wants of the membership by playing with the pavilion to the side. With unimpeded sight-lines behind both wickets, the seedy movement of screens and people, common on some Test grounds, was and is avoided and batting was and remains unhindered.

The last quarter of the century had formulated the traditional working-class culture, much beloved, in caricature, of the novelist and the television producer. The Great War did little to change that. It is true that the prosperous advance of the upper cohort of that class had been halted, and the economic cracks, started in late Victorian England, were to grow more overt. The General Strike, in the warm spring of Lancashire's first post-war triumph, was one signal. The depression of the 1930s would soon be the 1860s cotton slump writ large. For the time being, however, the professional cricketer was the genuine epitome of the respectable topside of the proletariat. Stable, watchful, complacent and a little self-satisfied, they knew their place and preferred it. They were tradesmen, skilled and decently paid. They would stroll, in their good boots, watch-chains across their waistcoats, around the wintry streets of their spinning or weaving homelands, un-pressurised by the stress of the mill hooter and admired by their peers. In the summer evenings they would sink their pints and smoke their pipes in the quiet, second-grade hotels of Worcester or Canterbury, and then, off again by train, to Taunton or to Gloucester. The motor car, the cinema and the dance hall had not yet exerted their socially magnetic pull.

They could be awkward and temperamental, and Major Green would sort out any nonsense behind closed doors, for the honour of the regiment. Presumably they had marital tiffs and certainly one or two succumbed too adoringly to the arms of Bacchus. No newspaper reporter would have deigned to write nor any news-paper to print such yarns, and few cricket readers would have cared to read them. Manchester had its own reputable newspaper, the *Manchester Guardian*, and, in Neville Cardus the professionals of Lancashire found their Boswell. It is fashionable now to scoff that his portrait of the thick-accented Lancashire 'pro', canny in approach, dry in humour, is sentimental and idealised. Neville Cardus was assuredly more interested in the truth of character than of fact, but it would be wrong to jump to the conclusion that the pictures he etched had no base. That solid and ironic culture existed, the stolidity and the irony visited oftentimes by their near-neighbours, ponderousness and smugness. Neville Cardus asked Richard Tyldesley why, when batsman and umpire agreed he had made a clean slip catch, he insisted that he had not, and the ball had touched the grass. His answer was, 'Westhoughton Sunday School, Mr Cardus, Westhoughton Sunday School'. Whether or not Richard Tyldesley actually said the words, and he well may have done, they were, in effect, the real explanation.

With obliging tidiness, halfway in time through this history, while county cricket was yet a popular, two-class sport, this was the prototype of the cricketers who, with Cardus as their Pepys or Evelyn, were ready over three seasons to carry Lancashire cricket to its mightiest heights yet or since.

*1926 . . . 1927 . . . 1928*

Leonard Green and his Magnificent Eleven won the Championship in 1926, and then enjoyed the sensation of two sequels, losing only three games in that brave spell.

The start was none too auspicious: four draws through some drizzling days, and then a Charlie Hallows century helped defeat Derbyshire, and a Harry Makepeace century Leicestershire. Lancashire lost at Whitsuntide to Yorkshire at Bradford and, next, drew with Kent. Surrey were beaten after Lancashire had been 95 behind on the first innings. Makepeace was in strong form. His two good innings against Northamptonshire, assisted by 8 for 15 from Dick Tyldesley, gave Lancashire a fourth win, and there followed a promising victory over the strong Nottinghamshire combine. First, Makepeace carried his bat, with 92 out of 159, and, second, Leonard Green and he put together sufficient of a stand for McDonald to weight in with seven cheap wickets. Lancashire drew with Middlesex in damp weather at Lord's, and beat Gloucestershire; and then, at Ashby de la Zouch, a purportedly weak Leicestershire side thrashed Lancashire by 144 runs.

After this game, sensationally, Parkin was dropped and returned to the leagues from whence he came. Somehow the Lancashire team sloughed off its unease, and never lost again. Having won eight of the first score of games, they won nine of the remaining 12. Much was due to the venomously accurate pace of E. A. McDonald. Thirteen wickets at Birmingham and 12 at Dover, including a hat-trick, secured two useful victories, although rain salvaged Sussex and Somerset, there was a draw at the Oval, and Essex, in one of the select Nelson fixtures, fought gamely for another draw. Lancashire, despite the improved quality of their play and their demeanour, had still only won eight games, and the season seemed wellnigh over.

Demonstrating stern character, Lancashire won at Taunton against Somerset, and against Derbyshire at Chesterfield, where, after Frank Watson and Charlie Hallows reached centuries, Richard Tyldesley heaved and appealed his massive way to 5 for 17 and 5 for 18. Derbyshire were all out for 46 in their second innings. Makepeace pored for five hours over 140 at Leyton against Essex, and then, at Old Trafford, there was a drawn match with Middlesex.

Finally, Lancashire ended with five stout victories. Glamorgan and Northamptonshire both perished at Blackpool, Worcestershire were well beaten, Hampshire, caught after a thunderstorm on a drying wicket, were disposed of by McDonald and the young Jack Iddon, who took 5 for 9, and big centuries at Old Trafford by Makepeace and Tyldesley overwhelmed Nottinghamshire. Although Yorkshire had not lost at all, Lancashire's 17 victories guaranteed them the Championship, by a short head.

It was even closer in the moist summer of 1927, when Lancashire were separated from Nottinghamshire by 0.9 per cent, a narrow shave indeed. Nationally, less than half the county games were finished that year, and Lancashire drew no fewer than 17, winning only ten. However, they lost just once – to Sussex – and scraped home not too convincingly. The batting erred on the side of caution, and there was an overdependence on McDonald.

It was the reverse of the previous season. This time Lancashire made a forthright beginning. Iddon, who first played in 1924, took 6 for 22 and Warwickshire were all out for 64. They drew the return match at Birmingham, but beat Somerset, Frank Sibbles now making his mark with 12 wickets in the match. At Ilkeston, needing 106 in an hour, Lancashire flopped riskily to 68 for 7 in a futile endeavour; and then they drew, at Old Trafford, versus Gloucestershire, for whom a youthful Hammond famously made

187. But there followed five good wins. Hampshire were rolled aside by heavy batting at Liverpool and Glamorgan were wiped out in two days. Worcestershire, Gloucestershire and Yorkshire, against whom McDonald took 11 wickets, were all decisively beaten.

Unluckily, the rainy season set in, and Lancashire found maximum points in only one more game of the remaining 14 and that against Hampshire at Southampton. Hallows spent five hours over 118 to save the Sussex match, and Iddon scored a century, his first for the club, as a score of over 500 was assembled against Surrey. Thereafter a mix of frustrating rain and some grim fighting-back by eager opponents led to one draw after another. Nottinghamshire actually won 12, two more than Lancashire, but they had an edge in first-innings leads, 11 to Nottingham's eight. Lancashire, late on in the season, found the going at Trent Bridge difficult. Collapsing to 148 in reply to Nottinghamshire's 420, Lancashire followed on, but Hallows batted over two hours until the rains brought safety. He scored seven during this vigil. After losing to Sussex and drawing with Leicestershire, Lancashire had to await the outcome of Nottinghamshire's last match. Newcomers Glamorgan, thumbing noses at the form-book, skittled Nottinghamshire for 61, and Lancashire were champions a second time.

1928 was a glowing warm summer of hard-baked wickets. Hallows's thousand runs in May foreshadowed much run-making all season, and it was Lancashire's good fortune that McDonald had perhaps his most hostile year, taking 178 Championship wickets. As token for the season, Hallows's benefit match against Surrey produced 1155 runs for the loss of 13 wickets, Surrey 567 and Lancashire 588 for 4. Frank Watson's 300, not out, was then Lancashire's best-ever score, MacLaren's 424 apart; it overtook Johnny Tyldesley's 295 in 1902 to become the highest score ever attained at Old Trafford, and this stood until 1964 when Bobby Simpson made 311 for Australia. In concert with Tyldesley, the second wicket accrued 371, a Lancashire record for any wicket.

Frank Watson began the season with 223 against Northamptonshire, who were severely trounced, and, now opening the batting with Charlie Hallows, the two enjoyed five opening stands of over 200 and another seven over 100 during the season. Glamorgan were also clearly beaten, and soon Essex and Sussex. Nevertheless, draws at Swansea, at Lord's, at Birmingham (despite

Iddon taking 8 for 50) and elsewhere meant only four wins in the first ten matches. Other counties were finding batting simple, too. Kent were pressing hard, and, in Tich Freeman, they had a leg-spinner superbly capable of taking full advantage of the hard wickets.

E. A. McDonald then commenced a long and punishing phase of bowling. It began with 11 wickets at Colchester, where everyone had severally to assemble on the third day while Lancashire scored two runs for a ten-wicket victory. Some rare rainfall halted the Warwickshire match, but Tyldesley's batting secured another victory at Southampton, yet then Worcestershire held Lancashire to another annoying draw. McDonald bowled on. Suddenly there were four wins, over Hampshire, Essex, Surrey, where, at the Oval, Iddon got 184 not out, and Kent. During this quartet of successes, McDonald, took 35 for 526.

There were a couple of draws with the powerful Nottinghamshire and Yorkshire teams, then, after Middlesex were beaten at Old Trafford, there followed a crucial contest with Kent, also at Old Trafford. Woolley dominated the early hours of the Kent innings, and they seemed to be cruising, healthy and optimistic, at 262 for 4. McDonald, supported by Frank Sibbles, who was now a regular member of the eleven, abruptly shot out the last six for only 15. Watson and Hallows produced, inevitably, a start in the grand manner, and then Ernest Tyldesley made good the ground with Hallows. Lancashire declared at 478 for 5. McDonald proved an extremely hazardous proposition, and Kent collapsed for 113, the Australian taking 15 wickets all told.

Kent were destined to be runners-up. Rain interfered with the Leicestershire match and it was drawn, disappointingly, after a huge, unbroken stand by Iddon and Tyldesley of 300. It epitomised the season that, as a finale, the batting of Tyldesley and the bowling of McDonald caused the downfall of Sussex at Hove. Lancashire, unbeaten, and with 15 solid victories, won probably their most clearcut Championship of them all.

Oddly, they always seemed to go off the boil at season's end. In 1926 they were subjected to a merciless harrying by the Rest in the Champion's match at the Oval. Woolley raced to 172 in two hours, and Lancashire lost by the humiliating margin of 374 runs. In 1927 the rain characteristic of that year assisted them, not forgetting a Hallows century, to a draw, but their 1928 record was tarnished by a single defeat, again by the Rest at the Oval.

Lancashire started well, but slumped to 296. The Rest's total was a towering 603, scored in less than six hours, and they won by an innings and 91. A friendly encounter with Wales at Blackpool at the end of the same season also gave them a shock. The veteran Sydney Barnes, in his mid-fifties, returned to haunt old colleagues with a cheap haul of six wickets, but Hallows, yet again, paved the way to victory with a century.

The machine ground on in 1929. 1929 was a summer of larger stumps, a county ban on press articles by professionals and the most rational Championship yet, all counties being obliged to undertake 28 fixtures and points replacing percentages. Major Green had business demands, and another 'natural' leader had to be discovered, another well-to-do amateur to do his duty and officiate over the 'pros'. Peter Eckersley was appointed. He was only 23, but had made his debut when he was 19, and had learned some of the job at Green's elbow. He was, above all, an enthusiast, and he captained the county for seven seasons. He was much the same calibre as Green as a batsman, if he lacked something of the older man's civic virtue of command. He scored 4500 or so runs, and scored one century, at Bristol in 1927. P. T. Eckersley became Conservative MP for the Exchange Division of Manchester at the 1935 General Election, and, sadly, was killed on active service with the navy in the summer of 1940.

The well-drilled combat unit inherited by Peter Eckersley gave a firm account of itself in his first year as skipper. Lancashire tied for second place with Yorkshire behind Nottinghamshire in first place. They won 12, and lost only three, to Nottinghamshire, Sussex and Gloucestershire. Age and staleness had withered the dominant character of Lancashire cricket, but the sheer mastery of technique and the long hand of experience disguised most of the inner failings.

Creaking they may have been, but, over yet another horribly dank summer, this highly trained band of journeymen cricketers grafted away to another Championship. 1930 was a season of plentiful draws – Lancashire counted 18 – but they ensured no one beat them, and contrived to chalk up ten conquests over the weaker vessels. It was a very astute performance.

Lancashire banked high points in the opening and rather dryer stages of the season. There were wins over Gloucestershire, Northamptonshire twice, Glamorgan, against whom Ernest Tyldesley scored two hundreds in the match, and, after rain marred the

Middlesex fixture at Lord's, a crushing defeat for Leicestershire. In between times, Lancashire drew twice with the Australians, and, at Aigburth, the ageing McDonald had the pleasure of bowling the stripling Bradman.

Five draws followed. Rain was universal. It was July before Lancashire won again, but they chose their victims sagely. It was Kent, at that juncture the Championship leaders. Tyldesley, in his early forties, belaboured the Kentish bowlers for 206 in three hours, and McDonald took 11 wickets. Bill Farrimond, Duckworth's perpetual understudy, had seven victims in one innings, six caught and one stumped, an all-time Lancashire record and the equal of the English county record. Lancashire won by an innings and 49. McDonald got his third hat-trick for the county at Edgbaston (he had previously performed the feat in 1925 and 1926 against Sussex and Kent, respectively) and this was another win. The return match at Old Trafford against Warwickshire was narrowly and irksomely drawn, and marked by a glorious 256, not out, by Tyldesley, his career's best.

More rain and more draws: eight in all, and Yorkshire pushed themselves to the head of the table. However, Lancashire finished as powerfully as they began, with three out of five wins. Dick Tyldesley took 12 wickets against Leicestershire; the double was completed over Kent, at Dover; and Essex were swamped by 174 runs at Blackpool. Predictably, the Rest beat the champions quite easily at the Oval.

## The Structure of the Championship Team

Champions in four out of five years, and only an ace away in the fifth year: this was the zenith of Lancashire cricket. It was not the cavalry charge of MacLaren and Spooner. Perhaps the Great War had left a mark, for these conquests had more of the attrition of trench warfare about them. Because of its calculating fashion, it is a success which is tellingly illustrated by statistics. The robot-like consistency of these skilled professionals may lack the glamour of the Edwardian era, but one must perforce admire the assurance and the control. When fine brass bands of the time, like Black Dyke Mills or Foden's Motor Works, sat down in the bandstand, they had no fears that they might not play cogently and melodiously. The Lancashire cricketers of the 1920s similarly lacked self-doubt. They were as adept at their trade as any engineer a few hundred yards away in Trafford Park: they reduced to a minimum the margin of error and the scope for failure.

In the Championship years of 1926–30, Ernest Tyldesley's runs for the county numbered 2432 (average 62), 1610 (50), 2467 (77), 1506 (45) and 1904 (49). Charlie Hallows's tally was 1406, 2119 (73), 2564 (66) and 1265, with something of a dearth in 1930. Harry Makepeace scored 2340 (49) in 1926 and 1351 in 1928. Frank Watson's series of totals was 1420, 1536, 2541 (63), 2137 and 2031, an amazing run, second only to Ernest Tyldesley. Jack Iddon scored 1066 in 1926, 1353 (52) in 1928, 1739 in 1929 and 1352 in 1930. J. L. Hopwood also passed a thousand runs in 1930. Lancashire batsmen have scored 2000 for the county on 25 occasions: eleven of those occasions were in the years 1922–30.

There were stands and centuries galore. There were 25 stands of over 200 in the same period, while in 1928 alone there were 34 centuries. In the triple Championship years, Frank Watson had 14 centuries, Charlie Hallows, 20, and Ernest Tyldesley, 23. In 1928 ten of the team averaged over 20.

Teamwork was no idle shibboleth for this hardworking gang of runmakers. Tactics were carefully considered. Batsmen would be selected to take certain bowlers or to eschew self-aggrandisement for other reasons, such as the need to accelerate or decelerate the tempo. There is no doubt that Makepeace and Watson were slow, and that the elegant Hallows, not naturally in the Barlow tradition, adjusted his style along similar lines. It was all about the solidity of the base. Risks before lunch were against the rules of Lancashire's game, not as a symptom of weakly defence, but to tire and demoralise the opponents. Indeed, a minimum of 400 in the day was the target, and it was frequently met, with the rate gradually lifted until, in the last overs of the evening, runs came furiously. That construction, not just of an individual innings, but of a complete innings, was an architectural triumph. Here were the master-builders.

Protected and insured by the bounty of runs, their allies, the bowlers, were equally talented and encouraged to assail the enemy at all times and by all methods. Central to this scheme of things was the classic pace of E. A. McDonald. In these five years of Lancashire predominance, he took 175, 150, 190, 142 and 108 wickets, an average of 150 a year. To the sharpness of this knightly lance, Dick Tyldesley, like some archer at Agincourt, added the wiles of his devious trajectory. His spin-bowling was the suitable counterpoint to the speed of the Australian. In that quintet of famous years, his sum of wickets ran as follows: 128, 100, 104, 154 (at an average of 15) and 133, a total of 619 to add to the 765 of his partner. With Iddon and Sibbles and, latterly, Hopwood offering decent support, it made for a balanced attack, if lacking the range of Hornby's team and, that ancient Lancashire failing, a second top-class opening bowler.

The fielding was sufficient. Specialist bowlers and batters of this merit were not likely to allow opportunities to slip through their fingers by poor fielding. It was a safe fielding team, but it was not electrifying. These were careful, thoughtful men, several old-timers by sporting criteria, and they did not rush about too much. In fact, there was some slowness of motion in the field, and, unusually for the county, there was no outstanding cover point. They situated themselves with precision and held their catches, none more so than Dick Tyldesley, a Billy Bunter or Friar Tuck at first slip, voracious in his appetite and pouching most catches, including six – a county record – against Hampshire in 1921.

There was a memorable exception to this lack of glamour in the field. George Duckworth first played in 1923, and was capped for England the following year. In 1928, the season of Lancashire's most convincing title win, he became their first wicket-keeper to register a hundred first-class victims: 107, 30 stumped and 77 caught; 97 in the county matches, and still fourth in line of most dismissals in a season. His ebullience and proficiency made the somewhat pedestrian fielding look sharper, and Duckworth proved to be a major influence on Lancashire's progress. He did not conceive of wicket-keeping as a defensive role: he was always a spirited attacker, so that batsmen were as worried about the enemy at their rear as the one approaching them. Moreover, his grasp of cricket was profound, and he was well placed to detect chinks of weakness in a rival batsman. Alongside Harry Make-peace and Ernest Tyldesley, he soon became part of the kitchen cabinet which, rather after the manner of the Yorkshire senior professionals of the same era, kept cerebral watch over seemingly physical activity. He made a most salient contribution to Lanca-shire's celebrated seasons.

Lancashire people hugely enjoyed the yearly exploits of this cricketing task-force. Membership was now over 4000 and the ladies' subscriptions were nearly 1400. £10,000 profit was made in 1926, and stands were built or extended. In 1926 76,617 fans attended the Yorkshire match at Old Trafford, the third-largest attendance in the history of county matches, and the largest since the First World War. These are the measures of prosperous success, and a number of aspects help explain it. There was the moral view, beloved of the establishment, that cricket's exemplary virtues created its own pure and attractive ethic. There was the aesthetic principle, enunciated mellifluously by Neville Cardus, with the bowling of McDonald, for instance, in parallel with what the Hallé Orchestra was achieving a mile or so north at the Free Trade Hall. For those who found this a little ripe and ornate, there was the sense of identification with vigorous battle and definite success, an element which has grown much stronger over the last 50 years, but was, of course, present in the 1920s.

The fourth ingredient was also apparent then, and should not be underestimated. People wanted to be entertained. Cecil Parkin was the jester supreme, and it is said there were hundreds who turned their back on Old Trafford after his departure. But the others had a trick or two to play. The crowds chuckled and groaned in mock-horror as Makepeace and Hallows, down there in the engine room, determined on reducing speed from dead-slow to stop; they chortled gaily as fat Dick Tyldesley wheezed his heartfelt appeals both to unfeeling umpires and the fates that conspired to mortify him; they waited expectantly for and, with a similar familiarity, laughingly delighted in George Duckworth's shrill and assertive claim, as they would for the catch-phrase of a popular comedian.

The crowd would disperse and, on the Saturday evening, might assemble at the Palace, Manchester or the Hippodrome, Hulme or the Empire, Salford to enjoy the antics and sallies of Sandy Powell or Billy Bennett. The tradition of a fixture or two at Stanley Park, Blackpool, usually at the season's back-end, during the final wakes' weeks, was properly established in 1923. After a day at the cricket there might follow an evening at the Central Pier or the Winter Gardens, where Clapham and Dwyer might be opening the batting. The Lancashire professionals were old-headed and self-aware. Instinctively, they understood the culture in which they operated. They had the wit, first, to spot their own foibles, and, second, to exploit them for the delectation of the crowded terracing.

However, this strong team was already beginning to disintegrate.

It is convenient to examine more closely what in the variety theatre might have been called their bill matter.

## Cecil Parkin

Right away one starts with Cecil Parkin at the top of the bill, for he was probably the most consciously funny man the game has known. After producing sensations with Church in the Lancashire League, he made his début for Lancashire in 1914, when he was already in his late twenties. It was 1922 before his league commitments allowed him to play full-time for Lancashire, and, as we have noted, a little into the 1926 season, and although he had taken 39 wickets at an average of 16, he was dropped. He was shocked. After all, he was the star. Major Green, weeks into his captaincy, was determined to brook no ill-discipline, and may even have been over-keen to seek out a punitive example. He may, too, have soon realised that his military training offered no assistance in coping with this awkward squaddie. Cec Parkin made a dramatic appeal to the committee: 'God has given me,' he began, 'these hands to work with ...' It was one of the most steadfast assertions by a cricketer that the labourer is worthy of his hire, although, with Parkin, one wonders whether, even at that moment, he was burlesquing a little. Back he went to the leagues, where he played another 11 years, and thus he was not really part of the five years of consistent success.

A low Anglican, rather solemn deity was worshipped in our house, five minutes' train ride from Old Trafford. That was for the sabbath. For weekday adoration, the household gods were Johnny Tyldesley, Billy Meredith and George Formby, senior. Billy Meredith was the legendary 'Welsh Wizard', the precursor of Stanley Matthews, who played outside-right for Manchester City and Manchester United. George Formby, senior was probably the only comic to convey deep-seated melancholia with the firm conviction that everything was dandy, and, alongside Gus Elen, he was one of only two artists Marie Lloyd would deign to watch. This trinity attracted the childhood hero-worship of my father, and so, by the time he was a young man, there was an addition to the litany. Post-war comedians were held in some contempt and, sorrowfully, Manchester United made manifest no household gods between the wars: thus it was left to Cec Parkin to play the role which, in the Christian persuasion, is taken by St Paul.

Hour after hour we would listen enthralled to the tales of his wonders, like the good citizens of Corinth or Ephesus clinging on to every last word of the latest epistle. How he went as opposing speaker to a serious cricket debate, agreed entirely with the first speaker and did card-tricks instead; how he palmed an orange and, pretending to pick up an impossible drive, splattered it into Duckworth's gloves; how, a tall and dextrous man, he would attempt suicide runs, yet somehow leaving his bat touching the inside of the crease, thereby inducing hasty shies at the wicket and subsequent overthrows; how his mock catching of fast shots to the boundary, complete with self-congratulatory throw-up and catch, would send persuasible batsmen half-way to the pavilion; how, chatting volubly to mid-off, he would stroll toward a rolling ball and it would spring exactly into his hand off his boot; how, in general, he could reduce an opposing field to dislocation and near-anarchy by his Groucho-like approach to batting, or opposing batsmen to disbelief by the varied and experimental science of his bowling.

Missing the point by miles, Pelham Warner, and others, felt he was more interested in trying something different with each ball than in bowling *per se*. Cec Parkin had the more authentic grasp of what the game meant to the spectators. For those who find Yorkshire's tedious insistence on indigenous talent a trifle wearing, perhaps Parkin's most amusing sting was to play for Yorkshire, although born in Egglescliffe, County Durham. In those his younger days, he was beanpole-like and stringy, scarcely nine stone in weight, and, in spite of his obvious faculty for bowling, Lancashire were initially loath to engage him. Eventually, on his début, he took 14 for 99 against Leicestershire, and, in all, 34 in six matches.

After the war, he had to be inveigled back from Rochdale, itself the home of such fine comics as Gracie Fields and Norman Evans. He was being paid £15 per week by the club, and its chairman, Jimmy White, talked of paying him thousands to remain. Returning to the Lancashire ranks in 1922, he took 172 wickets, average 17, in the Championship, his best figures being 14 for 73 against Derbyshire. In what amounted to little more than four full seasons, he took 901 wickets for Lancashire, at an average of 16, in 157 matches, a striking rate of six wickets in a match. His best innings performance was 9 for 32 against Leicestershire at Ashby in 1924 and his best match figures were 15 for 95 against

Glamorgan at Blackpool in 1923. His idiosyncratic batting produced just under 2000 runs, but his true merit lies in the fact that, despite so brief a sojourn in the county game, he stands as high as thirteenth in the register of Lancashire bowlers.

Whatever the forebodings of the establishment, such talent could not be gainsaid, and, on his first-ever visit to London, he took nine wickets for the Players. He played in ten Tests and took 32 wickets, but, during the 1924 South African tour, he was too trusting of his ghost writer, and found himself responsible for a newspaper attack on A. E. R. Gilligan, his England skipper, during a Test match. Although privately Gilligan and Parkin were reconciled, he was never forgiven in public.

Cec Parkin was, of course, gifted enough to play the Cheeky Chappie, and carry it off. He enjoyed batting with Richard Tyldesley, and that rotund worthy would be alarmed to find Parkin trotting alongside him as he tottered between the wickets. At Lord's once, batting with Tyldesley, he created one of his moments of panic, and, as the ball whistled away for more overthrows, he shouldered his bat, marching back to his crease, whistling 'The British Grenadiers'. Cecil Parkin, the Max Miller of cricket, would croon as he ran up to bowl: 'The sky is blue,' he warbled, 'and I love *you*,' with the accent on the final syllable as the ball was delivered. In a literary exchange in the 1921 Test at Old Trafford a spectator, bored with H. L. Collins's sloth while batting for Australia, bawled out to Lionel Tennyson that he should 'read him one of your grandfather's poems'. Out lbw to Parkin soon afterwards, Parkin explained to the spectators that he had taken this advice, and Collins, falling asleep as a consequence, had been easy meat.

He bowled trickily at medium pace, extracting a lot of work from the ball with his conjuror's fingers. Dark-haired and slim, he returned in later years to help coach bowlers at Old Trafford. It must not be thought he took cricket less than seriously, for it was the rationale of his being. In the old cricketer's favourite profession of publican, at the Northumberland Hotel, on the Chester Road, near Old Trafford, and, later at the King's Head, Droylsden, he would yarn happily for hours about the game. What he refused to do was cast cricket in an unnecessary solemnity.

He died, during the Second World War, in the June of 1943, when he was only 57. A final ghoulish jape was to have his ashes spread on the wicket at Old Trafford. As a boy, the first action I observed on my first visit to the county ground, when matches were resumed there in 1944, was Cec Parkin's ashes blowing up and around the faces of the mourners, as a prelude to a game between the North of England and the Royal Australian Air Force. This piece having begun on a religious note, it is fitting to end it similarly, with Cecil Parkin's most celebrated aphorism. As, time and again, the batsman essayed unChristian heaves at the weaving ball, yet still managed narrowly to survive, he rolled his eyes heavenward and exclaimed, 'And they send missionaries to China.'

## Makepeace and Hallows

The opening duo whose names flow on the tongue as easily as a firm of solicitors or ships' chandlers is rarer today, but, once, there was an automatic assumption that Hobbs and Sutcliffe, or their county equivalents, would stay in business for ever.

After Hornby and Barlow, Makepeace and Hallows are Lancashire's most fondly remembered opening pair, with Washbrook and Place a respectable third. They became a byword for persistent defence. Neville Cardus tells of leaving Old Trafford, with Makepeace and Hallows arrived at the crease, in order to get married at All Saints Register Office, returning to find the score elevated to 17, chiefly in leg-byes.

It is true they were obdurate bats. Between them they carried their bat through ten innings, and, in 1926, they opened with hundred partnerships in both innings against the Australians at Liverpool. Makepeace, especially, had learned, in part from the Australians, that the sapping of a bowling attack, prior to withering assault, was the most profitable strategy. Like Ernest Tyldesley, he understood the need to watch particular bowlers, or keep an eye out for the approaching interval, or to counter the threat of the new ball. Unlike some slow batsmen, he was essentially a team batsman.

There was a basic difference. Harry Makepeace was innately cautious, while Charlie Hallows was nurtured into due care. Makepeace took a Calvinist attitude to his batting, eschewing all mortal error in the hope of divine grace, reducing his earthly acts to the minimum compatible with survival. Hallows was more the high Anglican, reluctantly acceding to the demands of the Puritan revolution. There was the whiff of incense around his batting. A slinky off-drive from about middle and leg, or a gossamer-like leg glance from off his middle stump: these hinted at the priest rather than the preacher, the sacristy not the kirk. Sometimes the flamboyance would be overrife, and 'Shake' would stride down the wicket to 'Flight' (to mention both their odd nicknames) and scold him, John Bunyan rebuking Cardinal Newman.

They only won six England caps between them, although Makepeace scored 117 on tour in Australia, 1920–21, but the parochial fan found this agony bearable, as it meant they were in constant deployment for Lancashire. Critics said Hallows's fielding was poor by international standards. Hallows played 370 games between 1914 and 1932; Makepeace 487 between 1906 and 1930. Charlie Hallows came, like his uncle Jimmy who did the double for Lancashire in 1904, from the Bolton area, while Harry Makepeace was, as if to abet those who believe in regional characteristics, originally a Yorkshireman. They consistently scored their thousand and more runs a summer, Makepeace 13 times (twice reaching 2000) and Hallows 11 (thrice reaching 2000). Makepeace recorded 43 centuries, all but his single Test hundred for Lancashire, while Hallows had 55 hundreds, all but three for the county. Two hundred and three at Worcester in 1923 was Makepeace's best, whereas Hallows's tallest innings was 233 not out, at Aigburth in 1927 against Hampshire.

So were their careers parallel, until, eventually, their separate spirits are revealed. Charlie Hallows was the more dramatic. In 1928 he became one of only three batsmen to score a thousand runs in May, joining W. G. Grace and W. R. Hammond on that pedestal. Tom Hayward, Bradman (twice), Bill Edrich, G. M. Turner and the prodigious young Hick required a fragment of April to complete their thousands. It took Hallows 27 days from 5 May to 31 May, and his series ran: 123, 101 and 51 not out, 22, 74 and 104, 58 and 34 not out, and, finally, 232 from some sympathetic Sussex bowling. It was extremely precise, ending on May's last day with exactly 1000. His average, 125, was higher than that of Grace or Hammond. One might be forgiven for saying he walked on hallowed ground. He scored ten centuries that summer, perhaps Lancashire's best-ever season, and this included 123 and 101 not out, in the Warwickshire match at Birmingham. He had previously achieved this against Leicestershire at Ashby de la Zouch in 1924. He was lucky enough to take his benefit against Surrey just after the completion of his springtide thousand, scoring 36 and collecting nearly £3000, Lancashire's largest benefit until after the Second World War.

Not for Makepeace were such shenanigans. However, in the ultimate analysis, the doggedness enduring over many years sets him above his defter partner. With 25,207 runs stored, squirrel-like, over the seasons, Makepeace stands fourth behind the Tyldesleys and Cyril Washbrook. His average is 36. Hallows just touched 20,000 runs, with an average of 40. Between them they scored only 1376 other first-class runs in all those manifold seasons. They were trusty and well-beloved servants of the club.

Harry Makepeace played right-half in the Everton team behind Jack Sharp on the wing when they beat Newcastle United, 1–0, in the 1905–6 Cup Final at the Crystal Palace. A double international, like Sharp, and with a cupwinner's medal to add to a century against Australia, his is a rare collection of sporting attainments. He was born in the August of 1881, and, having become deputy coach and then recalled to the colours, he was 49 in his last playing season. He followed John Tyldesley as coach, whereas Hallows, perhaps to Lancashire's disbenefit, sought coaching work elsewhere, before returning home as coach in 1965. Makepeace remained as coach until his death just before Christmas 1952. He was then 71. Charlie Hallows died in November 1972, aged 77.

It was unkindly remarked of Makepeace that he coached the bowlers to bowl off the wickets and the batsmen to leave them alone. What is true is that he endeavoured to instil basic tenets into young players, and to imbue within them some of his own virtues of watchful patience. It was not unknown for him to appear on the Old Trafford balcony wielding three stumps as an *aide-mémoire* to an inexact bowler of his target. Over 40 years of dedicated service carved out for Makepeace a specific niche in the stones of Lancashire cricket. Charlie Hallows, always the more elegant, with his dash of what Makepeace probably thought of as amateurism, was his most valued foil. The one was robust and craggy in build, with a flattened nose and the makings of a scowl. The other was tall, good-looking, and with his black hair sleekly plastered. Makepeace was all right-handed cussedness; Hallows had the left-hander's grace to moderate his own regard for self-preservation.

As Makepeace aged, Frank Watson was drawn more into the frame, and a subsidiary opening partnership of Hallows and Watson ensued. Frank Watson leaned more to Makepeace than to Hallows in demeanour. If Harry Makepeace had an outstanding trait, it was fortitude. He refused for over 20 seasons to flinch, and he looked for equal courage in his trainees. The defiant Watson was on a par. Less marked as a public figure and thus less spoken of over the pints in the pubs and club bars, he nevertheless proved a titanic batsman. He was born in 1898, dying, aged 77, in 1976, and he came into the Lancashire side in 1920 to play 456 matches between then and his retirement in 1937.

During this time he was an unsung hero who garnered almost 23,000 for Lancashire, fifth in the list, just behind Harry Makepeace, and, with 37, a better average. He scored 50 centuries, all but one for Lancashire, and his 300 not out, against Surrey in 1928 is Lancashire's third-highest individual total. In season after season he laboured to his thousand runs, 12 times in all, and, in a triple spell of success, 1928–30, he scored 2000 each year. In 1928 he shared in an extraordinary dozen opening stands of over a hundred with Charlie Hallows. F. B. Watson, never spirited away to play for England, although he joined a minor MCC tour to the West Indies, rarely failed. He was involved in no less than 15 stands of over 200, five of them with Hallows in 1928. Four times, including the Lancashire second-wicket record, these partnerships totted over 300.

All these runs were acquired with virtuous husbandry, his only curtsey to unseemliness being a productive late chop, particularly useful, perhaps, against leg-spin, the playing of which he found relatively simple. To all this merit there must be added the 400 wickets he took for Lancashire as a somewhat expensive change-bowler – his average was 32, not far from his batting average. Still, it amounts to one of the most solid careers in the county's lengthy history. This is a tale dotted with brief encounters with brilliant stars who failed or vanished, and thus some emphasis must be given to Makepeace, Hallows and also to Watson, for, among them, they played over 1300 matches for Lancashire.

These three built the foundation for Lancashire's prime triumphs, with a fourth, Ernest Tyldesley, making an even more notable contribution.

## Ernest Tyldesley

The most productive and businesslike batsman in Lancashire's history is Ernest Tyldesley, and a cricketing equivalent of the *Financial Times* Share Index is required to suggest even a modicum of his prodigious industry. His diligence and acumen brought him 38,874 runs, 34,222 for the county, and that is the highest total gathered by a Lancashire player. His county average of over 45 is also Lancashire's best, although Clive Lloyd has a superior average when all matches are considered. Ernest Tyldesley is the twentieth-most successful run-getter of all time, and he is one of only 21 batsmen to have scored a hundred centuries, 102 in all, 90 for Lancashire. He is the only Lancastrian to have passed that supreme test, and they range from his 107 against Surrey in 1912 to his 137 against Sussex in 1935.

The yearly dividends declared by this most profitable of enterprises were unfailingly consistent. He reached a thousand runs on no less than 19 occasions, and only Cyril Washbrook, with one more, has surpassed this for Lancashire. In five of these seasons he scored more than 2000. In 1928 he amassed 3024, the only Lancashire player, other than John Tyldesley, ever to have scored 3000 in a season.

He seven times scored double centuries, and his highest innings was 256; not out, versus Warwickshire in 1930. A further record is his 166 half-centuries for the county, while, in 1926, he established a world record of ten consecutive half-centuries, a remarkable feat not equalled until Bradman managed a similar run in the 1947–48 and 1948 seasons. From 26 June to 6 August 1926, his scores were: 144, 69 and 144 not out, 226, 51 and 131, 131 (for the Players), 106, 126, 81, 44, 139 and 85. Another paltry six runs to that 44, and it would have constituted a run of 13 half-centuries. The series included four consecutive hundreds and eight in all, while Ernest Tyldesley scored 1128 runs in the nine innings which fell in the month of July. Cricket reveals few instances of such intensive mastery of its batting science.

An intriguing sidelight, illustrating the solidity and careful teamwork of Lancashire's batsmen then, is the number of productive partnerships in which Ernest Tyldesley, like many another shrewd business tycoon, was involved. Invariably batting first-wicket down, he shared in no less than 27 stands of over 200 for Lancashire, including the county record for the second wicket, 371, with Frank Watson, against Surrey in 1928, four other stands of over 300, three of them with Watson and the last with Jack Iddon, and, happily, stands of 218 and 224, both in 1919, with brother John. Ernest headed the main Lancashire averages seven times and was one of *Wisden*'s famous five for the 1919 season.

One might have expected to find Test honours strewing the path of so competent a batsman, but this was not to be. The co-existence of prime middle-order players, such as Patsy Hendren and Frank Woolley, in the 1920s and the rumour that his nerve might be suspect at the very highest level told against Ernest Tyldesley. He played in 14 Tests, and, in fact, he is by no means disgraced by the resultant figures. He scored 990 runs and made three centuries, and, curiously perhaps, his average of 55 leaves him seventh in the English Test averages and second, behind Eddie Paynter, in Lancastrian Test averages. His most successful foray into Test Cricket was when he played in all five Tests of the 1927–28 tour of South Africa and scored hundreds in the Johannesburg and Durban tests. Many thought he should have been granted a much more regular international place, and it scarcely adds up to a record of failure.

Ernest Tyldesley was born in Worsley, at the Manchester end of the Bridgewater Canal, on 5 February 1889, and he made a startling début for Lancashire in 1909. Batting with MacLaren, he raced to 61 out of 128 in 90 minutes, but, thereafter, his activities were a trifle more circumspect: in 1923, for instance, he tarried five hours over 236 at the Oval. He became settled in the Lancashire side, with the first of his myriad 'thousands', two years before the Great War, and, like all his compatriots, lost four frustrating seasons, which would have added remorselessly to his already fine figures. He was unluckily afflicted by appendicitis part-way through the 1925 season, but he still preserved intact his regularity of scoring a thousand runs in every possible summer from 1913 to 1934: he just managed 1010, at an average of 48. In 1934 he talked of retirement, despite his 2487 runs and an average of almost 58. In 1935 he played only 14 innings, and, although he contrived again to top the averages, he was now 46. He played a game or two as an amateur, but his career was effectively finished.

Like his brother, Ernest Tyldesley made a substantial contribution to the status of the professional cricketer, and his standards, not just of play but of manner, were widely recognised and appreciated. There can be no more genuine evidence of this than the move to make him the Lancashire captain in 1936, when Peter

Eckersley resigned. Amateur standing was, in the minds of many, a matter of birthright, and not something that could be assumed, and the concept of a professional turning amateur to become skipper was not entirely welcome. Ernest Tyldesley's age may also have ruled against him, for his rival for the post was the 24-year-old Formby amateur, W. H. L. Lister. Nevertheless, committee voting of 11 to 6 against indicated a firmness of support that, in those pre-war days, was positively avant-garde. It is said the membership at large had favoured Tyldesley, even as a professional, and the inexperienced Lister had gallantly volunteered to serve under him. After the Second World War, Tyldesley joined the committee and was the first quondam 'pro' so to do. He was chairman of the cricket committee and later a vice-president, again a first for a onetime 'player'. For the benefit of professional cricket, these little political victories were probably more important than Ernest Tyldesley's proud record of unerringly profitable batsmanship. He died, aged 73, on 5 May 1962.

The sheer accrual of Ernest Tylesley's batting inevitably evokes the image of commercial success, with scoreboards totting up his mounting account like great cash registers. That business-oriented metaphor could be misleading, for it might be thought to betoken a soulless approach. Now business has no automatic requirement to be dour and relentless. In the pages of *Nicholas Nickleby* there appear not only Ralph Nickleby, the dark-flavoured villain, but those kindly philanthropists, the Cheeryble Brothers, based, incidentally, by Dickens on a pair of Mancunian businessmen. Both firms seem capable of making boundless profits, but we hate the one and we love the others, who exemplify, as Ted Heath remarked, the acceptable face of capitalism.

Ernest Tyldesley illustrated in fine detail the acceptable face of run-accumulation. Not for him, nor his admiring watchers, the arid or awkward style of some mechanical collectors of countless runs. What he did was to bring unusual concentration to the deployment of a comprehensive range of shots. He was charmingly correct in method and could play any shot with befitting efficiency. The outcome was a sedate and pleasing performance, replete with assurance and underpinned with exceptional mental stamina. Ernest Tyldesley was not so dramatic as his brother at the crease, but he was never boring: his orthodoxy was based too closely on classical foundations for him to be other than always attractive.

It was business, indeed, it was big business, but it was business with a human face, with the bright, user-friendly presentation of the best-managed and responsible service industries.

## Ted McDonald and Dick Tyldesley

The tradition of bowlers hunting in pairs has usually meant unity of type: Lillee and Thomson or Laker and Lock. Lancashire have not often managed to pull off this Romulus and Remus trick of uncovering twin pace- or twin spin-bowlers. They have made do with the odd couple, like Mold and Briggs or, briefly, Statham and Tattersall. With the disappearance of Parkin, Lancashire sought comfort in the happy mixed marriage of Ted McDonald and Dick Tyldesley. The Championship years of the 1920s owed much to this togetherness.

Dick Tyldesley is fourth in the Lancashire all-time averages, with 1449 (1509 in all games) wickets, averaging something over 16. E. A. McDonald stands eighth with 1052 (1395) and an average of a little over 20. Tyldesley took a hundred wickets a season ten times consecutively, 1922–31, and McDonald did the same for six seasons, 1925–30, including 205 (198 for Lancashire) in 1925, the fifth and last Lancashire bowler to achieve 200 wickets. Even in the soggy wetness of 1927 he obtained 150 wickets, occasionally slowing down almost to an off-spin variation. Their joint totals in the happiest years of Lancashire's life were as follows: 1925, 335; 1926, 303; 1928, 294; 1929, 296; and 1930, 241. It is powerful and consistent, in sum, 1719 wickets over six jubilant years.

It follows that they both registered a series of impressive analyses, McDonald taking eight wickets in an innings four times and Tyldesley six times. McDonald took 15 for 154 against Kent at Old Trafford in 1928, while Tyldesley enjoyed three very special outings: 8 for 15 against Northamptonshire in 1926, 7 for 6 against the same county in 1924, and astonishingly, 5 for 0 against Leicestershire in the same year. In 1929 he captured four Derbyshire wickets in four balls, whereas McDonald had three hat-tricks for Lancashire, and, three more times, three wickets in four balls.

All in all, it adds up to some of the most profitable bowling ever undertaken in the County Championship, and, splendidly though Lancashire's supreme quartet batted, all would have been as dust without the Midas touch of Ted McDonald and Richard Tyldesley. There, however, in equally admirable statistics, the symbiosis ends.

E. A. McDonald, with 11 Australian caps and 43 Test wickets in 1920 and 1921, was a feared pace bowler when he came to Nelson in the Lancashire League, the enterprising club that also found a home for Learie Constantine. In company with J. M. Gregory, he had formed one of those same sibling dualisms over which this essay earlier mused. By the time he was residentially qualified for county cricket, he was in his mid-thirties, having been born in March 1891. He had already been billed as one of *Wisden*'s famous five.

R. K. Tyldesley was included in that envied quintet in 1925. He was then 28. He was born in 1897, and had begun playing for Lancashire in the post-war season. He played until 1931, taking part in 374 fixtures. McDonald played in 217 games from 1924, also to 1931. In 1924 and 1930, Tyldesley gained seven England caps, and took 19 Test wickets, several years after the end of the other's international career. Tyldesley had the edge as a batsman, with 6000 runs, over against McDonald's less than 2000, but both, rather bizarrely, managed a century, the Englishman against Nottinghamshire in 1922, the Australian against Middlesex in 1926, both to the mingled joy and disbelief of their colleagues. McDonald was a fleet outfielder, Tyldesley a most stationary slip with 328 catches to his credit.

Ted McDonald hailed from Tasmania for whom he played before, in 1912, he first played for Victoria. Such exotic locations, those thousands of miles away, must have seemed remote indeed to Dick Tyldesley who probably found it something of a trial to effect the short journey from Westhoughton to Stretford. Each epitomised a regional prototype. Tall, beautifully built and tanned, McDonald was a regular Bondi Beach Democrat. Weighing in at 17 stones, one of the heaviest first-class cricketers there has been, Tyldesley appeared to have been force-fed on Bolton trotters, with sideplates of cow-heel. With the kind of stomach that the comedian, Dave Morris, was wont to describe as a Watney's goitre, he was typical of the rotund Lancashire man found in every workplace and cricket team. Tubby Turners all.

Next, one was silent, the other noisy. Ted McDonald was a dour and reticent man, given to an occasional moodiness, but basically phlegmatic. His action was effortless and his speed, stiletto-like, liable to test the quickest reflexes, his fame assured from the summer of 1921 when Gregory and he had destroyed England's batting. His balance was such that his run-up was soundless, and umpires spoke of not sensing his approach. Wilf Mannion, the Middlesborough and England inside-forward, was scornful of defenders whom he could hear coming. He would have admired McDonald, and groundsmen perhaps appreciated that the repair work was less than when bowlers were in operation who left Yeti-like footprints. He seemed not to get flustered, inequable or sweaty, and good batsmen tended to lift his pace and exactitude. It was Italianate in form: he could have opened the bowling for the Borgias.

Dick Tyldesley probably preferred lesser batsmen, for he extensively relied on what, in the vernacular, is termed kidology. Years of practice had rendered him very accurate, and the arc of his delivery was one of tempting allure. There was not much leg-spin, but the wickets came. Protesting, plaintive, perspiring, he trundled painfully up to the wicket, and, with an exaggerated demonstration of creaking arm and revolving wrist, the ball would present itself for examination. As the batsman pondered on the likely outcome of this contorted wizardry, the ball went, as Dick Tyldesley himself explained with an engaging disregard for conventional simile, 'as straight as a whistle'. If not bowled, there might be a rapping of the pads, and the reedier tenor of Duckworth would combine with the anxious baritone of Tyldesley, after the fashion of Flotsam and Jetsam, the premier male duet of the age.

He was the male counterpart of the ITMA character, Mona Lott: 'It's being so cheerful as keeps me going.' In another manifestation of working-class culture, Tyldesley was the one supporting the burdens of an ill-fated world on his massively complaining shoulders. When he stopped taking as many wickets, he blamed the batsmen, complaining that they had stopped playing back. He exited, complaining about his contract and wages, to the leagues, where, his impeccable line and length wavering and his high pace waning, McDonald also retreated for the 1932 season. One can almost hear Tyldesley echo the worldweary, careworn phrase of the fat man from the state of Georgia: 'this is a fine mess you've got us into'.

Who was there to assist and follow the tall, sharp-eyed pace-bowler and the overweight, mournful spin-bowler, the Abbott and

Costello of Lancashire cricket? Most importantly, there was that fine all-rounder, Jack Iddon. He came from Mawdesley, near Ormskirk, the son of a cricket professional, and he enjoyed a long career with the county. With his handsome strokes and occasionally unplayable left-hand spin, the slim and stylish Iddon played from 1924 to the outbreak of war. Rather like Jack Sharp's, one scrutinizes his achievements with enjoyable surprise. He played 483 games (only five, including Sharp, have played more) and, after Briggs, must be regarded, again with Sharp, as one of Lancashire's finest all-rounders. Without fuss, he assembled not only close on 22,000 runs, average 37, but collected 533 wickets. Forty-six centuries, all for Lancashire, the highest, 222 against Leicester in 1929, and a proud run of a thousand runs in every season from 1928 to 1939, he obviously contributed much with the bat. Nonetheless, some of his bowling was decisive: 8 for 50 versus Warwickshire in 1928, 9 for 42 at Sheffield in 1937, 5 for 9 at Bournemouth in 1926; these were the kind of returns that placed him among the 26 Lancashire bowlers with over 500 wickets. He was a dashing fielder, but his five Tests in 1935 proved none too successful.

Frank Sibbles from Oldham was much more the specialist bowler, for he scored not much more than 3000 runs in his 13-year career. His exact and brainy medium pace earned him satisfying gains. F. M. Sibbles captured 932 wickets (average 22) in the Lancashire cause, leaving him twelfth in the county list, an excellent reward. His best seasons were 1932 (131 wickets) and 1937 (107), and his two most dominating spells were 8 for 24 against Somerset in 1927 and 5 for 8 against Essex in 1937. It should be remembered that he bowled invariably on the well prepared squares of the 1930s, that he suffered a severe arm injury, and that he remained perpetually calm and amicable.

Frank Sibbles became a partner in a Manchester sports emporium, and he died, aged 69, in 1973. Dick Tyldesley, doubtless moaning about the sugar ration or the blackout, died in 1943. He was only 45, and he had always worn new flannels for the Yorkshire match. By a macabre coincidence, McDonald and Iddon both died in road accidents. McDonald was killed in the summer of the coronation year of 1937, and he, too, was still quite young, only 46. Then, in the April of 1946, when there was pre-season talk of this charming all-rounder becoming an amateur and Lancashire's captain, Jack Iddon was also killed in a car crash. He was only 44.

*George Duckworth*

George Duckworth kept wicket for Lancashire in 424 games, that is, in a seventh of all the first-class matches Lancashire have ever played. He caught 634 and stumped 288, and his total of 922 is almost twice that of the next nearest in number of victims, R. Pilling with 486, and Farouk Engineer with 464. He twice, in 1926 and in 1936, had six victims in an innings, and he twice, in 1928 and 1936, had nine in a match. In five seasons he harvested more than 70 stumpings and catches, with, in all matches, his 107 in 1928 being his highest yield. A hundred dismissals has only been achieved 12 times. On behalf of Lancashire, he faced, at a crude estimate, half-a-million balls in a career spanning from 1923 to 1938. In spite of the competition of L. E. G. Ames, who batted with infinitely more accomplishment than George Duckworth, he won 24 caps and obtained 59 Test wickets. He only scored 4000 or so runs for the county (indeed Ames, statistically, was eight times as accomplished) but his contribution was intangible as well as arithmetic.

The Lancashire fielding in many of these years bordered on the ordinary, and, with his enthusiasm and aptitude, George Duckworth pushed it to the limits of its potential. He was a small, chubby, active man, with podgy features and quick hands, born, in 1901, in Warrington, so basically a Lancastrian town which now, unaccountably, is part of Cheshire. He died in 1966.

During his lifetime he became a knowledgeable and voluble conversationalist and commentator on a broad range of topics from rugby league and current affairs to pigeon-racing and temperance, a subject about which some of his colleagues provided unsolicited evidence. In the affable tones of Albert Modley, 'Lancashire's favourite Yorkshireman', or Harry Korris, Mr Lovejoy of 'Happidrome', he would discourse on any theme at the drop of a cloth cap. More directly, he had the most acute comprehension of the interstices of cricket. With Harry Makepeace and Ernest Tyldesley, he completed Leonard Green's advisory council, a kind of cricketing Witan. His playing career over, he loaned this acumen to several touring teams, his intense concentration and grasp never failing him, no more than when, during a Middlesex innings of 465 in 1934, not a bye escaped.

He made agile catches off the fast, and razor-sharp stumpings off the slow, bowlers. Throughout all this time, Bill Farrimond, yet another from the Bolton area, was the ungrudging understudy, happy to label himself 'Lancashire seconds and England', for he had four caps and nine Test dismissals to his credit. Entirely reliable as a wicket-keeper, his unassuming livelihood occupied him with Lancashire from 1924 to the coming of war. He contributed 2000 runs, and, for all their irregularity, in his 134 matches he mustered 297 dismissals, including, when the spot became entirely his own, 84 in 1938 and 72 in 1939. He was 36 when war broke out, and he died in 1979.

Neville Cardus bestowed upon George Duckworth the felicitous title of 'The Chanticleer of wicket-keepers', and there was certainly a crowing note to his defiant appeal. In fact, it was not questioning enough to rank as an appeal. It was judgemental. With one accusative arm raised high aloft as if commanding divine endorsement, the shrill, long howl was the closing statement for the prosecution. 'Quack, quack,' the crowd would bay in riposte.

George Duckworth did not jabber appeals repetitively like some modern wicket-keepers and close fielders. This was partly because he was a fair man and only appealed on conviction. It was partly because he knew it was counterproductive, inuring the batsman and, as importantly, the crowd to its surprise value. George Formby never said, 'It's turned out nice again,' as often as one's impression is.

Cockerel he may have been in voicing an appeal, but there was a glee about his activities which broke that image. He splattered the wicket, when attempting a stumping, with the zest of a little boy kicking over sand-pies. Some wicket-keepers – the Australian, W. A. Oldfield, for one – clip a bail off apologetically, murmuring a civilised query to the square-leg umpire. Duckworth did not entertain such Sir Percy Blakeney delicacy. It was rampant devastation. And should, to his open-mouthed astonishment, the case be dismissed on referral to the higher tribunal of the umpire, then the batsman was only reprieved. Just a slip, and the tumbrils would rattle, the drums roll and the Guillotine crash. Demolition and din lurked two feet behind.

George Duckworth was maybe a stumper rather than a wicket-keeper, a distinction as subtle as that between the butty and the sandwich. It was the unsettling gusto of his presence and his attack which produced the goods. It was like fighting on the front line with an intrepid resistance movement in the immediate background. Freed from his labours, George Duckworth would tell and retell his tales, most of them of that apocryphal brand which makes you fondly wish they were authentic. It was George Duckworth who related the yarn of the cricket pitch on a Pacific island through the middle of which ran a time-line, so that, he concluded, 'you were batting on Monday and bowling on Tuesday'.

George Duckworth. The very name might have been coined for this very character in some Walter Greenwood comedy of Lancashire life. It is tripe and onions or lashings of Lancashire hot-pot, with pepperings of ee bai gum. Len Hutton was one of several to affirm that, to be in Duckworth's presence for more than a few minutes without realising where he came from, was to be guilty of gross geographic illiteracy. There is no more pleasing conceit in the history of Lancashire than that, at their zenith in the 1920s, a crucially salient figure was a personification of the Lancashire myth.

For the neutral admirer, however, the perpetual half-memory may owe more to Mr Punch, clattering down the stumps with the big stick and crying, swazzle-voiced, something not too far removed from 'that's the way to do it'.

# 5. The Years of Paynter and Washbrook

## The 1930s and the 1934 Championship

By the early 1930s the great depression had dropped its dead hand on the British economy. International trade and money markets had collapsed, and the Lancashire textile industry, already feeling the draught of overseas competition, reeled. Manchester, with the diversity of a large and sprawling city, fared better, but engineering was also hit badly and there was unemployment and poverty.

In parallel, the systematically triumphant Lancashire team was in process of disintegration. McDonald, released from his contract a year early, Dick Tyldesley, protesting about the lack of guaranteed salary, left, while Makepeace and Ernest Tyldesley were at the veteran stage. Hallows and Watson lost form or suffered illness or both, and, eventually, Duckworth gave way, as was right, to Farrimond. Iddon and Sibbles prospered, and, as war threatened, Washbrook, Oldfield, Paynter became the major Lancashire bats of the 1930s, but, in a nutshell, it was a story of one team waning and another not waxing quite quickly enough. In the four pre-war seasons, Lionel Lister, the promising amateur and Oxford soccer blue, captained the team.

The weather was as depressing as the economy. The summers of 1931 and 1932 were especially drab, and it seemed that it never rained but it poured. The dreary coincidence of poorer cricket, poorer weather and poorer customers was discouraging. In the 1931 season a loss of £3600 was suffered, and, among other measures, the professionals accepted a ten-per-cent cut in wages. The top counties had agreed soon after the First World War to a maximum of £440 match fees for a full schedule of 28 matches, exclusive of bonuses, so the cut probably pushed the Lancashire 'pros' under £400 for a summer's work. On the other hand, most of the general liabilities had been paid off during the more prosperous 1920s, and, in 1934, a final £4000 was found to clear the main debt.

The county membership underwent periodic fits of insularity, urging, in 1935, that birth rather than residential eligibility should be the key. The committee agreed to proceed accordingly 'as far as possible', while stating that it was 'undesirable' that those who were housed permanently in the county should be excluded. It was an unsettling time, with people perhaps forgetting that, not only McDonald, but Parkin, Barnes and Makepeace would have been excluded from Lancashire teams.

Manchester itself exhibited another, more progressive, aspect. Its satellite estate, Wythenshawe, was developed to the south-east, with a population approaching 100,000, and the city's population was now well in excess of half a million. Certainly Lancashire's share of world trade in cotton piece-goods had sunk from three-quarters at the start of the century to less than a half, and the Chamber of Commerce had dropped its long cherished credo of free trade. Perhaps there was an answering echo among Lancashire members as they espoused protectionism for cricketers. But, as well as commercial diversification and because of it, there were advances. The town hall extension of 1938 and the opening of the Central Library in 1934 are token of this, along with the location of the northern headquarters of the BBC in Piccadilly. There were great changes in transport. From 1930 to 1938 at Barton and thereafter at Ringway there was a municipal airport, whilst electric trams and motor buses grew in number and routes. One of the nation's first electric overground services ran from Manchester London Road to Altrincham, pouring out its customers at Warwick Road Station a yard or so from the Old Trafford turnstiles. It was three old pence for the trip from London Road.

Despite the pressures, then, Manchester deserved and could sustain a top-rated county team, as it could its two famous football teams, with Manchester City rather catching the eye in the 1930s, its orchestra and its grand theatres. Nor were Lancashire a feeble team. It was more that, by the fierce yardstick of the previous decade, they seemed to lack both lustre and stability. Apart from the shock season of 1934 when, against the form book, Lancashire won the Championship, they were never in the first three. Eleventh in 1936, their worst performance for 22 years, and ninth in 1937, they were sixth three other seasons, fifth once and fourth twice.

In 1933, for instance, the brightest summer since the smouldering days of 1921, Lancashire lost only once, but contrived to draw 18; conversely, in the rainy season of 1938, and although they led the table for a while, only six wins in the last 20 matches were achieved.

There were some satisfactory individual performances, with Paynter in the van. Buddy Oldfield scored a thousand runs in each of the five seasons before the war, scoring 7000 in all for the county. Cyril Washbrook also began to score heavily. Dick Pollard took a hundred wickets in the last four pre-war seasons, and W. E. Phillipson in two of them. Three wicket-records stem from the 1930s: for the third wicket, 306, by Paynter and Oldfield at Southampton; for the fifth wicket, an undefeated 235, by Oldfield and A. E. Nutter (another all-rounder of promise) in 1939 at Old Trafford against Nottinghamshire; and for the sixth wicket, when, against Sussex at Old Trafford, Iddon and H. R. W. Butterworth, a 22-year-old amateur, gathered 273 in 1932. Despite the downpours of 1939, which produced six games with no result in the middle of the season, there were some batting performances which would have augured well, had the future been less catastrophic. Iddon and Hopwood centuries led the way to a barnstorming 385 for 4 at Southampton, and then, with a deficit of 88 on the first innings, a large opening stand by Washbrook and Paynter at Trent Bridge assisted Lancashire to 324 for 4 in the fourth innings.

Two names worthy of mention must be Len Hopwood and Len Wilkinson. Hopwood was on the Lancashire staff from 1923 to 1939, played almost 400 matches, scored 15,519 runs, and took 672 wickets with his left-hand spin. A highest score of 220, against Gloucestershire in 1934, and 15 for 112 match figures in the same year against Worcestershire were his best performances, and the year is an interesting one. For, in 1934 and 1935, J. L. Hopwood did the double, with 1660 runs and 111 wickets in the former and 1538 runs and 103 wickets in the latter season. Cuttell and Jimmy Hallows were his only predecessors in this regard: no one has emulated him. After a longish apprenticeship, this highly competent all-rounder made steadfast claim to a place in the first eleven throughout the 1930s, and he played for England twice in 1934 without luck. Concentrating his chief work into those few seasons, he deserves congratulations for he is one of only three Lancashire players – Briggs and Iddon are the others – to have scored 10,000 runs and taken 500 wickets for the county.

Len Wilkinson, a product of the Bolton League, was the revelation of 1938. Gauche and awkward-looking, he turned his leg-spinners from a lanky height, and, on the pacy wickets of that year, he turned them with zip and at acute angles, throwing in a fair googly to add to the motley. He took 145 wickets, a little dearly, as is the fashion of the leg-spinner, at 23 apiece, but it was the highest bounty of victims since 1929. He was immediately shipped over to South Africa for the winter, taking seven wickets in three Tests, before returning home, and, no longer the novelty, and on the soaked grounds of 1939, he did less well. In all, he took 232 wickets in 63 matches over only three seasons, and looked like the spinner Lancashire required.

Before his advent, however, Lancashire had won another Championship, and Len Hopwood, with one of his doubles, contributed manfully to that rather surprising success. It was something of a curio, this 1934 title. Yorkshire more or less monopolised the Championship in the 1930s, only being tumbled from their throne in this year and in 1936, when Derbyshire won. In 1934 Yorkshire provided several members of the Test teams against Australia, and this, evidently, was one reason they dropped to fifth. Lancashire were also abnormally fortunate with the toss. They batted first in 24 out of 30 fixtures, and, with efficient batting, were able to declare no less than 18 times. Thus, in spite of bowling that rose little above the level of utility, they manufactured 13 victories, and lost only three.

Preserving the Lancashire habit of headlong rush or trouble-strewn crawl at the beginning – and, alternatively, at the end – of the season, the team won only one of its first seven games, and that against a weak Somerset eleven. Yorkshire trounced Lancashire comprehensively, and the venerable Hobbs ensured a draw for Surrey in Duckworth's benefit match.

On tour in June, things improved, with wins over Gloucestershire, Worcestershire, Hampshire and Nottinghamshire. This last match proved to be one of the most epic in the county's story. Fresh from his controversial exploits in the bodyline series in Australia, Harold Larwood, against Lancashire, took wickets and inflicted wounds with equal abandon. Lancashire were six wickets for one run on the first morning: it is said that five slip-catches were dropped, and a shaky 119 was cobbled together. Larwood next proceeded to add the insult of 80 in 45 minutes to this grievous injury of his bowling, and Nottinghamshire reached 266.

Then Ernest Tyldesley, in his cricketing dotage, played what many regarded as the most splendid innings of his career, in the season when he passed his brother's total runs to become Lancashire's heaviest scorer ever and when he became Lancashire's one and only centurion of centuries. Against violently hostile bowling, he exhibited great valiance in reaching the ninety-ninth of his hundreds. Watson and Lister half-centuries and useful knocks from Eckersley and L. W. Parkinson produced a total of 394 for 7. Hopwood now took six wickets, and, in a melodramatic last over, Iddon's third appeal for lbw was upheld, Nottinghamshire were dismissed for 146 and Lancashire won by 101 runs. It was a courageous victory, but there had been storms over Larwood's tactics in the dressing rooms, where the exchanges had been, as they say of diplomatic talks, frank and fearless. Indeed, fixtures with Nottinghamshire were temporarily dropped as a result.

Heartened, if bruised, the walking wounded pushed on from Trent Bridge. Glamorgan were beaten at Liverpool and Northamptonshire were twice defeated, at Blackburn and at Peterborough. After shoddy batting gave Worcestershire a first innings lead of 108 at Blackpool, Lancashire rallied and won, and Pollard's earliest forays assisted in wins over Gloucestershire and Leicestershire. Hopwood took 13 wickets in the defeat of Derbyshire. Earlier Hampshire had drawn with Kent and beaten Lancashire, and, at Lord's, Middlesex inflicted a damaging ten-wicket defeat. Back at Old Trafford, Lancashire bounced along, scoring 167 in just over two hours, to wreak a little vengeance on Middlesex and, at the same time, overtake Sussex at the head of the table. Lancashire kept their heads over the last four matches of a short southern tour, and finished champions. It seems otiose to add that they were then defeated, as usual, by the Rest of England at the Oval.

The batting had proved to be extremely strong, with two (Tyldesley and Iddon) scoring over 2000, Watson, returning to form, almost there with 1857, and with Hopwood and Paynter easily reaching the thousand-mark. This fivesome amassed almost 10,000 runs. The bowling lacked pace and devil, and this must be one of the few Championships won without benefit throughout of a genuine opening bowler. Apart from Hopwood, F. S. Booth took a hundred wickets. He played irregularly over ten or 11 seasons, taking 457 wickets over that time. It was a team of elder statesmen at the crease and mixed striplings with the ball. With

Duckworth keeping wicket, Eddie Paynter in the covers and a sprinkling of keen young men, the fielding was excellent, probably more enthusiastic and surely more athletic than in Major Green's time. It seems uncharitable to be less than gushing over a perfectly worthy reward, but, somehow, this must be evaluated as Lancashire's least convincing Championship.

This is mainly to do with the intangible element of personality rather than the mathematics of the county table. This particularly applied to the bowling, which tended to be anonymous and, that death-knell for excitement, reliable. There was no Briggs, no Parkin, no McDonald. The falling gates of the 1930s remind that entertainment as well as success is sought. Of course, the slump had a hand in this, for money was not as readily available in the North-West during these grey years. Nonetheless, it was, unlike the economic collapse of the 1980s, a low-wage, low-price depression, and the football grounds and variety theatres were by no means empty. The Saturday crowds at Old Trafford were reasonable, as were, it is salutary to remark, many of those on the league grounds, but insufficient spectators were attracted in the week. Unemployed men, for instance, sought cheap solace elsewhere, and the middle-class members presumably were finding other matters to distract them from the travails of business.

Some argued, and some will always be found to argue, that county cricket was not, overall, as skilled as in days gone by. The Yorkshire team of the 1930s, it must be confessed, stood a class above the other counties, but, in the late 1930s, Middlesex blossomed, and, with the likes of Wally Hammond and Joe Hardstaff about, there was no definable shortage of talent. Lancashire's basic problem was that, possibly for the first time in their history, they lacked a couple of three-dimensional characters of vivid gifts. The exception was Eddie Paynter, the one cricketer of stature who arrived, made his mark, and departed in the 'thirties.

## Eddie Paynter

He was known to his team-mates and friends as 'Ted Paynter'. This makes him sound like the leader of a 1930s dance-band, working on a localised scale around Rawtenstall or Accrington, or perhaps the regional branch secretary of one of the textile unions of the same era. One is inclined to run but a cursory rule over the *Wisden* article about him entitled 'Edward Paynter', suspecting it to be the obituary of the treasurer of Leicestershire or some such worthy. The isolated 'Paynter' renders him anonymous. Eddie adhered to Paynter more unyieldingly than Hutton's Len or Hardstaff's Joe. In the inter-war years, perhaps only Patsy Hendren enjoyed that same adhesiveness of diminutive to surname.

It is often the case that this form of identification implies deep affection, and Eddie Paynter was very popular indeed. His countless wry tales and his penchant for performing handstands and allied acrobatic feats at Crewe Junction, or at other termini where 1930s cricketers found themselves hanging about around midnight, made him equally a favourite among his colleagues. He was keen and good-humoured, the decent child of uncomplicated working-class Oswaldtwistle.

Some cricketers – David Hughes for his twilit exploits against Gloucestershire in the Gillette Cup match of 1971 – find their fame exclusively engaged in a single feat. Often it becomes something of an albatross, so overtly hung around them as to preoccupy the gaze and make the watcher forgetful of other deeds. Eddie Paynter's 83 at Brisbane during the controversial leg-theory series of 1932–33 has such a quality. Bidden by Douglas Jardine, like some Arthurian wizard, to rise from his hospital bed, where he lay stricken with a feverish throat ailment, Eddie Paynter heroically responded. Swinging totteringly from near-swooning collapse to the striking of dashing boundaries, his saving of the side has taken on the flavour of historical reference and schoolboy yarn. The dual struggle with illness and enemy occasionally turns up in the history books, with El Cid, shoulder pierced by arrow, a colourful example. Napoleon's piles at Waterloo and Anthony Eden's encroaching sickness as he presided over the absurdity of Suez are less romantic illustrations, and were less visited with success than Eddie Paynter's bravery at Brisbane.

Valour is important, not least because, in cricket's rolls of honour, it has perhaps been overly ascribed to the glorious amateur. But it is not enough. Extremely ill, and batting in a climate rather warmer than that of his native habitat, Eddie Paynter had to demonstrate shrewd expertise in order to notch up his significant score. He was small in stature, in the pleasing tradition of nimble left-handers, and he was not a powerful man.

He was not entirely orthodox, although he drove straight as a die. It is rumoured, for example, that he thought nothing of playing the hook shot with both feet off the ground. He also delighted in what he called his 'fancy cuts'.

Yet he frequently played long innings, and has several tall scores on his ledger. The key to his method was timing, a chronological sense that owed much, possibly everything, to his sharpness of eye. Triangular of countenance, his features seemed a trifle sizeable for so small a man. Ears of which Prince Charles might have approved, nose edging in stature towards the Jimmy Durante category, mouth wide and partly-open – and yet the eyes dominate the facial scenery. They were big, still and piercing, and, in his photographs, they appear to be penetrating the distant horizons. This radiographic trait enabled Eddie Paynter to play late. All fine batsmen play late, but he carried this aesthetic unpunctuality to such a finesse that the ball had performed all the trickery of which it was capable before he determined on his shot.

Such avian ocularity also helped Eddie Paynter to grace the covers in what, happily, has become something of a Lancashire art form from the earliest days to the present. The relish with which he fielded gave Old Trafford crowds as much delight as his batting, and another asset he possessed was speed. Running between the wickets or running after the struck ball, he had few equals in his generation.

Born on Guy Fawkes Day 1901, Eddie Paynter found his career crushed between two circumstances, catching him like the hero in the horror movie facing rapidly closing dungeon walls. On the one hand, the Lancashire batting in the late 1920s was exceedingly strong, with Ernest Tyldesley, Frank Watson, Charlie Hallows and Harry Makepeace the most constant of performers. Indeed, only the statesmanlike persuasion of T. A. Higson, an influential grey eminence of Lancashire cricket, prevented Eddie Paynter from seeking his fortune in the leagues which then attracted huge followings.

It was 1931, when he was 30 years old, before Eddie Paynter had real chances, and scored the first of his 45 centuries, against Warwickshire and New Zealand. He distinguished himself by his 45, not out, against Yorkshire, and then, following on, a further 87 not out, without his having taken his pads off between innings. In 1932 he consolidated his position with five centuries, by far the most appealing a crusading 152 against Yorkshire. This included four sixes off Hedley Verity, which was akin to an England goalkeeper of the time, such as Frank Swift or Harry Hibbs, letting in a dozen goals. Frank Sibbles took 12 wickets, with Yorkshire all out for 46 in the first innings, and Lancashire won by a comfortable innings.

On the other hand, and after only eight full first-class seasons, the alternate wall to Ernest Tyldesley *et al.* was provided by the Second World War. Eddie Paynter was 44 when it ended, and, although he played a little first-class festival cricket, he decided to concentrate on a league career. He was unfortunate enough not to have a benefit, and a relatively small grant of £1000 was paid him in 1945. He wreaked something of a vengeance for first-class life so attentuated on the Bradford League bowlers during the 1939–45 conflict. There were no easy pickings. In 1943 70 first-class cricketers, including 14 Test stars, were playing in that league. Eddie Paynter scored 4426 runs in the six wartime seasons, and a host more in many top-class charity matches. He was one of the war's most compellingly successful batsmen.

Sir Walter Scott asserted that 'one crowded hour of glorious life is like an age without a name', and Eddie Paynter, as if unconsciously aware of a curtailed career, batted like an express train, apropos both of speed and distance covered. He crammed 20,000 runs into his brief sojourn in top-class cricket, at an average of just over 42, only Clive Lloyd, Ernest Tyldesley and Cyril Washbrook bettering this from among Lancashire's ranks. He scored a thousand runs in every season for Lancashire alone, including 2016 in 1936, 2626 in 1937 and 2020 in 1938 for the county. He also passed 2000 runs, all games considered, in 1932.

For so attacking and compulsive a player, he certainly played high-scoring innings and participated in many major stands. Cyril Washbrook and he have three opening stands of over 200 to their famous names and Eddie Paynter joined in half a dozen other Lancastrian compilations of over 200. In 1937 he scored 322 against a hapless Sussex attack at Hove, thus becoming one of only three Lancashire players to score a triple century. It is, in fact, the second-highest individual total after Archie MacLaren's 424. Eddie Paynter also scored 266 against Essex in 1937, and then just missed a second three hundred with 291 against Hampshire the following year. All in all, he had seven double hundreds to his credit, a very high striking rate, for only J. T. Tyldesley surpasses, and Cyril Washbrook matches, that record, both of them with many more centuries over long playing spans.

Indeed, Eddie Paynter's par of nearly six centuries a season shows immense consistency and concentration.

He crowned his efforts for Lancashire with sterling feats for England, for whom he played 20 times. In 1938 he managed to find himself sharing in both England's fourth- and fifth-wicket record stands against Australia: 222 with Hammond at Lord's; 206 with Compton at Nottingham, only for him to score one as Hutton soldiered toward his magnificent 364 at the Oval. In the Nottingham game Eddie Paynter scored 216 not out. Then, in the winter series 1938–39, he indulged in his most heroic vein, with 653 runs, a record for England in South Africa, in the series. He scored a century in both innings at Johannesburg, the only Lancashire player to accomplish this, and at Durban he scored 243. His average was almost 82.

An uncommonly registered fact about Eddie Paynter is that he stands fifth in the world's Test averages with a commendable 59.23. He is second, after Herbert Sutcliffe, in the English Test averages, with the likes of Wally Hammond, Jack Hobbs and Len Hutton trailing a little behind. What is more, when talk turns to his 83 at Brisbane, few now recall he won the match in his second innings with a hit for six.

His post-cricket path was not strewn with roses, with menial jobs and little luck coming his way. He played occasional testimonial matches, even until his late sixties, and travelled to Australia for the Centenary Test celebrations there in 1976. He died on 5 February 1979, aged 77, and there passed away the batsman who could pick out Tiger O'Reilly's faster ball 'because he shows his teeth'.

## The Post-War Years

The Royal Engineers requisitioned Old Trafford at the onset of war, and most of the staff joined the forces and civil defence or became munitions workers. Nearly a score of players were in uniform, and, apart from Peter Eckersley, three second-eleven players, J. M. Barrell, A. Kershaw and H. Robinson lost their lives. After use as a transit depot following the retreat from Dunkirk, the ground was taken over as a Ministry of Supply dump for vehicles and other equipment. Occasionally, one noticed sheep grazing, while, on nearby land, a barrage balloon was moored. Early in 1941 there was bomb damage to the pavilion, two stands, the groundsman's shed and even the sacred turf, and a sentry was killed at the main gate during this bombing. The carpets were evacuated to North Wales and the heavy roller conscripted for active service in the Western Desert in the construction of air-strips.

Captain, later Major, Rupert Howard, the secretary, kept the club afloat from T. A. Higson's city office, and loyal members ensured an income of £2000 or so each year. An ambitious appeal for £100,000 was launched, and, soon after the war, about half had been attained. There was no cricket at the ground until 1944, but with German prisoners of war recruited to paint and mend, the Victory Test of 1945 attracted over 72,000 spectators. The crowds were certainly ready for post-war cricket.

The players were half-ready. Unlike the previous war, when cricket had been halted in its tracks, there had been plenty of cricket during the Second World War. Indeed, Lancashire had proposed a regional county competition, which, with hindsight, was probably a sensible scheme. Left to their own devices, many counties, including Lancashire, floundered rather, but there was an outcrop of service and other cricket. Apart from the enterprising Lord's programme, the amount of cricket played in the North-West, sometimes with Lancashire committee-men at the helm, was more than in most areas, and goodly sums were raised for wartime charities. This meant that almost all the Lancashire players were enjoying regular cricket of the one-day kind, or entertaining crowds in the leagues, the Bradford League proving specially attractive. On occasion, a Lancashire eleven was fielded which was tantamount to those selected in the pre-war years.

The rule is proved by the exception of Wilkinson. Stationed in distant parts, he played little cricket and the sensitive control required for leg-spin deserted him. Everyone else was in reasonable shape, although frustrated at the major loss of six seasons. However, Farrimond and Paynter returned to the leagues, and Norman Oldfield and Albert Hunter went to Northamptonshire, each of them seeking improved financial pickings as his career entered its last stage. With Iddon dead, W. H. L. Lister and T. A. Higson junior unavailable, Jack Fallows, son of J. C. Fallows, the county treasurer, stepped into a widening breach as captain. With qualification rules slackened, mercenary troops were engaged, the most successful proving to be G. A. Edrich, brother of W. J. Edrich.

With Edrich, a suddenly blooming John Ikin and an always dependable Winston Place in support of Washbrook, with Pollard and Phillipson in quick-bowling harness, and Bill Roberts to deliver orthodox left-hand spin, it was soon a team not to be taken lightly. Ken Cranston replaced Fallows in 1947 and 1948, and then Nigel Howard, son of Major Howard and an ex-Rossall schoolboy, captained the team for a further five years. He led the MCC tour to India in the winter of 1951, and captained England in four Tests, the last Lancashire player to do so.

During this period Lancashire enjoyed some reward on the field and, with other counties, shared in the post-war boom of spectatorship. Although slipping to eleventh in 1949, they were third five times and fifth once, as well as sharing the Championship with Surrey, then embarking on their long series of successes, in 1950. Throughout these years, the four leading bats consistently notched their thousand runs, and, from 1949, Ken Grieves brought his tough, unyielding craft to maintain that flow. There was a surfeit of left-handers: Bill Roberts, Eric Price, Malcolm Hilton, who startled the cricket world by dismissing Bradman twice in the 1948 match with the Australians, and Bob Berry. In 1948 Roy Tattersall came into the side, and Lancashire, with the versatile exception of Parkin, never fielded a more dangerous bowler of off-cut and spin. Finally, as Pollard tired, Statham's world-famous career began.

It was a difficult team to dislodge. For the opening months of 1946, Lancashire led the county table, but then lost twelve tosses in a row and, with that, some momentum. They made two gallant essays to regain control: faced with an Essex target of 299 in 185 minutes, they lost by 15 runs; and then, in an effort to procure 212 runs in 150 minutes against Hampshire, they lost by 29 runs. Lancashire finished a strong third, as they did in the glorious summer of 1947, when the batting of Washbrook and Place was rumbustious and fruitful, and Pollard took 137 wickets at 19 runs each. In the hard-fought contest of 1948 Lancashire, while fifth, were only 20 points behind Glamorgan the winners, and Washbrook, because of injury, played only 14 games, yet accumulated nearly 1500 runs and an amazing average of over 86.

In the early 1950s this solid progress continued. J. T. Ikin and Geoff Edrich remained sturdily proficient as retinue to Washbrook and Place, while Tattersall, Hilton and Statham carried on their varied assault on Lancashire's sometimes baffled opponents. In

1953, for instance, a very damp season, Bob Berry took all ten Worcestershire wickets at Blackpool for 102, the third and last Lancastrian to enjoy that distinction, while Somerset were defeated in one day, with 55 minutes to spare, on the alliterative occasion of Bertie Buse's benefit at Bath. Tattersall took 13 for 79. The same year Lancashire hit 253 in under three hours to beat Hampshire, and pressed hard for the title. Both in 1951 and 1952, John Thomas Ikin, bearing the forenames of the illustrious Tyldesley, did well, topping the averages, and, in the latter year, Edrich passed 2000 runs in all first-class innings.

This immediate post-war eleven was, therefore, a well-equipped one of brave batting and balanced bowling. It rarely caved in, and, in those first eight post-war seasons, Lancashire lost only 25 matches. Their opportunity fell in 1950. The committee decided not to use the heavy roller and to ration the watering of the square. With Tattersall on one's books, that was an alluring temptation, and, not for the first nor final time, it appeared that pitches were prepared to suit the home team's bowling. For some, this dimmed the glory. On the other hand, Lancashire's opponents had bowlers of a similar type, and prejudiced pitch preparation has two edges. Moreover, Lancashire won nine of their 16 victories away from home, while Washbrook, batting half the time in this purportedly difficult environment, ended with an average of 56. Six batsmen topped the thousand-mark. Thus Lancashire should not feel any shame about this their twelfth, albeit shared, and, sorrowfully, latest Championship.

The season opened calmly with three draws, and then, with Winston Place carrying his bat for 101 out of 244, Warwickshire were defeated. A promising omen, Yorkshire were narrowly beaten by 14 runs, but Surrey, despite Tattersall's eight wickets, drew, Middlesex won, and Gloucestershire also drew. In among this, Tattersall took 12 for 68 in the home match against Gloucestershire to give the county three wins.

Lancashire were gathering strength. Their strategy of brisk runs, to allow time for the contemplative arts of spin-bowling to be practised, began to pay off. Derbyshire held them up with a draw at Buxton and an unexpected win at Old Trafford, but this was Lancashire's last defeat. Kent were crushed by an innings at Old Trafford and in two days at Tunbridge Wells, while Somerset were vanquished by Statham. There was a controversial match at Old Trafford with Sussex, which led to their captain, James

Langridge, formally complaining about the pitch. His brother, John, carried his bat for 48 out of 101, before Edrich, that bonny fighter, scored 89. Sussex, all out for 51 second time around, lost within the first day. This time Tattersall was not the avenger, all the wickets falling to Malcolm Hilton (11 for 50) and Peter Greenwood, a young off-spin bowler (9 for 67).

A Washbrook century and 12 wickets for Tattersall were too much for Essex to contend with at Colchester; Glamorgan fell twice, a hundred from Ikin propelling them thence at Blackpool; and there was a double over Nottinghamshire, the first a low-scoring game at Liverpool where Edrich and Grieves dominated. Malcolm Hilton took ten wickets in the match as Middlesex toppled at Old Trafford, while Tattersall had 12 for 94 as Worcestershire joined Lancashire's growing list of victories. There was the temporary hitch of draws with Yorkshire and North-amptonshire about this stage of the season, but there was also a fine win at Bournemouth. Lancashire, asked to bat first, scored 281, and then removed Hampshire for 96 and 109 for a comfort-able innings win. Leicestershire were polished off in two days, and only irksome showers saved Warwickshire. After Washbrook's century, Tattersall bowled brilliantly, taking 7 for 29, and Warwickshire were all out for 80.

That frustration was costly. It left Lancashire needing just four points for the title as the last game of the season started. It was against their nearest rivals, Surrey, and, after the sparkle and bustle of much of the season, it was a drab encounter. Washbrook and Place both failed, and Lancashire took a long time over relatively few. Surrey passed Lancashire's total of 211 and were all out for 287. Batting again, Lancashire concentrated on denying Surrey 12 points for a win, and it was 203 for 4 at the close. Seven hundred and eleven runs in three days, only slightly interfered with by rain, was neither imaginative nor venturesome. Surrey needed to beat Leicestershire in their last fixture to share the spoils, and this they duly did. As if to underline the bias in favour of spin, Lancashire also lost twice in 1950 to the visiting West Indians, historically associated with the names of Ramadhin and Valentine.

It had been an agreeable and harmonious team effort. Wash-brook, Edrich, Grieves, Ikin, Place and the captain, Nigel Howard, scored a thousand or more each. Statham had begun his career with *élan*, and Geoff Lomax and Peter Greenwood had lent dependable aid. Malcolm Hilton took 127 wickets at an average of 15, while it was 22 years, away back to the time of McDonald, since anyone had reaped such a harvest as Tattersall did in 1950. He took 171 wickets for Lancashire, average just over 13, and 193 in all first-class games. No one since has approached that total. Eight for 60 versus Surrey was his best haul, and sometimes he was unplayable.

The teamwork was emphasised by the fielding, which was perpetually excellent and often miraculous. Cyril Washbrook now wielded authority in the covers, a supreme expression of that most exciting of Lancashire traditions, and the outfielding, especially when Wharton and Statham were in the side, was effective. What was startling was the close fielding, for, with Tattersall making the ball fizz from the off on helpful wickets, a fearless and secure leg-trap was most necessary. Ken Grieves, although often at first slip, John Ikin, Malcolm Hilton and Geoff Edrich provided this asset in a wondrous fashion never surpassed at Old Trafford, and few counties can have been blessed with so acrobatic a troupe. Only three times have Lancashire fielders taken 50 catches in a season: Ikin, with 55 (45 for Lancashire) in 1946, Grieves, with 54 in 1953, and, the most of all, Grieves again, 63, in the Championship year of 1950. In 1951, against Sussex, Grieves first equalled Tyldesley's six catches in an innings, and, in the same game, became Lancashire's only fielder to catch eight in a match.

Although lacking an outstanding wicket-keeper, it was a side as challenging in the field as any Lancashire team since as long ago as Hornby's powerful team, and the length of the batting was another substantial bonus. With Statham a late and, as yet, unripe entrant, the bowling over the season lacked in devastating pace, but the combine of Hilton with the hugely successful Tattersall made as engaging a spinning pair as Lancashire had known. Nigel Howard had his critics, and his critics were sometimes right. He was green, over-reliant on external advice and unwilling or unable to seek counsel from the experienced men in the team. Yet he batted gamely and encouraged youngsters, and, whilst not a leader in either the tradition of Hornby or Leonard Green, he is undeserving of some of the faults pressed against him. After all, a Championship is a Championship, and Lancashire have not enjoyed the luxury of one since.

For several, this single success came early in their careers, but it is, nevertheless, a convenient moment to subject Lancashire's first batch of post-war players to more personal scrutiny.

*Cyril Washbrook*

The post-war years at Old Trafford were dominated by the lordly strut of Cyril Washbrook, said by Len Hutton to be his favourite opening partner. Born in December 1914, a month or so after the start of the First World War, he first played for the county in 1933, and only slowly edged his way into a powerful batting line-up. Although he scored his initial century in 1933 (152 against Surrey) it was 1935 before his first thousand in a season was recorded. Thereafter he never failed to cross that threshold until 1956, including his most authoritative phase of 1946 and 1947 when, in those two seasons, he scored over 5000 runs. His roll-call of a thousand runs in 20 seasons is a Lancashire record; only the Tyldesley brothers and Clive Lloyd compiled more than his 76 centuries; and, with 34,000 runs and an average of 42, he is, after the Tyldesleys, Lancashire's most prolific batsman. With the important exception of Clive Lloyd, he has, far and away, been the county's most valuable batsman of the modern era.

Having made himself Eddie Paynter's regular partner and having tasted Test cricket, replacing the injured left-hander for one match against New Zealand in 1937, the war disturbed Cyril Washbrook's advance. He was, however, relatively fortunate, in that his RAF service allowed him to participate in much of the high-level cricket the Second World War witnessed. He seemed supercharged and assuredly ready for the post-war seasons, scoring heavily and entertaining mightily. Had it not been for the dual phenomenon of Denis Compton and Bill Edrich in the unsubdued sunniness of 1947, Cyril Washbrook's exploits might have been trumpeted more vociferously. In those first two post-war seasons, he averaged over 68, and scored a thousand runs alone in July of 1946. With Winston Place, he shared in no less than four opening stands of over 200, two of them in 1947 against the wilting Sussex bowlers.

The first of these onslaughts was at Old Trafford. Cyril Washbrook signalled the commencement of the assault, rather like a field officer blowing his whistle for the charge over the top, by hooking the very first ball of the innings for six. Unbeaten on 350, the pair were just 17 runs behind the Lancashire first-wicket record, and a sizeable crowd assembled on the third morning hopeful of seeing it tumble. They were disappointed by a declaration, then cheered by a Lancashire victory just prior to rainfall. There have been only 11 stands of over 300 in Lancashire's history; and this was the fourth-highest, and the only unbroken one of the set. It could, then, be said to be Lancashire's most successful stand ever, and Cyril Washbrook's share was 204 not out. Later in the season, he scored 251, not out, against Surrey, another of his six double centuries, and his highest-ever score.

Cyril Washbrook made six centuries for England, for whom he opened the batting regularly and satisfactorily for several summers and winter tours after the war. Although he found the Australians at their most lethal, especially with Lindwall and Miller at their peak, and although he was later faced with Ramadhin and Valentine as the West Indies matured into expert opponents, he had a splendid Test career. He totted up over 2500 runs in 37 international matches, after Statham, Lancashire's most-capped Englishman, and his average of 42 is genuinely creditable. No other Lancastrian has scored 2000 runs for England. The 359 he shared with Len Hutton against the South Africans at Johannesburg on the 1948–49 tour survives as England's record opening stand ever, while, on duty in Australia in 1946–47, the same pair managed stands of over a hundred in three consecutive Test innings. They also opened with 168 and 129 at Leeds against the Australians in 1948. Throughout these years, the quartet of Hutton, Washbrook, Edrich and Compton performed strikingly well: unluckily, and apart from Alec Bedser, the bowling was never of the same quality.

Few will need reminding that Cyril Washbrook crowned his fine international career with a memorable comeback at Leeds in 1956. Aged almost 44, he was, in fact, a selector, who absented himself from the meeting, while the England captain, Peter May, apparently argued against his inclusion. At 17 for 3, however, Peter May was generous enough to confess that he could imagine of no more reassuring sight than that of the doughty Washbrook, tramping down the Headingly pavilion steps to join him. Cyril Washbrook batted with May throughout a long first day, and his dismissal, early the next morning, for 98, added the piquancy of a near-miss to the sentiment of an efficacious return.

If Cyril Washbrook was a doyen of one of Lancashire's specialisms, that of opening the batting, he as fluently adorned another, the position of cover point. Acknowledged as the safest and swiftest exponent on the English scene, with only Neil Harvey from abroad to rival him, he patrolled the cover territory with brooding aplomb. Unfailingly tidy in pick-up or catch, unfailingly accurate and arrow-like of throw, Cyril Washbrook was a diamond link in a bejewelled chain joining Vernon Royle with Clive Lloyd.

Cyril Washbrook played on, perhaps a little reluctantly, until 1959, and, indeed, notched up his twentieth thousand in 1958. He was resolute in response to a challenge, and, then as earlier, knew he was expected to and could make a contribution to Lancashire cricket. His phase as captain, six summers from 1954 to 1959, was not a joyous one. It came too late. It would have made better sense to have given him the post earlier, while a younger man, such as Nigel Howard, was nurtured for the task. The ancient prejudice against the professional skipper persisted, and, quite properly, Cyril Washbrook saw no reason why he should become an overnight repentant and espouse amateurism.

He did not fail as a captain, certainly not when comparisons are drawn with later years. Lancashire were normally occupying positions around sixth or seventh in the table, and in 1956 they were second to all-conquering Surrey. It was the mood that was a little dreary and defensive, with young hopefuls scarcely seeming to be encouraged, and the overall urgency of a collective mission rarely to be remarked.

Later Cyril Washbrook was to be one of the first of cricket's managers, but that, too, was not very successful. In the longer term, his service on the county committee has been estimable, and he proved also to be a competent businessman in the field of sports equipment. All of this was helped by his overwhelming benefit, when he was generously allowed the Australian match at Old Trafford in 1948. The public gratitude and admiration was enormous, and his £14,000 tally was then, and by many pounds, an all-time record. John Tyldesley's £3,000 was the next Lancashire best.

Cyril Washbrook addressed the crowd during his benefit match, and, for the ordinary spectators, it was perhaps the first time, they had heard one of their heroes speak. It was rather surprising. Cyril Washbrook spoke in a well modulated, calm and controlled bass. There was little hint of a northern accent or a working-class twang. It could have been an amateur. After that, calling him 'Washy' was decidedly impertinent, rather like cheeky schoolboys nicknaming a stern teacher.

There was something schoolmasterly about Cyril Washbrook,

predictably so, perhaps, as his great career was prolonged and as he himself evolved into elder statesmanship. It certainly affected his captaincy, for, eventually, a whole decade opened up between his colleagues and himself. It was also a post-war decade that separated them, and some of the values had changed. He could not be avuncular, and it has been written that some young players regarded him with fearful awe rather than respect. He had been permitted to become isolated.

But that was in later years. One must concentrate on the nine or ten seasons from the end of the 1939–45 war. Cyril Washbrook was a stockily built bat, military in carriage and with a chest that appeared inflated, so pouter-like was it in dimension. High-shouldered and immensely confident, foot cocked at the crease and with a proud follow-through of the bat, cap – and his very own cliché must be again deployed – at a jaunty angle: this was Cyril Washbrook, a domineering batsman and an imperious fieldsman.

He assailed bowlers with panache, undeterred in his belief that he must command them, and not they, him, with the flourish of his run-getting. It is appropriate that, when people reminisce of Cyril Washbrook, they whisper in hushed tones of the arrogant dispatch of his square cut and the mountainous trajectory of his contemptuous hook. Cyril Washbrook had, of course, been tutored in a strict college of professionalism, when the award of a county cap was tantamount to a knighthood, and when that accolade was no guarantee that anyone would ask your opinion on matters arising. Nonetheless, there was an additional element to Washbrook's stern discipline, and that was his awareness of the cricketer as entertainer. It was partly a question of temperament, for, by disposition, he preferred to unseat the enemy with the rapier of Archie MacLaren rather than the bludgeon of Harry Makepeace. Each fielding side would dutifully post a deep square leg for him, and Cyril Washbrook would duly note the placement. Then he would attempt to out-hit that fielder, and often, not always, he succeeded. He was, above all, a spectator's batsman, and, in the parks of Manchester in the late 1940s the youngster's cry was 'Bags me Washbrook', when the coats were recruited for wickets and an impromptu Test match began. He was one of the last and one of the greatest of the cigarette-card heroes, bowing out before the onset of one-day cricket and the termination of the players and gentlemen convention.

Thus he was no authoritarian figure. He was his own independent man, as the giveaway snake-clasp he kept on his belt after higher authority had ordered him to jettison it, recalls. He was certainly a person of authority, but the zeal to entertain moderated any puritanical images. When the young men of the 1950s failed to meet his exacting criteria, it was probably not only because, in preparation, attitude and, thus, performance, he found them lacking, it was also because, related to these insufficiencies, they were not much worth watching.

Finally, that buccaneering spirit saved Cyril Washbrook from the offence of autocracy. If he was monarch of all he surveyed, he was a pirate king, piratically remorseless with himself and with his subordinates. One is tempted to think of him as Captain Hook, and my own first unfading memory of Old Trafford was made the more indelible because Cyril Washbrook swashbuckled 133 for the North of England against the Royal Australian Air Force as, in 1944, cricket hesitatingly resumed there. Cyril Washbrook was, as Israel Hands reverently said of Cap'n Flint, 'the flower of the flock'.


## Dick Pollard

It has been said that, were the Lancashire committee invited, although it seems unlikely, to choose the cast for a medieval morality play, Dick Pollard would surely get the role of 'Toil'. With a run-up longer and at a speed faster than was then the English norm, he bowled over after uncomplaining over for the county. Although the high pace of Lindwall and Miller in 1948 placed this in fiery perspective, Dick Pollard was, before and after the Second World War, one of the most aggressive and hardworking bowlers around.

Like many born prior to or about the time of the 1914–18 war, his career was truncated by army serivce in the 1939–45 war. Joining the staff in 1933, he only made certain of a place in 1936, and, by 1949, his career was on the wane. He finished with the county the following season. Thus, surprisingly for one who appeared to be very much part of the furniture, he only managed to pack in eight or nine seasons.

He made the most of it. Memory suggests that he bowled virtually non-stop, and he became the seventh Lancastrian to take a thousand wickets for the county. His first-class haul, all told, was 1122 at an average of just over 22. This included a couple of hat-tricks, and key performances of 14 for 126 against Middlesex in 1946 and, his best innings figures, 8 for 33 against Nottinghamshire the following year. In six of his handful of seasons he passed a hundred wickets, and he also played in four Tests, one each against India and New Zealand, and the other two against the 1948 Australians. In the Old Trafford Test he is remembered for the on-drive which dispatched S. G. Barnes, truculently sledging at silly mid-on, for medical care and attention. In the Leeds Test he is remembered for taking two early wickets in one over on the last day, only for Australia to recover and score 404 for 3, their highest-ever fourth innings.

In those seasons sandwiching the Second World War, Dick Pollard formed a profitable and aggressive partnership with Eddie Phillipson, and they played together in one or two of the Victory Tests in 1945. Eddie Phillipson, two years Pollard's junior, was unlucky with injury and stomach ailments, and his career was even shorter than his stable-mate's. He took some 500 wickets, but was a more useful bat than Pollard, averaging 25 from his 4000 runs. Taller and thinner than Dick Pollard, he was a quick, accurate bowler. He later became an umpire. Lancashire have not often had so penetrative a duo to open their attack.

Dick Pollard was barrel-chested and broad-bottomed, with hair inclining to ginger and countenance to beetroot. He bowled with an incessant honesty, and was rewarded with a mean of something like four or five wickets in each of the 266 matches he crowded into his brief allotted span. Feet soon sorted at the beginning of his run, he lengthened his stride considerably, before his strong shoulders yet again whirled, right to left, and what the Victorians referred to as the cherry was pinging once more around the batsman's midriff. With the new ball and given appropriate climatic conditions, he would bowl the most outrageous away-swinger, perhaps pitching centre pitch and ballooning away toward second slip. His shirt might become dislodged from his hardly svelte waistband, and he would perspire liberally. His only lazy gesture stemmed from his loathing of bending down, so that, if the ball was returned to him along the ground, he would toe-end it to mid-off like a full-back back-passing to his goalkeeper. And then he would bowl again, and again.

Cricketers enjoy subtle degrees of admiration, ranging from grudging respect to rank adoration. Dick Pollard, quite simply, was popular. He was exceptionally popular with the popular side. Flocking from the factories of near-at-hand Trafford Park and from the mills in districts a little more distant, the working men on the ring recognised a mate in Dick Pollard. He came from the spinning areas and, like them, he did his time as an army private. He bowled through unremitting hours as if marked by the factory card-clock and buzzer, a solid journeyman, certainly automatic and a little regimented in action, but with an inner conviction of the worthiness of his craft. He was a working man who had transferred his allegiance from mill to pitch, and, after his retirement, he was to be discovered toiling as assiduously in a small floor-covering concern.

If today's cricketing biographical anthologies are to be believed, every single player has a nickname, however contrived or banal. Dick Pollard is one of few cricketers who had two sobriquets which were in common parlance on the Old Trafford terraces. He was variously known as Westhoughton Dick, as if he were some fancy gunslinger like the Wyoming Kid, and T'Owd Chain-horse, after, for industrial illiterates, the tough, old horses which dragged laden barges along the canals of the North-West. To be so likened by his admirers was a token of his popularity and of their understanding. He was one of them, but one who happened to be slaving away at something rather more interesting and colourful. Had the Pennines not intervened to grant him Yorkshire residence, Jesse Oldroyd, of J. B. Priestley's *The Good Companions*, might have been compared with Dick Pollard. He, too, left the factory-system of Bruddersford, but sustained the same values when embarked on a life in the entertainments industry, as help-meet to a concert party.

Dick Pollard was born, in Westhoughton, near Bolton, on 19 June 1912, and he died, aged 73, on 16 December 1985. Whether the concept of demanding just one more over from a flagging bowler survives upon the Elysian Fields is a topic for theology rather than cricket history. T'Owd Chain-horse would, one can, however, be assured, comply with that despairing request, be it human or divine in source.


## Ken Cranston

The romantic heroes of British films in the late 1940s were

inclined to be dark and swarthy, after the model of James Mason and Stewart Granger. Ken Cranston, handsome, sleek-haired and cravatted, might easily have been taken for one of them. His publicity photograph would not have disgraced the collection of stills in your local Gaumont or Odeon, while the dramatic tale of his brief but stirring first-class career might, indeed, have been scripted for portrayal on those very screens.

He appeared, so it seemed, from nowhere, batted and bowled with insouciant flair, forced his cavalier way into eight Test sides, and then, after two colourful seasons, disappeared as mysteriously as he had arrived.

The salient element of these heroics is beyond question. In 50 county matches, over those two seasons of 1947 and 1948, he took 142 wickets, including five wickets on ten occasions, and he scored 1928 runs, for an average of 40. In his eight Tests, he added 209 runs and 18 wickets, including a bravura four in six balls against South Africa at Headingly. As well as three Tests in 1947 against the South Africans, he then toured West Indies the following winter, and actually captained England in the first Test, because of G. O. Allen's indisposition. He played in just one Test against Australia in the next summer.

Truth is not invariably stranger than fiction, and some of the surrounding matter was a little more mundane. Ken Cranston, born in 1917, trained in dentistry at Liverpool University and learned his cricket in the Liverpool Competition. He made some noted contributions to wartime cricket, serving as a dental officer in the Royal Navy, and was thus not entirely unknown.

Nor was his assumption of the county captaincy handled with the finesse which J. Arthur Rank would have enjoyed watching in one of his films. Poor Jack Fallows, who helped Lancashire out of a deep hole by captaining the side in the first post-war season, discovered news of his removal through a press leakage. His professional colleagues were very shocked. Jack Fallows, while without pretensions as a top-class player, had proved a popular and shrewd skipper. In that difficult summer of 1946, he had managed such practical matters as transport and hotels with quiet skill, providing Solomonite judgements about, for instance, when bowlers or batsmen should have the rare fried egg for breakfast. That kind of man-management, scarcely ever publicised in the public prints, is, of course, most important in first-class cricket, where the long togetherness of lengthy playing time and constant travel is a chief characteristic. Beyond that, Lancashire had had a tremendous season, especially in regard of its depleted stock of players, and Fallows had earned much credit for his leadership. He leaned properly but carefully on the advice of his senior professionals, who were left themselves feeling highly insecure by the sudden, discourteous and summary dismissal of their captain. It is said that relations between committee and staff deteriorated from that juncture, and a gap was created which lasted many years. Fallows, born in 1907, died in 1974, after giving exemplary committee service to the county.

Ken Cranston, something of an innocent abroad in these higher reaches of cricketing politics, was not to blame for a foolish committee, but he did perhaps make the mistake of continuing to listen overmuch to it during his two-year spell as captain. Although there was never any overt animosity between the players and himself, he never truly earned their confidence or took their sagacious counsel. It has to be said that he was an impoverished captain, unable to plan a co-ordinated campaign or command his unit effectively. The continued good form of the early Lancashire batsmen and, in particular, of Pollard with the ball, saved the county from undue distress. However, after winning 15 games in 1946, it was a little disappointing to drop to 13 in 1947 and then to only eight in 1948.

Whereas the likes of Washbrook and Place could soldier on and score their runs, it was perhaps in attack where this inadequacy of coherent oversight counted. The left-hand spin-bowler, Eric Price, has been mooted as one who rather faded, after an initial firm impression, because of lack of skilled advice and encouragement. Cranston never promised to play for more than a couple of years and he himself claimed no special expertise as a leader, so that, on the debit side of the account, it must be recorded as something of a loss. He returned, in the autumn of 1948, to his dentistry practice on Merseyside and to the delights of club cricket and golf – although, in 1949, he pleased the festival crowd at Scarborough with a splendid 156, not out, for the MCC against Yorkshire.

It proved, yet again, that captaincy is no simple task. Harsher judges have said that Cranston's lack of a first-class apprenticeship also told when he had to face superior opponents, such as the 1948 Australians, and that perhaps his prowess was as superficial as that of the matinée idols on the silver screen.

That is an abrasive assessment. Kenneth Cranston's glittering career burst like a cascading firework over Old Trafford, and it was good while it lasted. He was a naturally gifted cricketer, and he approached close to a spectacular double in his first season. Amid the greyness of the post-war years, a good-looking 30-year-old athlete of dashing mien, was an attractive proposition, and his exploits were much enjoyed. The advantage of his lack of grounding was that he did not pace himself too patiently, as if determined to cram as much as he could into the two summers he had allotted himself. He batted eagerly, scoring runs with quick and evident glee; he bustled keenly into his astute seam-bowling; he fielded with verve; he was a cricketer on the attack, bringing the more brash enthusiasm of the Saturday afternoon player to inform the potential of a Test player. However sadly one might pen a critique of his captaincy, there must be no gainsaying the unalloyed pleasure he gave to Lancashire spectators over that all too short span. Would that he might have stayed longer and served, and developed, under the mature captaincy of another.

Here, then, was a man who played for England after only 13 first-class matches, and who was assessed by Harry Makepeace, never the one to permit of hyperbole, as the most gifted boy he had ever coached. In all matches, he scored over 3000 runs, took 178 wickets and held many catches, and older members daydreamed a little of the likes of Reggie Spooner. That undeniably, is the case to set against Jack Fallows, with his paltry 171 runs in 25 matches. Cranston even completed the schoolboy story by hitting the winning runs in his last match against Kent. It was not quite the epic tale of a Clark Kent turned Superman, leading Lancashire to Championship honours, before returning from the Metropolis of Old Trafford to the Smallsville of a suburban dental practice. But it was as near as one might realistically hope for in real life – and it seemed to us so peculiar that a cricketer who could give such pleasure was professionally engaged elsewhere in a pursuit which brings, in legend and, unfortunately, in fact, such pain.

## Winston Place and Alan Wharton

Winston Place was born in the winter after the outbreak of the Great War, his parents perhaps enthused by Churchill's deeds as First Lord of the Admiralty. But he was never a Churchillian figure, being much too careful, even too stealthy, a figure for that. He came from Rawtenstall and learned his cricket in the Lancashire League during a time when cricketers of major prominence were engaged as professionals. He appeared first for Lancashire in 1937, but it was after the war, as Washbrook's partner, that he really came to the fore and quietly enjoyed a most satisfactory career until he bowed out in 1955. With a nest-egg of £6000 from his benefit, he established himself in a little shop somewhere in Lancashire, content to sell the newspapers and placidly count his blessings.

He scored over 14,000 runs in almost 300 matches, at an average of 36, and passed a thousand runs in the first eight post-war seasons. In 1947 he scored 2408 runs for the county, at an average of nearly 69. He scored 36 centuries, ten of them in the prolific season of 1947. These included his highest score – 266, not out, against Oxford University – and two hundreds in the same match versus Nottinghamshire. He scored a century for England in the West Indies on the 1947–48 tour, when the absence of star names allowed him a glimpse of international experience, and he won three caps.

Place was an orthodox batsman, somewhat in the Makepeace mould of pedantry, but with his grave technical aptitude relieved by the unleashing of a graceful off-drive or the execution of a fragile late cut. In personality and power he was subsidiary to Washbrook, and accepted that with equanimity, but it was a question of degree rather than of subordinate status. He played Little John to Cyril Washbrook's Robin Hood.

He was taller than Washbrook, and as powerfully built across the shoulders. His homely face always seemed to be in repose, his Lancashire cap pulled, like Washbrook's, toward the left ear, but somehow without the same cockiness. He had a long reach, playing deliberately forward with due gravity, occasionally appearing a little leaden-footed, but with the sheer flawlessness of his method ensuring that he never looked awkward. Few doubted that, on poor wickets, his correctness rendered him Washbrook's superior. Time and again, in those colourless post-war years, Winston Place helped give Lancashire heartening starts and pleased the crowds, so eager to be lifted. He reached fifty over a hundred times, and he would mark the occasion calmly, raising his cap politely to acknowledge the applause, revealing his sandy hair for a second or two.

Peter Tinniswood, a schoolboy watcher of Lancashire in these years, obviously took a shine to Winston Place, for he is honoured liberally in 'Tales from the Long Room'. Peter Tinniswood, like Alan Bennett, has a sensitive feel for the byways and tributaries of Northern life, and he doubtless found in Winston Place something of whimsy. Without word or overt gesture, he certainly conveyed a wryness, whether batting or fielding, as, in the outfield, he did with a sort of grudging competence, taking catches safely but not in textbookish manner. Peter Tinniswood's character from his amusing novels of South Lancashire life, Uncle Mort, has the same tendency. Near to death, his vision of heaven is of a whist drive attended by 'me mother and father – having a bloody good row as usual – there was C. B. Fry and Ranji, there was Lottie Besant, who got electrocuted that time, there was Fred Foreshaw, Billy King, Tommy Handley, me Uncle Asa . . .'

Winston Place appeared to have this same mordant humour, and it was said of him that he was well versed in the ancient Lancashire folk-game of evoking an aggressive argument and then stealing silently away. He was, no doubt, a cricketer of brain, not brawn, thinking about and examining bowlers with shrewd acuity, and he served his county with sedate application.

Younger than Place – he was born in 1923 – but merging into this first post-war generation was Alan Wharton. He played first in 1946 and, until he moved to Leicestershire in 1961, his urgent excursions were an eye-catching part of Lancashire's play. By 1952 his place in the team was consolidated, and, in eight seasons, he made a thousand runs. Such was his punishing approach that he scored almost 18,000 runs for Lancashire, more, that is, than Paynter, MacLaren, Clive Lloyd and Hornby. The best of his 25 centuries was his 199 against Sussex in 1959.

All this betokened a similar kind of consistency to that of Winston Place, but the nature of it was different. Sharp-featured and gaunt, Alan Wharton looked manic alongside the meditations of Place. He wore an enormously peaked cap that gave him a Yankee appearance, as though he were aping Spanky MacFarlane in Our Gang. His frenzy would not have been out of place on the baseball diamond. Apart from the energetic batting, chiefly off the front foot, which places him tenth in the list of Lancashire run-getters, he hurtled himself through a busy action to take 225 wickets and he darted keenly around the outfield, his cap giving some impression of a startled partridge.

His single appearance for England in 1949 against New Zealand was unremarkable, and, like Place, he never quite aspired to international heights. However, his all-round soundness, in particular the unremitting regularity of his batting was self-evident. If the fraction be excused, he exceeded fifty in every four and a half innings he played for the club, and that warrants admiration and praise that, somehow, never quite came Alan Wharton's way. He was also a fighter for improved conditions and thus something of a shop steward; indeed, his grasp of affairs might have caused Lancashire to have found some useful position for him with the club.

We could enjoy the phlegm of Winston Place and the antics of Alan Wharton, like Place, a product of the leagues, in relaxing fashion. In recalling the memory of Lancashire in the 1940s for us, through the medium of artful wordplay and gentle parody, Peter Tinniswood is possibly the nearest to a genuine inheritor of the Cardus mantle.

## John Ikin, Geoff Edrich and Ken Grieves

They came from far afield to capitalise on the investment of Washbrook and Place and to poach catches off the tantalising deliveries of Tattersall. Johnny Ikin, born in 1918 in Bignall End, Staffordshire, for whom he played fore and aft of his first-class career, was on the ground staff before the war, and was a regular member of the eleven for ten or so seasons afterwards. Geoff Edrich, hearing of Lancashire's depredations in 1946, came from Norfolk, after arduous war service, accompanied by his brother, Eric, a balding and lively wicket-keeper-batsman. Like Ikin, he was born in 1918. K. J. Grieves was younger – he was born in 1925 in Australia – and he was the Rawtenstall professional before playing for Lancashire in 1949. He was a goal-keeper with Bury, Bolton Wanderers and Stockport County in the winter months.

They came together like the Three Musketeers, the tough loyalty of Porthos in Edrich, the martial shrewdness of Aramis in Grieves, and the self-effacing introversion of Athos in Ikin. Together, as close fielders, they were, as has been mentioned, conspicuously agile. If poetic licence permit the unlikely shift of site from Gascony to Werneth, then a young d'Artagnan, Malcolm

Hilton, arrived to complete the ring and also to unsettle Bradman, as if he were the Cardinal. Unaided by the modern trappings of helmets and protectors, they outdid fiction in their uncanny anticipation and prehensile catching, a sporting equivalent, if you will, of Dumas-style fencing. Jack Ikin may, by a fraction, have been the pick of this foursome who would not have been out of place in the sawdust of George Lockhart's circus across the city at Belle Vue. Ikin rested between deliveries, squatting, one hand on knee, head lowered; gradually, he adjusted himself without fuss to a watchful, never tense, pose. His prediction of angle and pace off the bat was enviable and perplexing. Scarcely a match passed without heads being shaken in disbelief over another miracle catch or stop.

Like the Musketeers the three were fearless, not only as close fieldsmen, but as batsmen. Geoff Edrich, small and sturdy, applied himself to orthodox method expressed through relentless courage. It made of him a happy run-scorer on good and an immovable ally on bad wickets. He scored almost 15,000 runs for Lancashire at an average close on 35. His 24 centuries for the county were part of this fine achievement, his 167, not out, at Nottingham in 1954 being the highest. He later captained the second eleven with good sense and pragmatic judgement. Characteristically, he refused to inform on youthful culprits after a silly prank in a hotel, and this cost him the job. Committees are apt to choose wrongly when faced with a clash of conflicting loyalty. Lancashire could ill-afford to lose as principled and steadfast a man as G. A. Edrich, who, like Alan Wharton, might have proved of value to the club at the highest level. Edrich left in 1958 to pursue an equable life in minor cricket and schools coaching.

Ken Grieves, who had played for New South Wales, brought the pugnacity and the street-wisdom of Sydney to Old Trafford. With the possible exception of MacLaren at his best, he was the dandiest slip Lancashire have known, and, casual air hiding know-how, his leg-spinners earned him 235 wickets. Although in his mid-twenties when he made his début, the stubble-haired, rangy Australian played in 452 matches for Lancashire. In 1962 he took himself off to the Central Lancashire League, only to be called back, in crisis, to captain Lancashire in 1963 and 1964. As with Washbrook, the invitation might have been made earlier, say, in 1958 or 1959. Little went right, and, some weeks before the end of the second season, he learned that his contract would be terminated. Back he went to the welcoming arms of the Central Lancashire League.

Over the years, however, he battered the bowling to some purpose. Tall, capless and upright, he strove mainly to sway on to the back foot and crack the ball away square and into the covers or force it in an arc from mid-wicket to fine leg. He scored 26 centuries for Lancashire, 224 against Cambridge University in 1957 being his best effort; a thousand runs in each of twelve seasons, including 2253 in 1957; and, in full sum, 20,802 runs for the county (22,454 in all matches) average of 33. Proudly he stands between Hallows and Iddon, eighth in the county list. At Old Trafford he replaced, in effect, B. P. King, a Yorkshireman with experience with Worcestershire, who like the Edrich brothers and the Glamorgan wicket-keeper, T. L. Brierley, had been drafted in to fill the war-torn gaps. Ken Grieves, while not as spectacular in impact as his antecedent, McDonald, gave long and sterling service to his adopted home.

Of the three, Jack Ikin was the only international. Thrust a little precipitately into Test cricket in his first full season, subjected to the Australian onslaught in all five Tests during the tour of 1946–47, he never settled comfortably. He won eighteen caps, scored just on 600 runs and never took a wicket. At the same time, his cool disregard and stubborn defence in face of both Australian and South African fast bowling won him well earned praise. Harry Makepeace had dinned into a willing student the capital virtue of courage, and no braver man played the game.

In more relaxed mood, he was a charming left-hander, moving easily, dispatching lissomely, providing restful pleasure. He was a handsome-looking cricketer, dark and neatly proportioned. He scored 14,327 runs for Lancashire at an average of nearly 38, and he scored nearly 4000 more in other first-class games. His highest innings was 192 at Oxford in 1951: that was one of his 27 centuries, 23 of which he scored for Lancashire, and he passed the thousand-target ten times. Like Grieves, he was a leg-spin bowler, although he adopted a busier approach than the passive Grieves. As a change-bowler, he took 278 wickets in his 288 games for the county.

John Ikin died in 1984. Injury and illness had plagued his career, and now, aged only 66, this popular sportsman was the first of the post-war echelon to die. It was a sad moment because of that, and because of another reason. Somehow, not only those who knew J. T. Ikin intimately or even casually, but most of those who watched and admired from the stands, decided that he was a most courteous and civil man. When the conversation turns, over lunch at Old Trafford or in the evening in one of Lancashire's scores of clubrooms, the epithet that always occurs is that Johnny Ikin was a real gentleman. To many he was in cricket what Bobby Charlton became in football, a sportsman whose attitude was innately humane. In these years when sportsmen find it difficult to recognise, let alone reach, reasonable standards, that may be judged a richer epitaph than 18,000 runs and a bagful of impossible catches. J. T. Ikin could not question an umpire, show dissent or, perhaps most important, exhibit unfriendliness toward an opponent. Sincerely, naturally and without primness, it was *toujours la politesse*.

## A Quartet of Left-Handers

In the heyday of the County Championships, and until the coming of one-day cricket, it would have been as unthinkable to enter a match without a left-hand spin-bowler as for a man to wear his hat in church. In the immediate post-war summers, Lancashire, almost absent-mindedly, found themselves with four. Each of them would probably be preferred to any left-hander playing today.

Eric Price, arriving from Middleton, played only two seasons, 1946 and 1947, and the wiseacres claimed he was not looked after properly during the Cranston regime. He was considered good enough to earn a Test trial at Canterbury, but he moved to Essex, for whom he took 92 wickets over a couple of seasons. E. J. Price was already 27 when he made his first-class debut, and played 35 matches for Lancashire, taking 115 wickets, average 20. He was no batsman, but he did manage one fifty, whilst his best bowling was 6 for 34.

Perhaps his best performance was in 1947 when Lancashire inflicted upon Middlesex their only home defeat of that glorious season. Ikin bowled Compton around his legs, and Price was successful in placing strict restraint on all the other batsmen, including Bill Edrich. It was my first visit to Lord's, and a happy one.

Bill Roberts was a little older, having been born in 1914, and he had been on the ground staff prior to the war. He was a most orthodox bowler. Eric Price was of the high-stepping variety: fair and slightly built, his last pace before bowling was a goose-step which would have done the Wehrmacht credit, and his delivery was correspondingly high. W. B. Roberts was more conventional, running smoothly and turning his fluent arm in the classic tradition. He was very accurate: indeed, adverse commentators insisted that he 'bowled them in', his lack of variation a disbenefit, as opposing bats eased themselves into the groove against predictable length. He played over a hundred matches, principally in the first four post-war seasons, and he took 382 wickets at a cost each of 21. In 1949 he took 8 for 50 against Oxford University, his best performance.

Against the powerful 1948 Australians, he came on late at Old Trafford and then bowled unchanged throughout most of Saturday and took six wickets, including Bradman's. On Sunday the Test team was to be announced, and some thought Roberts might have earned a cap. It was not to be.

He was not one to fret, for a more cheerful soul would have been hard to find. His was a casual and unworried approach, and maybe his lack of serious aplomb disadvantaged him. He scarcely seemed to bother about the state of the game and regarded batting as an undignified adjunct to the more sophisticated art of bowling. Just once, however, spectators arriving late at Old Trafford were surprised to see a batsman driving freely, as if the ghost of Spooner had descended upon his shoulders. It was Bill Roberts, the nightwatchman, cutting loose and notching his solitary fifty. His frame was medium-sized and portly, but it did not prevent him being a surprisingly efficient boundary fielder, and, red-faced and grinning, he saved many runs. He died, suddenly, sadly, in 1951, only 37 years old.

Bob Berry was born in 1926, and came from the Lancashire and Cheshire League to Old Trafford, where he played from 1948 to 1954, before transferring first to Worcestershire and then to Derbyshire. He found it difficult to command a place with so many spinners around. He played in two Test matches against the West Indies in 1950, taking nine wickets, and he also toured Australia, where he found the going hard, as, later, he did on English wickets as they became more soundly prepared. In 93 games he took 259 wickets, average 23, and, in the Worcestershire game in 1953 when he took ten wickets in an innings, he completed his tally at 14 for 125. His batting was slapstick in the Harold, rather than the Clive, Lloyd mode, and afforded much amusement.

A tiny, rotund figure, yet a brilliant outfielder, he flighted the ball more expansively than his colleagues. Because of his own smallness, the height he tossed the ball gave an illusion of being almost at hand-grenade level. He rolled the ball rather than spun it with his fingers, relying more on the bamboozlement of a sky-high flight-path. He was always a jolly and blithe cricketer to watch.

Malcolm Hilton was the most enduring of the four, playing from 1946 through to 1961 and participating in 241 Lancashire matches. He also took fifteen wickets for England in his four Tests, and, because of his acute fielding, he was sometimes in demand to act as twelfth man for the England side. He took a hundred wickets in seasons 1950, 1951, 1955 and 1956, and he is Lancashire's thirteenth wicket-taker, with 926 dismissals, average 19. Other games considered, he just passed a thousand wickets in his career, a most creditable display. He was younger than the other three, arriving at Old Trafford an eager teenager more or less straight from school, and after some experience with Werneth in the Central Lancashire League.

Thus he was barely 20 when, in 1948, he first bowled Don Bradman for 11, and then, when Bradman decided to whack him, he had the Australian maestro stumped for 43. It became a *cause célèbre*, and Hilton learned quickly how the man who shot Liberty Vallance must have felt. Malcolm Hilton was an extremely assured cricketer, a little, some opined, in excess of a necessary confidence, but no one denied that he found cricket a most enjoyable occupation. He bowled faster than the other three, depending on biting spin from a normal length, and it was not uncommon to find this slimly framed and fair-haired young man opening the bowling. Had he been allowed, he would have opened the batting, too. He scored over 3000 runs for the county, his proudest day being in 1955 at Northampton when he hit an undefeated century. His best bowling was at Weston-super-Mare in 1956 when he took 8 for 39 in an innings and 14 for 88 in the match versus Somerset. At Old Trafford in 1958 he took 8 New Zealand wickets for 19, a demonstration of his extreme danger on a helpful pitch.

No left-hander has seriously challenged Hilton's claim to be

Lancashire's most effective bowler of that mode in the modern era. In fact, only Johnny Briggs and Harry Dean, whose career was chiefly confined to the Edwardian period, stand above him in quantity of wickets taken.

The fact that there was always one and often two slow left-hand bowlers in any Lancashire eleven of the late 1940s and early 1950s meant that one delight was ever in store. Now what left-handers there are seem to dip the ball in somewhat at the batsmen, and the batsmen seem unready to advance and be recognised. There is much bat and pad scrabbling, with armoured guards crouching inches from the bat, hoping that the next hesitant prod will produce a bat-and-pad catch. It is unlovely. Then the left-handers would flight the ball more richly, pitching on middle and off, with a crescent of fielders from mid-off to first slip, and frequently no more than a lonely twosome on the leg side. Batsmen picked up the gauntlet, driving and driving again into the packed arc, searching for the gap through or over, and providing one of cricket's most decorous and exciting spectacles. This is exactly what Bill Edrich did at Lord's against Eric Price in the warmth of a late summer morning. He scored fifty or so, and then, marginally misjudging the length, he towered a ball into the waiting covers. A fair contest, with both players, one would imagine, reasonably pleased.

For a moment, in memory's vale, nostalgia overwhelms.

## Roy Tattersall

Roy Tattersall was born on 17 August 1922, and Jim Laker on 9 February 1922. In cricket lightning does strike twice in the same place. There will be half a dozen magnificent opening bats or fast bowlers in one decade, and none the next. Whether it is conductive circumstance or unproductive coincidence need not concern us, but it speaks more for Tattersall's class that he made 16 Test appearances (and Bob Appleyard of Yorkshire, another virtuoso of off-side bowling, 19) in the Laker years than if he had won double that number of caps in a Laker-less period. When the saloon bar selectors pick a world XI to challenge the galaxy all-stars, Jim Laker is the only racing certainty. He has a place, with no rivals for the off-spin spot.

Tattersall, a product, like so many, of Bolton cricket, must be a chief contender for that same niche in an all-Lancashire eleven. Curiously, the main competitor would be Cecil Parkin, than whom no more different cricketer in temperament could be discovered. Carl Jung would have been gratified to have sat Cecil Parkin and Roy Tattersall side by side for his demonstration lecture on extroversion and introversion. That, at least, was the image transferred to the intrigued spectator, and it is likely that their dispositions were similar in what might be called real life.

Roy Tattersall appeared to be withdrawn to the point of monkishness. One could not easily visualise him singing a merry air as he ran up to bowl, or whistling a stirring march on the route back. An austere note of Gregorian plain-chant would have been the most for which the music-lover might have hoped. Personality flowed over into approach to bowling, with Parkin instinctively versatile and inventive, and Tattersall pensive and methodical.

Had Julius Caesar been captain of Lancashire, he would not have asked 'Tatt' to bowl' 'Let me,' he would have abjured, perhaps tossing the ball to Dick Tyldesley, 'have men about me who are fat.' Cassius had 'a lean and hungry look; he thinks too much: such men are dangerous.' Roy Tattersall was also guilty on all three counts.

Firstly, he was dangerous. In a career lasting from 1948 to 1960, he took 1168 wickets (1369 all told) at a cost each of 17 in almost 300 games, and stands seventh in the list of Lancashire bowlers. In eight years on the run, 1950 to 1957 inclusively, he reached a hundred wickets, his 171 dismissals of 1950 constituting a post-war Lancashire record, and requiring the archivist to dig back to the days of McDonald for parallel, when Roy Tattersall was but a toddler. His best figures were in 1950, 8 for 60 against Surrey; in 1952, 8 for 28 against Kent and 8 for 71 at Portsmouth against Hampshire; in 1953, at Birmingham against Warwickshire, 8 for 54; in 1956, 8 for 43 – 14 for 90 in the match – against Yorkshire at Leeds. Most remarkable of all was, in 1953, when he had seven Nottinghamshire batsmen out for no runs, including the hat-trick, finishing with 9 for 40, and 14 for 73 in the match. In that prime phase, 1950–57, Lancashire bowlers otherwise only six times reached a hundred wickets. He was often the sole avenger, and the shared Championship of 1950 must largely be attributed to him. He took 58 wickets for England, including 12 for 101 at Lord's in 1951 versus South Africa.

Secondly, he was very lanky, a beanpole of a bowler. His black hair was neat and his face was still, unsmiling but not grimacing. Like the Piper of Hamelin, 'he himself was tall and thin, with sharp, blue eyes, each like a pin'. But, although he surely lured many to destruction, it was not by pretty enticement. He stooped a little, and the resultant brooding question-mark gave him a donnish air. He strolled back to the mark at the turn of his length, curving run-up for all the world as if on the Backs at Cambridge, mentally wrestling with an abstruse point of Euclid.

Thirdly, then, he thought, sometimes, perhaps, too much. He was a mathematician's bowler, a boffin of angles of deviation and length of tangents. He probed and probed again for the batsman's weakness, employing both off-spin and off-cut and able, off his longish run, to increase pace considerably – and, in fact, he originally arrived at Old Trafford as a medium-pacer. He turned, a lonely, academic master, and ran smoothly and introspectively in, his right arm rather held at his side, grip disguised from his opponent. In spite of his thinness, he was strong in calf and thigh and bowled lengthy spells, so much so that he has a record of ten wickets in a match 16 times and five wickets in a match 83 times. He had long fingers as well, and used them to impart a lot of work on the seam, sometimes surprising with the leg-cutter or out-swinger for variation. He did not claim to be much of a batsman – though he did muddle his way to one fifty – and his fielding was only competent. He was a very specialised cricketer.

His diffidence was wellnigh contagious. He did seem a little remote and unemotional, and one thinks the gesticulation and hysteria that now greets even a minor inroad on the cricket field would have embarrassed him. He would be the shy collegian cringing at the rowdies. A batsman out was a part of the experiment finished, another section of the thesis completed. It was dispassionate and scientific.

His game seemed to disintegrate rapidly, so much so that he found even minor cricket a trial. One is surprised to find, on examination, that he did not vanish earlier: tricky memory suggests that he disappeared abruptly while still a young man, perhaps because he did not seem to age or fatten much. In fact, he last played for Lancashire when 38. However, he did not play regularly in his last years, nor do as well. Captain and committee seemed unable to utilise him fully, as the accent stressed the need for fast bowlers and the cry was for a partner for Brian Statham. Roy Tattersall maybe lacked the ambition or the zest to be authoritatively decisive in that atmosphere, allowing himself to be overlooked and misused.

It was as keenly felt as a bereavement to visit Old Trafford and find that his pensive lope was no longer a familiar sight for spectators. With his passing vanished, hindsight informs, Lancashire's last connection with the upper echelon of the County Championship.

# 6. Statham's Years

*Fifteen Years of Ignominy*

Without Brian Statham, it might have been nobody's years. After the collapse of the harmoniously balanced 1950 eleven, Lancashire never thereafter produced a team capable of winning or sharing the Championship title. Having, singly or with others, won 12 titles in the first 86 years of their history, Lancashire now negotiated the next 38 without a Championship win, and, worse, only threatened the possibility two or three exceptional times.

The playing aspect of the next 15 or so seasons may, in charity, be considered briefly, from the resignation of Nigel Howard in 1953 to the renaissance of Lancashire as a one-day cricket team in 1969.

Washbrook's uneasy incumbency lasted six years, and, save for 1956, Lancashire became a middle-table club. In the wetness of 1954 they were tenth, and Yorkshire beat them for the first time since the war, and, the following year, they were ninth, with both Ikin and Washbrook producing strong veteran performances. Lancashire rallied substantively in 1956 and were runners-up to the all-conquering Surrey. Wharton, Grieves, J. Dyson and Edrich scored a thousand runs, and the first-named became the first to score a hundred for the county versus the Australians since Ernest Tyldesley in 1934. 1956 and 1957 were Alan Wharton's most fruitful seasons for the county, and 1956 was also Hilton's best year, for he took 150 wickets, although Statham topped the averages with just under 14. The 1956 season was distinguished by a cheerful curio, accomplished three times on the subcontinent, but never elsewhere in first-class cricket. Lancashire beat Leicestershire without losing a wicket. Jack Dyson, from the Central Lancashire League, and Wharton added 166 without loss, replying to Leicestershire's 108. After the declaration, Leicestershire were dismissed for 122. There then ensued a brisk race with threatening rain, which Dyson and Wharton marginally won in chasing 66 runs. Incidentally, Geoff Edrich captained Lancashire to that shrewdly organised victory.

There was a bright start to 1957 with five clear wins, but with Statham and Washbrook absent on Test and selectorial duties, Lancashire fell away to sixth, and they were seventh in 1958 and fifth in 1959. Geoff Pullar, Peter Marner, Tommy Greenough and Ken Higgs were easing themselves, with apparent comfort, into the side. On the hard wickets of 1959's dry summer, three batsmen, Pullar, Grieves and Wharton passed 2000 runs, and the vigorous Marner obtained a thousand runs in consecutive seasons from 1958 to 1964. Statham, the leg-spinner Greenough and Higgs, now bringing relief to Statham's lone arm, all took a hundred wickets. The year previously, in 1958, J. B. Statham had 6 for 12 at Cardiff and 5 for 8 at Liverpool against Yorkshire.

It was mildly disappointing, not uniformly tragic, and, in 1960, Lancashire, captained by Bob Barber, the Ruthin schoolboy and Cambridge blue, were second again. This time Statham's 106 wickets cost him the easily remembered average of 10.66, the best average ever obtained by a Lancashire bowler in a season, using 40 wickets taken as a minimum. Greenough and Higgs again took a hundred wickets each, and five batsmen, led by Grieves with 1942 runs, reached a thousand. Yorkshire, the eventual champions, were beaten twice, the first time this appetising double had been accomplished since 1893. Pullar scored the third of his five centuries against the old rivals, a record for Lancashire in the roses matches, until Clive Lloyd's six in more recent years. Unluckily, four of the last six matches were lost, and the aspiration faded.

It was the next year that disappointment yielded to calamity. In Barber's second season, the county tumbled down the table to thirteenth, the lowest in its hitherto proud story. Six batsmen hit a thousand runs, but only Higgs, with 102, reached a hundred wickets. Eleven matches were won, but 18 were drawn and eight lost. 1962, the single year of Joe Blackledge as skipper, there was a further fall, to second from the bottom. with only two wins against 16 defeats. The batting was not too feeble, and Jack Bond followed his 1700 runs of 1961 with over 2000 in 1962. For the first time since before the First World War, that is, since the county competition had adopted a recognisable shape and quantity, no Lancashire bowler, no, not even Statham, managed to take a hundred wickets.

Ken Grieves was tried as captain for two seasons, 1963 and 1964, but only four matches were won while ten were lost in each of those seasons, and Lancashire finished fifteenth in the former and fourteenth – a dismal centenary for the club – in the latter year. Grieves and Marner sustained the batting as best they might, while Pullar and David Green offered some support. Statham was the only bowler of true hostility, and the outlook was bleak.

Brian Statham succeeded to the captaincy for the next three years, but no impression was made on the county's position. Lancashire were thirteenth in 1965, twelfth in 1966 and eleventh in 1967, and barely a dozen games were won in that time. Statham and Higgs remained the chief bowlers, but the experiment of signing Sonny Ramadhin for 1964 and 1965 cannot be judged a success. Graham Atkinson arrived from Somerset and scored a thousand runs in 1967, while Harry Pilling and Barry Wood did the same in their first full-run season.

The signs of maturing talent among such junior players, and a sense of improved atmosphere, was Statham's legacy to Jack Bond. He became captain in 1968 and hoisted the side to eighth place, which would have been regarded as a disgrace between the wars, but which now was received with adulation. Lancashire won eight, drew 14 and lost six, by no means a dominating performance, but it served to raise the county from the murky recesses of these double-figured places. The batting was a little woeful – only Pilling reached a thousand – while Ken Higgs, in his benefit year, was the leading bowler with 105 victims.

Jack Bond had captained Lancashire in a match or so previously, in Statham's absence, and it was noticed, at one point, he put a friendly arm around a bowler's shoulders by way of encouragement. It was noted because of its rarity value. Lancashire captains had not, for some seasons, been remarked for that sympathetic approach, nor had they, conversely, been able to enthuse teams after the sterner method of Hornby or Green. It was refreshing and prophetic, and a portent of Lancashire's thrilling successes of the 1970s.

Before embarking on an analysis of what had caused the problems of the late 1950s and the whole of the 1960s, by no means a swinging decade for the denizens of Old Trafford, it would be appropriate to detail more fully the outstanding career of Brian Statham, and of two or three others who attempted to support him in saving Lancashire from bleak despair.

## Brian Statham

When Yorkshire visited Old Trafford at the Whitsuntide of 1950, they batted first and were subjected to an epic assault. Brian Statham, splay-footed and tottering, collapsed in spectacular style on his approach to the wicket, not once, but two or three times. A copious application of sawdust, leaving the surrounds like a circus ring, restored his foothold, and he proceeded to blast out two or three Yorkshire batsmen. He finished with 5 for 52. Even the lordly Hutton appeared unduly hurried, and only an elegant century by Norman Yardley restored a semblance of transPennine sanity.

Brian Statham, born in Stockport on 17 June 1930, actually made his début on his twentieth birthday against Kent, but this roses match was his first big game. Later that season he contributed to the débâcle of Somerset. Statham took 5 for 18. At one juncture his figures were 5 for 5. Manchester journalists, faced with a longish stroll from press box to telephone booth, found the proceedings much too frenetic for orderly communion with their editorial office, such was the strength of the whirlwind.

If, like the Assyrian, the young Statham came down like a wolf on the fold, then possibly he was discomfited by the melodrama of these opening strikes. He quickly qualified, in terms of temperament, for membership of that fold, so lamblike was his disposition. It is conceivable that no great professional sportsman has conducted himself as unfussily and as diffidently as Brian Statham did, so much so that his reputation for the all but meek dignity of his sportsmanship was as high as for his immaculate accuracy and speed.

And that was mountainous indeed. When pure pace is under critical scrutiny, Brian Statham's name is always in the frame, jostling for a place in the best-ever England, even the best-ever World eleven. He must be judged, technically, as Lancashire's most efficient ever player. His 2260 victims (1816 for the county) meant that he had taken more wickets than any other Lancashire player. He headed the Lancashire averages, among bowlers with a haul of 40 wickets minimum, for 16 consecutive seasons, 1951 to 1966, an unprecedented record, and, like Arthur Mold before him, he took most wickets in a season seven times. He led the national averages or was second or third in nine seasons, and, with 70 Tests, he became Lancashire's most-capped English player.

Brian Statham is one of only seven English internationals to have over 200 Test wickets, and, until Fred Trueman overtook him, his 252 wickets were a world record. He is second in average after Trueman in that select septet. Having obtained his county cap in his first season, he was flown out, with Roy Tattersall, to reinforce an injury-prone and beleaguered party in Australia, and he made his Test début against New Zealand. During the West Indian tour of 1953–54 he assumed his rightful and permanent place in the English ranks, and, in concert with Frank Tyson or Freddie Trueman, remarkable deeds were wrought. In personal terms, his most effective international forays were reserved for the South Africans, against whom he took 7 for 39 at Lord's in 1955 and 11 for 97 at Lord's in 1960, his finest innings and match performances at Test level.

Brian Statham took five or more wickets in an innings on no less than 123 occasions, including four batches of eight and 15 lots of seven. His own best performance was 8 for 34 at Coventry against Warwickshire in 1957, and, with 15 for 89, this same game provided him with his most meritorious match performance. He took ten or more wickets in a match on 11 occasions. This betokened a consistency of titanic proportions, and his first-class bowling average – 16.36 – offers further sumptuous testimony.

Much stemmed from the flexibility of his rhythmic body. His only weakening to the vivid, and that unconscious, was the double-jointed manner in which he divested himself of his sweater, preparatory to bowling. It had the air of the comic contortionist about it, and, it was rumoured that, on West Indian duty, his limbo dancing was much admired. This natural elasticity allowed him, from breaking into his easy, unfaltering run to the momentum of his classic delivery, a bounty of grace and force that was demonstrably telling. It was a composition of style and control, the one heightening the degree of the other.

No wonder journalists turned to the kennels for metaphoric assistance. Statham was sometimes 'the greyhound', and sometimes 'the whippet'. Such sleekness and velocity seemed beyond human ken. It was this impeccable tuning and balance that permitted of unremitting accuracy at persistently high speed. It was this poise and cadence which caused Sir Neville Cardus to think of Mozart. It might seem shameful to translate so classical a construct into figures, but the statistics are amazing. A quarter of Statham's close on 17,000 overs were maidens, and he gave away barely more than two runs an over during his first-class career.

Brian Statham was an athlete in the purest sense, and thus was no slouch in the field. Not for him the respite of second slip or mid-on, or a chance to lean on the boundary fence between overs. That had sometimes been the undistinguished role of quicker bowlers, but Statham was bested by very few as an outfield fleet of foot and clean of hand. Greyhounds and whippets were once more conjured up in the press box as he sped around the boundary, while his effortless arm was a joy alike to spectators and grateful wicket-keeper. He held 231 catches, including 28 for England. It is said that he dropped only one catch for England, and that off Trueman, and that worthy clasped his soul-mate sympathetically around the shoulders, remembering the stunning catches taken rather than focussing on the one that got away.

Lancastrians, as payer and payee, figure in the two most generously modest compliments paid to cricketers. As Neville Cardus recalled, Archie MacLaren said of Victor Trumper that the Australian was thoroughbred Derby winner beside his own cab-horse. And Frank Tyson, writing of his glamorous and bloodcurdling feats in the 1954–55 trip to Australia, confided that it was Brian Statham's 'relentless pursuit' which led the batsmen to play desperately at the other end. 'It felt like having Menuhin,' wrote Tyson, 'playing second fiddle to my lead.'

Ironically, it was Lancastrian paying compliment to Lancastrian, for Frank Tyson, a native of Middleton, slipped through the faulty county net and found fame with Northamptonshire. Until, late on in his career, Ken Higgs arrived, Statham never enjoyed the strength from partnership of his halcyon England days. That was not until the late 1950s, when Ken Higgs recruited from the Staffordshire leagues, where he had been playing for Port Vale, joined forces with Statham. Something of a protégé of John Ikin and a townsman of Kidsgrove, he took over a thousand wickets for Lancashire and 1531 in first-class matches. In fact, Ken Higgs is, perhaps surprisingly, Lancashire's fourth-highest wicket-taker in all cricket. This included 71 wickets for England in his fifteen Tests. Ramrod stiff of back and spirit, the tall, fair-haired Higgs had Dick Pollard's unshirking measure of endeavour, and he was a most useful county player. After a spell as a west coast guest-house proprietor, where his dourness may have been less welcome than in his indefatigable approach to bowling, he went as player and later coach to Leicestershire.

The lack of a sparring partner left the Lancashire pace attack entirely as Statham's responsibility for much of his career, and, sadly, his first season, when Lancashire shared the Championship with Surrey, was, in a team sense, his only successful one.

Conversely, allied with the bombardment of Trueman or the ballistics of Tyson, his tenure in the national team was triumphal. The contrasts, either with the bellicose Yorkshireman or the abrupt, meteoric upsurge of the aptly named Typhoon, were striking. Fast bowlers are much given to aggression, disgruntlement and temperamental upheaval, and Brian Statham belied this image entirely. His bowling was never less than harmonious and his equanimity was always balmy. He scarcely bowled a wide and he never lost his temper. Asked by team-mates to wreak vengeance on a West Indian short-pitching bowler, Statham said, 'No, I think I'll just bowl him out.' As catches tumbled in the slips, as snicks to the wicket-keeper passed unseen by the umpires, as certain lbws were disregarded by these same arbiters, and as the proverbial coats of varnish accumulated into tinfulls, he was never at all ruffled. He never appealed like other bowlers. He might, occasionally, turn at the end of his poised follow-through, and risk a glance of polite and puzzled query in the direction of the umpire; but never more than that, never an anguished cry. In this he was the antithesis of the stentorian Duckworth.

This was, as his *Wisden* appreciation entitled him, 'Gentleman George', for he was known to his many colleagues as George throughout a lifetime in which he never uttered a word of complaint or enmity and, as rare, no similar words were cast at him. Stringent critics said he bowled too accurately, so that poor players failed to connect and brilliant players sometimes found the rhythm to play him with security. There is a story by Guy de Maupassant about a fairground knifethrower who found, when he tried to kill his errant wife and target, that he was incapable of deviating from the grooved pattern of hurling blades around her. Brian Statham could no more bowl a bad ball than Paderewski could hit a wrong note.

His career came to rest in August 1968, against Yorkshire at Old Trafford. He more than emulated his début in a roses match by taking 6 for 34 as Yorkshire reeled to an impoverished 61 all out. In the second innings, needing just over 250, Yorkshire did better. In his 16,810th over, Statham had Phil Sharpe lbw for 20, and that was his last wicket. Brian Close was obdurate, and finished with 77 not out. Brian Statham bowled the last over of the day, and the crowd hoped for an ultimate celebration. Close, of course, was not beguiled by such sentiment. Six times Statham ran in. Six times the ball pitched middle or middle-and-off, on a rational length. Six times Brian Close played forward and astutely deadened the ball. It was Brian Statham's 4,262nd maiden over, and, in one way, it was more apposite an ending than a wicket falling.

The picture of Brian Statham leaving Old Trafford for this final time is almost painfully revealing. Head lowered, shoulder ducked, embarrassed by excited youngsters, clapping adults and protective policemen, he hastened away as quickly as he could into the silent shadows.

## Geoff Pullar, Peter Marner and Tommy Greenhough

It was Geoff Pullar's misfortune to arrive at Old Trafford from the Werneth club, near Oldham, in 1954, just as Lancashire were on the wane, and to leave the county for Gloucestershire in 1968, just before the big times came again. He was born in 1935 and was 19 in the August of his first year in first-class cricket. Given the miserable and foreboding seasons in which he played, Pullar's record is significantly good. He scored 16,853 runs for Lancashire, more than either MacLaren or Paynter, and his average was 35. He totted up 21,528 in all cricket.

It was 1958 when he came first to prominence with a sturdy thousand runs, after a sound apprenticeship with Geoff Edrich in the second eleven. In 1959 he scored over fifty in his first seven innings, and completed the season with 2647 runs, including eight centuries, three of them against Yorkshire. His average was 55, and his aggregate, which helped gain him honourable mention in 1960's *Wisden*, has only been passed four times by Lancashire batsmen. He passed the two thousand milestone once more in 1961, and, in all, eight times reached the thousand-landmark for Lancashire. Of his 41 centuries, 32 were for Lancashire, including his top county score of 167, not out, against the 1966 West

Indians. One testimony to his value must be the fact that, in a
lean phase, Lancashire only enjoyed four stands of 200 in the
1954–68 period, and Pullar was involved in two of them: with
Brian Booth at the Parks in 1962 (272) and with Washbrook
against Glamorgan in 1958 (216).

Such yeoman consistency attracted the Test selectors. Between
1959 and 1963 he opened the batting for England, sanely and
cautiously, in 28 Tests, touring Australia, the West Indies and
India and Pakistan. Only four Lancashire players have more
England caps, and they are John Tyldesley, Statham, Johnny
Briggs and Washbrook, imposing personages every one. He
scored nearly 2000 runs, and his average of just under 44 is higher
than Washbrook's, J. T. Tyldesley's or MacLaren's. Using ten
matches as a minimal yardstick, only Paynter and Ernest Tyldesley
better him. He scored four centuries for England. His 175 against
South Africa in 1960 was his highest score in first-class cricket,
and, overseas in the winter of 1961–62, he scored 119 against
India and 165 against Pakistan. His 131 against India in 1959,
nonetheless, brought him most fame and a corner in the cricketing
quiz-books. He became the only Lancashire batsman to score a
century in a Test match at Old Trafford, something that neither
Washbrook nor MacLaren had produced.

The statistical portrait is an imposing one, and Geoffrey Pullar
made a genuine contribution to Lancashire cricket. A native of
Swinton, he was taller, at six feet, and heavier, at 13 stones, than
many batsmen, and his reach and strength stood him in good
stead. He exuded sureness. Dark and left-handed, he played
solidly, without much backlift, but capable of smothering difficult,
and pushing away easy, deliveries. There was mental as well as
physical stamina. He was a master-builder of innings. Even when,
in his later years, the one-day game appeared, he understood the
need to construct and pace an innings, adding the more reckless
shots gradually as the score mounted. Although he never aspired
to the elegance of Hallows or the dash of Paynter, he was never
ugly in deportment and he was always interesting to watch
because of his choice of technique. The dragged drive, between
gully and cover, and nudges behind the wicket on the on-side were
his favourite scoring strokes.

He was nicknamed 'Noddy' because of his capacity for instant
somnolence, a trait shared with some other first-class batsmen.
That placidity, which enabled him to sleep like a babe at a

moment's notice, was a key to his batting, for, like Washbrook before him, the ball before, whatever its hazards had been, was shut from his mind immediately. Psychologically, he may have exaggerated this equability into the vice of lethargy. Plainly he disliked fielding, and, standing on the rails, he would ask any amateur meteorologist in the crowd to offer a second opinion on the probability of rain. Rain meant the comfort of the dressing-room and another chance to indulge his obsession with Westerns. Perhaps he styled himself on Burt Lancaster as the Rain-maker, and he must have viewed his benefit match wryly in 1967 when not a ball was bowled because of rain. Perhaps, too, it was the Western genre which informed his image of the sheriff, sauntering out of the town gaol, to admonish the visiting, noisy cowpokes. His batting certainly had that air of resigned authority.

His counterpoint at this time was Peter Marner, a strong, ginger-haired young man from Oldham, who clouted as powerfully as Pullar more carefully turned and pushed. In 1952, aged 16 years four months, he superseded John Briggs as Lancashire's youngest-ever débutant, and, an efficient slip-fielder and bowler of military-medium to boot, he looked destined to an enviable career. Moreover, his size and style gave every sign of making him a popular crowd attraction, no small concern as audiences at Old Trafford dwindled. His powerful forearms caused him to strike the ball as ferociously as all but the most famous hitters in the game. He played 236 games for Lancashire, compared with Pullar's 312, and he transferred to Leicestershire after the 1964 season. He scored 10,312 runs for Lancashire, at an average of 29, and thus scrapes into the list of 25 batsmen to make that cut. It is commendable, but the feeling persisted that it was less than the potential. He passed the thousand-runs target six times, and scored just ten hundreds for Lancashire, 142 not out, against Leicester in 1963, being the pick of these. But P. T. Marner was the young white hope whose flame stuttered and was extinguished.

Their contemporary, Tommy Greenhough, also suffered some lack of career fulfilment. Possibly it was peculiar to uncover a leg-spinner in so unlikely a clime as Rochdale, far distant from the exotic reaches of India where such magicians frequently appear. As Greenhough, who played 241 times between 1951 and 1966, was said to occupy himself with a humdrum milkround in the winter, there was little of the bizarre about him. He was of nondescript

**11** Eddie Paynter, *above left*
**12** Cyril Washbrook, *above*
**13** Brian Statham, *left*

Standing (left to right) : R. Tattersall, M. Hilton, P. Greenwood, A. Barlow, R. Perry, K. Grieves.
Seated : G. A. Edrich, W. Place, N. D. Howard (captain), C. Washbrook, J. T. Ikin. Inset : B. Statham

**14** 1950: the last champions

**15** Ken Cranston
(*Barratt's Photo Press Ltd*)

**16** Roy Tattersall
(*Fox Photos Ltd*)

**17** 1969: a great one-day combination

**18** Clive Lloyd (*Bob Thomas Sports Photography*)

**19** Farokh Engineer

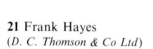

**20** Jack Simmons (*Mark Leech*)

**21** Frank Hayes
(*D. C. Thomson & Co Ltd*)

**22** David Hughes (*Mark Leech*)

build and rather horsy features, and it was his gait which attracted note. He walked smartly as if spring-heeled, his high shoulders bouncing as he marched along. When bowling, this tendency was accentuated, and, craving for the leg-spinner's necessary balance, he deployed a marsupial series of hops for his run-up, not much less kangaroo-like than the bounding D. V. P. Wright of Kent. All this, together with the expected fun and games when a leg-spin bowler operates, offered scope for both cricketing reward and spectator satisfaction.

It was not quite to be. Tommy Greenhough only played in about half the games he might have done. Pitches were often slow and damp; captains were often impatient for results and anxious about the extravagance of leg-spin attack; his stressful action caused damage to legs and hands; he had something of the leg-spinner's artistic temper and may have flowered with more sensitive nurture: all these elements made of his career a valley of minor sorrows. That said, he took 707 wickets at a cost of 22 each; his best return was 7 for 56, and his best summers were 1959 (102 wickets) and 1960 (119 wickets). This makes him one of Lancashire's bowling élite: a corps of 25 who have taken more than 500 wickets for the county. He played in four Tests, 1959 and 1960, and did reasonably well, taking 16 wickets. Happily, perhaps his most impressive performance for Lancashire was in the centenary match of 1964 with the MCC, when Tommy Greenhough baffled illustrious members of the old guard, such as Washbrook, Ikin, Frank Worrell and Denis Compton.

The determined application of Pullar; the ruggedness of Marner; the rarity-value of Greenhough: they should really have found more meritorious employment in a winning side, playing before crowded surrounds. They achieved satisfyingly as individuals, but Lancashire's slump was not to be halted by individuals.

## Lancashire's Decline

English politics from the banishment of Sir Robert Peel in 1846 to the ascension of Gladstone to the premiership in 1868 is known as the Confusion of the Parties. Over a similar period, a century on precisely, Lancashire cricket club underwent the same trauma. As comparisons go, this one flies not too fancifully. Gladstone and Peel both had Lancashire birth qualifications, the People's William born in Liverpool of merchant stock, and Sir Robert the son of a

Bury mill-owner, a member of that very *Schlottjunkertum*, that 'chimney-aristocracy', without whose support the Lancashire club would not have been formed nor patronised. Some Lancashire members, in their weariness, may, however, find an equally valid parallel in the Chinese period of history known as the Six Hundred Years Confusion.

The introduction piously hoped not to speculate about boardroom squabbles and back-stairs deals, and it is not intended to breach that tenet. There follows a more arm's length scrutiny of the topic, as it made itself manifest to the ordinary member or regular spectator.

First, as to the captaincy. Up to 1939 Lancashire had employed, in chief, nine captains for its 80 or so seasons of first-class play. Since the war, in some 40-odd seasons, there have been 14, par slipping from nine years to three. Both the nature and the number of these comings and goings reminded one of the presidential politics of a South American banana republic. Jack Fallows was replaced by Ken Cranston without due consideration or consultation; Cranston never got to grips with leadership, and left the post to Nigel Howard, when Washbrook might have been a preferred choice; Nigel Howard was rather a puppet leader, while his successor, Washbrook, found communion with the newly rising generation difficult. R. W. Barber captained the side in 1960 and 1961, when he was aged only 25 or 26. He was deliberately separated, olde-worlde style, from the professionals, and became isolated and disillusioned. An instinctive and bright athlete, he scored nearly 7000 runs and captured 152 wickets for the club, before uncovering the treasure trove of his gifts with Warwickshire and with England. He also blotted his copybook by his public chastisement of Cowdrey over his strategy for Kent.

The unhappy Joe Blackledge, a Northern League cricketer, was unexpectedly drafted and predictably failed. He knew no member of the team personally, and 1962 was a nightmare. In August Lancashire failed on five occasions to reach a hundred. Ken Grieves returned, but it was a belated and grudging move. The search for the oldtime amateur led to both Washbrook and Grieves being considered beyond the most relevant time. As with Fallows, press leaks informed all and sundry of Grieves's imminent departure, and then Statham tried, in spite of his own pacific temperament, to mould a new side. At the same time, Charlie Hallows was introduced as coach, with Norman Oldfield (who, in his day, had scored 7000 runs and 12 centuries for Lancashire and played in one Test) as his deputy. Stan Worthington and then Tom Reddick had both been coaches in the interim.

If Fallows was the Robert Peel, then John Bond was the Gladstone who stabilised the political situation with a five-year reign. Afterwards, the not so merry-go-round turned again, and a new shuttle of skippers began, but that is for the following chapter.

Secondly, it was Norman Oldfield, along with A. E. Nutter, Bill Farrimond and, albeit he was at the veteran stage, Eddie Paynter who first whirled another kaleidoscope. At war's end, they moved to another county or to the leagues, and thus began an intense mobility of players in and out of the county. Some of this was assisted by more lenient rules about qualification and special registration, but it was abetted, one must assume, by flaws in management. Gordon Garlick, Bob Berry and Eric Price, to be sure, left for, respectively, Northamptonshire, Worcestershire and Essex in the hope of a more regular first-team place, and, later, others (B. J. Booth, for instance, an opening bat and occasional leg-spin bowler, who went to Leicestershire) moved on for what seemed to be reasonable career chances. Movement was not always political.

But several appeared to disappear on grounds other than mobility and normal circumstance. Relieved of the captaincy, Bob Barber went to Warwickshire. Geoff Edrich and Alan Wharton, who went to Leicestershire, are other cases in point. It was so different from pre-war years when most players remained with the county for a stable period. Phrases like 'in the best interests of Lancashire cricket' became a catch-all for banished players. Peter Marner and Geoff Clayton, the wicket-keeper, were sacked in 1964, and signed for Leicestershire and for Somerset. This followed a semi-final in the Gillette Cup against Warwickshire, when an enormous audience watched Lancashire wilt feebly. Soon after Bond took over the captain's role, David Green and then Geoff Pullar departed for Gloucestershire. Of course, the reasons may have been sensible. Not only playing ability but general disposition in team terms must be assessed, and undue individualism as well as outright indiscipline can be hazardous to the enterprise. Nonetheless, this frequent rite of passage of vanishing cricketers made Lancashire followers fret over the likelihood that the induction and supervision of players was inadequate.

As well as those who got away, there were those who never came. Frank Tyson and Keith Andrew were two such notable Lancastrians, while, in the mid-1960s, and, as is famously known, Basil D'Oliveira was earmarked for Lancashire, but ended up with Worcestershire. At base, the problem was of long standing and concerned the county club's relationship with the outlying leagues. This had often been uneasy. The league clubs had attracted big names and big crowds in concert, and were able to pay good money for what amounted to a day's cricket and perhaps some ancillary coaching. The county scene offered first-class standing and the possibility of international duty, but it was a more arduous slog. When the linkage operated smoothly, all was well. Many Lancashire players sandwiched valuable first-class experience between league cricket as a promising tyro and a proved campaigner. In the case of Cecil Parkin and Ted McDonald, bargains had been struck to release the players for the county from their league engagements.

The immediate post-war period witnessed a surge of inter-national talent into the leagues, probably more so than in the 1930s. By residence, many of them could have qualified for Lancashire, and, it is whispered, as many of them would have done so, anxious to secure a year-round contact with first-class play and learn its English mysteries. To choose three from a dozen and more, Frank Worrell played with Radcliffe, Everton Weekes with Bacup, and Clyde Walcott with Enfield. It would appear that the Lancashire committee underwent a period of estrangement with the leagues, and closed diplomatic channels. It has been argued that Lancashire had agreed at national level not to seek advantage from the fortuitous bevy of gifts nearby, for fear of unbalancing the county system. As Lancashire sank to the foot of the table, one wondered whether this altruism had been overdone.

Of course, in essence, it was the same dilemma Albert Hornby had faced. Did the club exist to maintain the purity of cricket in and for Lancashire, or to provide an entertaining and successful spectacle? Usually, the half-conscious compromise had been to utilise Lancashire lads with a healthy sprinkling of outsiders. Some of these, in turn, became models of Lancashire myths: the dry humour of Parkin, or the grit of Edrich and Ikin. Hereabouts the wrong balance had been attempted.

These internal difficulties do, however, require to be set in perspective. There was, of course, a general slump in the fortunes of cricket, following the falsely beguiling post-war boom. Freed from the restraints of warfare but still existing in austere surrounds, the public flocked back to cricket matches to enjoy their pastoral charm and reflect that, as the song ran, 'this is worth fighting for'. But it was to be a brief chimera. Social changes abounded. The motor car liberated more and more people to seek other outdoor pursuits, often with the family, while the television persuaded them to stay at home. Other pastimes and the trappings of an expanding consumer society left behind the conservatism of county cricket.

Some commentators have spoken of a quickening tempo of life, with the leisured amble of cricket bypassed by speedier hikes through the social world. There may be truth in this, but it must also be accepted that, conversely, cricket slowed down. One has only to glance at the excellent over-rates of the Edwardian period and the mid-war years, as well as the swifter scoring of the likes of MacLaren and John Tyldesley, to observe that, since about 1950, Lancashire, along with their competitors, have bowled less and batted more slowly. Worse, perhaps, an anonymity shrouded much of Lancashire cricket. If character existed, it was not readily perceivable by the spectators, and, one must presume, as crowds fell away, character became even more disguised. Men and women do not read books or watch players only because of the unfolding plot, otherwise the last page or the denouement would be sufficient. It is not enough to know that the butler done it: one is eager to learn what kind of butler he is that should edge him to such resorts. The ambience of cricketer and crowd is as significant as that of entertainer and audience. Watching Lancashire play on almost empty grounds in the 1960s – and all the other counties, too – was like watching teams selected by the civil service. Nationally, crowds dropped from over 2,000,000 at the back-end of the nineteenth century to less than 750,000.

Altered social values changed players' attitudes as well. Lancashire's insistence on an amateur captain who, as in Barber's case, was socially segregated from the professionals was a throwback to a pre-war world. In the looser meritocracy of post-war Britain, the gentleman and player division, which, as MacLaren's career underpinned, had always been blurred and messy at the edges, was an anachronism. It grimly survived until 1962. Young players were not so biddable as those of the pre-war genre. They did not know their place. They were less happy about unrestrained authority being exerted over them, while the mill-owner mentality of the Lancashire committee struggled to maintain the old ways. This was destabilising. Not knowing your place, or, at least, not discovering another one, does not make for settled and coherent approaches. The gulf that opened between Cyril Washbrook and the youngsters coming into the team illustrates this. He saw them as undisciplined and ill-prepared to make the appropriate sacrifices, while they saw him as an old-fashioned tyrant. He could not, presumably, soften his method or find the argot to address them; they could not see the prize that lay in a more regulated concern for their cricketing welfare. In brief, it was, as Dickens almost called, with apt sarcasm, *Little Dorrit*, 'nobody's fault'. No appropriate style emerged in this era to bind the players in a relevant discipline all could accept.

Finance played its part. The minimum guarantee of £416 for capped players in 1945 was no great advance on pre-war levels, and was one reason for some players leaving. The war had, of course, boosted wages substantially. By 1953 capped players received a basic £262 plus £12 10s match fee and £10 expenses for away games. There was also talent money, and, in the end, the minimal wage of £463 and the maximal £650. It was not a great sum for well-known entertainers, and soon the shift from limited salaries for footballers would complete a tiny economic revolution from footballers being worse off than cricketers in the 1930s to the reverse in the 1960s.

It was all the more galling for Lancashire that, as their gates slumped, Manchester United, across the main road, were doing wonderful business in the most vivid years of that club's history. As with the other counties, Lancashire, enthused by the initial response to post-war cricket, failed to predict inflation. After all, in 1951, following their Championship triumph, membership stood at 10,000; there was a waiting-list, and the subscriptions alone culled £23,000, on top of pleasing gate-money. Twenty years later, the vicious spirals of upward costs and downward support left them, economically as well as sportingly, bereft. Again, it must be emphasised that Lancashire were not alone in this predicament. What was slightly different was that Lancashire had rich heritage and was unused, like some fellow counties, to the strain of wrestling for sustenance, and that, too, the playing side had declined to weakness. When Old Trafford was empty, it was forlorn and cavernous; rather more depressing than a similar plight at some of the smaller first-class grounds in the South. And not being in the top half of the table, let alone not being in the top three, was that much harder to take than for those who had lingered around the lower depths for most of their history. The further one falls from grace, the bumpier the landing.

# 7. Clive Lloyd's Years

## The Modernisation of Cricket

First-class cricket was on the verge of bankruptcy. Private benefactors, like A. B. Rowley, were less willing to pay off the debts. There was some bankruptcy of talent as a result, for young men, against the competing claims of well-paid jobs outside cricket and the fears of early and unqualified retirement from cricket, jibbed at the prospect. A Wigan coalminer, unlike his pre-war counterpart, earned more than an Old Trafford junior.

The establishment paused at the brink. Then it initiated a wholesale revision of the first-class structure, and, for a short span of seasons, Lancashire, in resurgence, became first inheritors of the new millennium.

The early signs had been the belated amalgamation of amateur and professional into a single category of player, and the introduction of 'special registration' provisions so that players might move more easily and without a residential qualification. However, the *annus mirabilis* was 1963, the first season of the Gillette Cup. It was not only the notion of one-day play which was significant: had not even T. A. Higson once warmed to the idea of the single innings game in the pre-war years? Nor was the knock-out cup a novelty: had not Lancashire, away back in the 1870s, resisted the mooted cup competition as the game 'requires no such encouragement' and might incite gambling? Both these aspects were of import, but the principal factor was the admission of sponsorship.

The acknowledgement that the commercial interest must be served changed county cricket overnight from pastime to business. Hard on the heels of Gillette followed the John Player Sunday League in 1969, the Benson and Hedges Cup in 1972 and the

Schweppes County Championship in 1977, as well as sponsorship for international matches. One of the first effects, in a move redolent of the switch to a more entrepreneurial approach, was the decision, from 1968, to offer substantial contracts to overseas stars.

The transformation at Old Trafford was dramatic and personal. T. A. Higson was chairman from 1932 until his death in 1949. This busy and domineering solicitor had gradually assumed dictatorial powers, and, whilst doing much to rebuild the club after the war, he was neither a progressive nor a democratic leader. Dr J. Bowling Holmes was, briefly, chairman, and then T. E. Burrows took over. He was much more open, he attempted to court the leagues, and, most important of all, he inaugurated the benefit programmes, based on year-round activities and outside efforts, which, beginning with Washbrook, made Lancashire beneficiaries the coveted ones of county cricket. In the meanwhile, Rupert Howard, as secretary, a man who had done his best to retain county contacts with leagues which themselves indulged in some rigidity, had been succeeded by Geoffrey Howard. Previously assistant secretary at Surrey, he did useful administrative work at Old Trafford, but never quite comprehended the complexities of Lancashire's wider cricket community.

Cedric S. Rhoades, a Manchester textile merchant, organised the rebellion. The last straw for many members was, as is the nature of such straws, tiny and piquant. Over the winter of 1964–65 the committee advertised in *The Times* for a captain, prior to the appointment of Statham. It was like the War of Jenkins's Ear, a silly incident that became a rallying cry for revolt. Geoffrey Howard also decided to return to Surrey. At a special general meeting, and with a new secretary, J. B. Wood, appointed, a vote of censure was passed on the committee, six Young Turks were elected to it, and the aldermanic and reactionary blockage of the vice-presidents was swept aside later by the new committee.

In due season, Rhoades became chairman, and his crucial task was to restore Lancashire's financial standing by investment in the real estate of Old Trafford. An ambitious three-stage scheme was designed, but, so successful was the first phase, that the need for the other two was lessened. Cricket grounds, white elephants for seven months a year, offer much scope for development, especially at Old Trafford which encompassed a second sizeable ground. Office blocks, tactfully named after MacLaren, Statham, Washbrook and Duckworth, were constructed, and catering and allied facilities developed, and, despite the ultramontane grumbles of the old school, estimated annual profits of £50,000 to £90,000 could hardly be resisted, when there were overdrafts and debts to pay.

The overall effect was by no means detrimental to the playing and watching facilities, and constant improvements to the ground – new stands, a new press box, an embellished pavilion, executive boxes – sustain Old Trafford as one of the premier arenas of world cricket.

This opportune venture, coupled with the assets of sponsorship, advertising, television fees and the like, revolutionised Lancashire's finances and put the county on a businesslike footing. Money-making schemes, including lotteries and pools and all manner of auxilary funding, soon became standard the country wide. Professional salaries could be guaranteed for the players: it now waited upon the players to produce some cricket worthy of the new stage.

## Lancashire's Series of One-Day Triumphs

Lancashire proceeded to create a side in the modern idiom under Jack Bond's generalship. In keeping with the enterprising commercialism of the new overlords and the razzamatazz of TV coverage and colourful sponsorship, it was, in cricketing culture, avant-garde. It was a one-day team, nothing less, and, as we shall note, little more. In its deportment and presence, it was as different from Hornby's team as the Beatles canon is from the Savoyard operas of Gilbert and Sullivan. And yet they can be compared. Just as *The Pirates of Penzance* was the urban folk-opera arising from and adulated by late Victorian society, so did *Sergeant Pepper* reflect the urban values of the 1960s and 1970s. The team of Hornby and Barlow was at one with its age in much the same way, and so was the team of Clive Lloyd, Frank Hayes and Barry Wood. Moreover, while the words and music of both the Beatles and Gilbert and Sullivan continue to enjoy popular acclaim, such is their fundamental and universal appeal, so is it possible to marvel over the annals of the 1881 champions and the 1971 cupwinners together.

Interestingly, Old Trafford was the venue for the first-ever Gillette Cup-tie, for the doleful reason that Leicestershire and the home team had been the bottom two clubs in the previous championship, and this was a preliminary round to reduce the numbers to a symmetrical 16. It was 30 April 1963, and Peter Marner's century gave Lancashire victory. They moved on to the semi-final at Worcestershire, only to be removed comprehensively by Jack Flavell for 59, the game all over by luncheon. In 1964 Warwickshire beat them by 85 runs in that infamous match which spelt the end of the Lancashire careers of Grieves, Marner and Clayton. Another five seasons passed, with Lancashire knocked out quite early, finally, by Yorkshire in 1969. Lancashire scored only 173 for 8 and Yorkshire won by seven wickets, Sharpe and Boycott both topping fifty. The exception was 1967, when Lancashire again reached the semi-finals, this time to be convincingly overthrown by Somerset.

1969 introduced the John Player Sunday League, and Lancashire became its first winners, their first taste of glory since 1950. After a satisfying start, defeating Sussex, then the one-day specialists, at Hove, a visit to Chelmsford proved shattering. Essex mounted a considerable barrage and reached 265, almost beyond belief in the second week of the competition, and Lancashire lost by 108 runs. Undaunted, Bond's team recovered and learned lessons. They won ten matches on the trot, excluding one abandonment, the Yorkshire match at Old Trafford, which, sadly, was destined to have drawn a great crowd. Nottinghamshire went down by 47 runs; Gloucestershire were beaten on a faster scoring rate in a curtailed match; Surrey lost to Lancashire by four runs in a close Old Trafford finish, and, the following Sunday, Derbyshire were beaten by five wickets. At Peterborough, Northamptonshire were defeated by six wickets, and, against the strong Kent combine at Blackheath, Lancashire scored their first 200 in the competition and won by 20 runs. Somerset fell by four wickets, and, at Southport, with the gates closed on a pressing crush, Engineer battled so blisteringly that Glamorgan's 112 was overtaken in 24 overs. Crowds were now flocking to see the wunderkinder. Middlesex, at Old Trafford, attracted a large audience, who were pleased to see Lancashire pursue their winning ways, and, next Sunday, Leicestershire crashed for 92. Another crowd complacently addressed itself in high numbers to the hunting of Hampshire, but, this time, Lancashire appeared lethargic, losing by 48 runs. Hampshire were now the nearest rivals, so that was a setback. Luckily, another 200 runs accrued at Nuneaton were overmuch for Warwickshire, and, despite a third loss at Worcester – a thrilling match, with Lancashire two runs adrift – Lancashire ended with 49 points to Hampshire's 48.

John Sullivan was the unsung hero. His all-round figures were 278 runs, average 35, and 19 wickets for 232, average 12. Indeed, he topped both sets of averages. Harry Pilling scored the most runs – 405, with a top score of 76 not out – while Lever, Shuttleworth and Higgs took over 20 wickets. Engineer did well, with 342 runs and 18 wicket-keeping dismissals. The fielding had left the crowds, home and away, gasping. It was urgent and spectacular, and also rewarding: an average of five catches a match were held. There were 11 fifties, five of these from Pilling, and two century partnerships, when David Lloyd assisted Engineer, who was 78, not out, at Southport, and at Nuneaton where Clive Lloyd and Sullivan put on 105 for the fourth wicket.

In 1970, confidence zooming, Lancashire monopolised the competition and won by the fair gap of five points. They lost only two matches, both lotteries of reduced overs because of weather conditions. First Middlesex, by eight wickets, next Leicestershire, by 92 runs, perished. In a controversial and argumentative contest at Beckenham, Kent were judged victors, but, up at Aigburth the following Sunday, Harry Pilling steered Lancashire home, with a well calculated 79, against Northamptonshire. Gloucestershire by 29 runs, Essex by 41 runs, Hampshire by 65 runs: these were the next three wins, the more pleasing because close rivals had been vanquished. Nottinghamshire were swept to one side, and Somerset suffered the indignity of a hundred-run loss. Pilling and Clive Lloyd added 182 for the third wicket, as Lancashire soared to 255. At Buxton, next Sunday, Derbyshire were humiliated; outbatted, outbowled, they lost by 114 runs. This was followed by wins at the Oval and at Hove, where Pilling scored 85 and John Sullivan was undefeated on 76, in a stand of 144. Glamorgan were again crushed, Clive Lloyd and Ken Snellgrove scoring half-centuries. After the Warwickshire fixture was abandoned after only three overs, Lancashire travelled to Dudley and beat Worcestershire by 37 runs. This all contrived to set up a stirring finale at Old Trafford, with Yorkshire the enemy, on 30 August. Approximately 26,000 were packed into a bursting stadium. Boycott held out determinedly for 81, but colleagues barely remained long, and, on a fine pitch, Yorkshire were all out for 165. After the early distress of Engineer's downfall, the composed Pilling, with 55 not out, and the bustling Sullivan, with 56 not out, passed that score with only three wickets down, midst scenes of exuberant rapture.

This performance had an even more definitive stamp than that of 1969. There were 14 fifties, including Clive Lloyd's 134, not out, against Somerset, Lancashire's first Player century, and his 90 against Gloucester. Pilling once more scored five fifties. He totalled 625, and in 15 innings suffered only one score below 23, an intense act of concentrated endeavour. Clive Lloyd, with 521, had an average of 58, and John Sullivan, with 364, and Engineer, with 340, were chief supports. Shuttleworth, Lever, Simmons and Hughes took over a score of wickets each, and 61 catches were gathered. After the miseries of the 'sixties, everyone found it breath-taking.

Well practised and assured in the techniques of so-called instant cricket, Lancashire began, in 1970, their exhilarating run of Gillette Cup successes. They started, in May, with a high-scoring contest against Gloucestershire, who were to be often matched with Lancashire. Played at Bristol, the two Lloyds, David and Clive, scored freely, and a final score of 278 for 8 looked way out of reach. Gloucestershire, with R. B. Nicholls scoring 75, did well to reach 251, leaving Lancashire winners by 27 runs. Lever and Shuttleworth skittled Hampshire at Old Trafford, and, with Barry Wood batting through for 63, Lancashire won by five wickets and moved into the semi-final with Somerset. Somerset were all out at Taunton for 207, and consistent batting – all but Hayes of the first seven scored 20 or more – produced a comfortable four-wicket victory.

On 5 September, Lancashire assembled their first-ever finalist team, and Lancashire supporters savoured that mixture of joy and tension which characterises the knockout system in any sport. Sussex batted first and never established a grip. Only M. A. Buss (42) and J. M. Parks (34) made a reasonable fist of it, against steady bowling and scintillating fielding which produced three run-outs. David Hughes took three middle-order wickets for 31, and Sussex were all out in the last over for 184. Lancashire approached their task pragmatically. Harry Pilling, who was nominated man of the match, batted without error, and was 70, not out, at the close. Joined first by Clive Lloyd, 29, and then by Engineer, 31, he steered Lancashire neatly home to a six-wicket victory, and there was much rejoicing.

Lancashire slipped to third place in the John Player League in

1971, losing six matches, one of them to Essex by 129 runs, a dispiriting occasion. The brightest Sunday was at Bedford in August when David Lloyd raced to an unfinished 103, and Lancashire were 246 for 3 at the end of the 40 overs. This setback, after virtually controlling the Sunday competition for its first two years, seemed not to affect Lancashire's special delight in the Gillette Cup. Although Roy Virgin batted through 60 overs for 106 and their opening stand was exactly a century, Somerset battled laboriously, and Lancashire overtook their 206 for 8 with time and six wickets in hand. David Lloyd batted throughout for 94. In the second round at Worcester, it was, if closer, rather the same pattern. G. M. Turner this time batted right through the innings for 117, but only 215 was mustered. Clive Lloyd, 83 not out, in company first with Wood, 58, and then Engineer, 37 not out, led Lancashire to another six-wicket win.

It was in the next game that Lancashire embarked on a series of schoolboy heroics that would not have disgraced the *Hotspur* or the *Wizard*. Matches became cliffhangers, with Lancashire, after the manner of Pearl White in the silent movies, extricating themselves from imminent doom with seconds to spare. Those of a nervous disposition, including, on occasion, some of the players, could not bear to watch, but there is no doubt that these Saturday matinée exploits did much to endear cup cricket to the public.

At Chelmsford, in the third round, Lancashire collapsed to 59 for 6, and all seemed finished. Clive Lloyd laid on one of his more pyrotechnic displays and crashed his way to 109, with resourceful aid from Simmons and Hughes. Two hundred and three for 9, however, was not a substantial amount. Essex started badly, then rallied, but the pace of Shuttleworth and Lever proved critical, and Lancashire scraped by with a dozen runs in hand. The semi-final with Gloucestershire at Old Trafford requires no retelling, for it is part of cricket's folklore. This was the game when David Hughes hit John Mortimore for 24 in an over as lights shone in pavilion, streets and railway station, and the clock stood at ten to nine. Procter, with 65, and R. B. Nicholls, with 53, enabled Gloucestershire to reach a competent 229. Lancashire batted soundly, but, as darkness encroached, overs were short. It was decided to persevere that evening rather than reassemble for a handful of overs on the next morning, and, of course, fielding in the twilight is no simpler than batting. Gloucestershire were, after Harry Lauder, roamin' in the gloamin', as Hughes wrote his folktale, but it should be recalled that Lancashire had to move swiftly in any event. They only had three overs to spare, as they won by three wickets, and prepared to face Kent in the final.

Just as Sussex had been pioneers of Gillette Cup action, Kent were now reckoned to be a formidable combination, and so it turned out. Lancashire, winning the toss, batted first on another day of early autumnal sunshine at Lord's. Wood was immediately lbw, although several, including, perhaps naturally, Wood himself, felt he had played the ball, and Lancashire faltered. Clive Lloyd imperiously swung and drove for 68, and David Lloyd battled away for 38. Lancashire ended with 224 for 7. Lever and Shuttleworth began dangerously, and Kent were 19 for 2. They then batted sturdily through their middle order, with Asif Iqbal catching the eye of anxious Lancashire spectators, as he glided and off-drove with silken eloquence.

Jack Bond then literally adopted the escape-clause of the schoolboy annuals. With one mighty bound, he leapt like a dolphin to catch Asif Iqbal at extra cover, as glum Lancastrian and thrilled Kentish eyes had focussed already on the Warner Stand boundary. Credit, too, for Jack Simmons, who had forced Asif to drive ever more relentlessly and, eventually, uppishly; credit, as well, for Peter Lever, who, amid the excitement, remembered that three more Kent batsmen had to be dismissed, and cleaned up with two wickets. Lancashire won by 24 runs, and pent-up relief and joy were alike unconfined.

As a postscript to that jubilant win, one should note that, when Asif was out, Kent were 197 for 7. Of course, a catch of that priceless value deflates the opposition and the match was as good as over. Nevertheless, at the same stage, Lancashire had been only 179 for 7. The difference there lay in the unbroken eighth-wicket stand of Simmons and Hughes. They added 45, in an engaging display of improvised batting against deep-set fields. With old-headed ingenuity, they contrived to score off practically every ball of the last five or six overs, thereby pushing wider the margin that even Asif Iqbal could not close.

In 1972, Lancashire lost seven John Player League matches, and dropped further down that league to eighth. They pulverised Nottinghamshire in the first match, 251 for 3 against 62 for nine, but, although there were some close finishes (Leicestershire, for instance, were beaten 91 for 9 to 90), Lancashire looked rather ordinary on many occasions. It was the first season of the Benson and Hedges Cup, but Leicestershire beat Lancashire in the quarter-finals.

Yet Lancashire continued to dominate the Gillette Cup with their flavour of high adventure. The first two matches were both full of runs and incident. Lancashire, at Old Trafford, scored a wholesome 243 for 9, Clive Lloyd once more the top scorer, with 86. J. M. Kitchen, for Somerset, hit 116, but, with an over to go, they were all out for 234, and Lancashire won by nine runs. B. A. Richards, the South African star, led a strong Hampshire challenge at Bournemouth in the quarter-final. He made 129 out of 223 all out. Lancashire responded with regular and well judged efficiency, Barry Wood scoring 66, and, with two overs remaining, they emerged as victors by four wickets. The semi-final was at Old Trafford against Kent, and Pilling, with 70, orchestrated another effective performance. Defending 224 for 7, Kent batted brightly, only to fade from, at one time, 155 for 3 to 217, all out. Nevertheless, it was an exciting finish, with the last wicket falling in the last over, and Kent but seven adrift.

A third final: this time against Warwickshire, with coaches and trains carrying Lancashire fans southwards to Lord's once more, and the ritual cry of 'Lanky-sheer rah-rah-rah, Lanky-sheer, rah-rah-rah' (with a downbeat on that third 'rah'), a sound now commonplace in St John's Wood.

Warwickshire batted first and established a strong position. Lancashire fielded only one fast bowler, Peter Lee, and relied on Clive Lloyd bowling 12 overs of medium-pace straight away. These tactics were not wholly successful. Whitehouse, 68, M. J. K. Smith, 48, and Kallicharran, 54, enabled Warwickshire to reach 207 for 4. It looked as if 300 was a possibility. It was here that the Lancashire fielding, especially that of Clive Lloyd, always a spicy feature of the county's play in cup-ties, erupted. Three Warwickshire players were run out, dramatically, consecutively, and, for Warwickshire, unprofitably. The Lancashire fans roared gleefully, welcoming each downfall like the old women knitting round the Guillotine.

Nonetheless, 234 was a steep enough target, always recalling that, doubtless because of the pressure, cup finals had tended to be relatively low-scoring affairs. Two hundred and thirty-four was the highest innings thus far in a Gillette final. Strong men wept as Lancashire began both slowly and badly. They were 26 for 2, with overs slipping away. It was now that Clive Lloyd played what some critics said was the most splendid innings ever witnessed at Lord's. When one considers the noble saga of Lord's that must seem a naïve judgement. However, against bowlers such as Willis, D. J. Brown and Lance Gibbs, and with time ever pressing, it must be agreed that it is well worthy of consideration for that honour.

Lloyd scored 126, only the second century in the 11 finals played. A gigantic figure, his heavy bat in resplendent flow, there was something of Gulliver among the citizens of Lilliput about his natural hegemony. He was particularly dominating off the front foot, with aggressive drives either soaring rows back into the stands or smashing back yards off the pavilion fence. It was an awesome display of cruel demolition.

Willis, with a slower ball, deceived Lloyd, with only 16 runs required, but Lancashire, with three overs to spare, won by four wickets. Pilling, 30, and Frank Hayes, 35, gave Lloyd the essential support and stability necessary for him to maintain his murderous assault. For the third time, a mellow September evening was filled with celebratory Northern shouts. Lancashire, the Houdini of the Gillette Cup trail, had escaped again.

That was not the end, but it was the high point, of their cup campaigning. John Bond relinquished the captaincy to David Lloyd and concentrated on coaching. A year later he left in 1974 to become player-manager at Nottinghamshire, and John Savage, after being chief scout under Norman Oldfield before sharing the coaching with Bond, then became chief coach. J. S. Savage had bowled his off-spin for Lancashire in 1967 and 1968 after years of service with Leicestershire. Under David Lloyd, Lancashire improved their John Player League position in 1973, rising to fourth, and were hindered by four matches of the 16 being abandoned. They won eight of the remaining 12, with Engineer the leading run-scorer, with 328, and with Lever, Lee and Sullivan all taking 20 or more wickets. For once, Lancashire progressed steadily in the Benson and Hedges Cup. Glamorgan were obliterated in the quarter-final. After a Pilling century had lifted the county to 227 for 5 in the allotted 55 overs, Glamorgan were all out for 68, Simmons taking 3 for 5 in four overs. The semi-final versus Worcestershire was as exciting as any of Lancashire's absorbing Gillette matches. Lancashire, at Old Trafford, were all out for 159, Gifford taking 5 for 42. Simmons opened the bowling but was unable to replicate that sort of spinning damage, and it was left to Wood, Lever and Lee to bring Lancashire back into contention. The last over was Gothic in its dark shocks and twists, but it left Worcestershire on 159 for 9, and they won on grounds, just, of having lost less wickets. That was the closest of all.

Lancashire had easy passage to the quarter-final of the Gillette Cup in 1973, scoring heavily against Bedfordshire and reaching 275 for 3, and, later, dismissing Staffordshire for 137, Lever and Lee taking three wickets each. The next match with Middlesex at Lord's was an intriguing one. Lancashire batted smoothly to total 224 for 6, Harry Pilling being the top scorer with 90. Middlesex enjoyed an opening stand of 135, and M. J. Smith, like Pilling, scored 90. Simmons and Hughes then made some inroads, but, in a nicely balanced finish, Middlesex won with four wickets and an over in hand. It was Lancashire's first Gillette defeat in 16 outings.

David Lloyd remained as captain in 1974. A veil needs must be drawn over the Player League, because Lancashire won only five matches, and fell into the bottom half of the table. The Benson and Hedges cup-run was again presentable, but Lancashire disappointed in the semi-final at Old Trafford against Surrey. The home side could muster no more than 130, a poor riposte to Surrey's not over-demanding 193 for 8.

Once more the Gillette Cup stimulated the Lancashire team to venturesome deeds, and, once more, the final was reached. Old rivals Gloucestershire were bowled out for 151 (Lever 4 for 29) after Lancashire had batted with steadiness to reach 201 for 6, in the opening round at Bristol. At Lord's, Middlesex were easily defeated. Wood and Lee demolished what appeared to be a powerful batting line-up for only 112, Lancashire having made 193 for 9. In a game at Headingley which ran into a second day Lancashire beat Yorkshire by 32 runs. C. H. Lloyd with 90 and Peter Lever with 4 for 17 were the main protagonists. There was no play on the first day of the semi-final at Worcester, that beautiful ground dulled by incessant showers. In dampish conditions on the Thursday David Lloyd (54) and Barry Wood (91) gave Lancashire a marvellous start, and their eventual 236 for 7 was too high a total for Worcestershire who lost by 28 runs.

The final was disappointing on two counts. Torrential rain destroyed any chance of play on the Saturday, and the match was played on the Monday in extremely wet and unfriendly circumstances, with the usual carnival air and spirit nonexistent. In a low-scoring, low-key game, Kent passed Lancashire's miserable 118 with six wickets down.

1975 saw Lancashire again fail in the Sunday competition, with eight wins and a tie against Worcestershire leaving them adrift in the table. Following promising wins in the Benson and Hedges zonal fixtures, Lancashire only scored 180 for 8 in the quarter-final, a total Leicestershire passed, not without a struggle, for eight wickets.

The Gillette Cup beckoned again. It was like the call of the wild for Lancashire. On a rainy July day, Northamptonshire were defeated at Old Trafford. Frank Hayes made a lively and undefeated 56, as Lancashire coasted to a nine-wicket win, after Lever had taken 4 for 18 and Shuttleworth 3 for 25. A crowd of 25,000 witnessed Hampshire's débâcle at Old Trafford. In amazed delight, they watched Barry Richards and Greenidge and company fall for 98. Bob Ratcliffe, swinging the ball in a helpful atmosphere, took 4 for 25, and, with Hayes again starring, the runs were easily knocked off. The semi-final at Old Trafford produced record Gillette receipts, except for the final matches, and Gloucestershire were once more the contestants. Sadiq Mohammad batted gloriously for 122 out of 236, a tall order for Lancashire, especially when Clive Lloyd was caught on the boundary for a single. Wood, with 69, officiated over a tense battle, and, with seven wickets down, Ratcliffe drove a four through the enclosing field, and it was back to Lord's.

The opponents were Middlesex. Competent bowling (Ratcliffe 3 for 25) and impeccable fielding restricted Middlesex to 180 for 8, not one batsman reaching fifty. In the prim and pragmatic style that had won them their first title against Sussex, Lancashire proceeded decorously to bank the runs. Andrew Kennedy scored 51 and Clive Lloyd was not out, 73. Lancashire arrived home by seven wickets. It was not a final of the classical sculpture of one or two earlier matches, but the Lancashire support was not in the mood to quibble over arcane quality.

1976 was the last of the clutch of good years, with the ugly omens of future failure already exhibited. The Player League produced the same pattern as 1975, with only eight matches won, and, again, Lancashire could not progress beyond the quarter-finals of the Benson's trophy. Warwickshire beat them by four wickets at Edgbaston, despite a fine 70 from Frank Hayes. Only the Gillette Cup remained for contemplation, and the Lancashire players were perked up at the prospect. Like fire-horses when the bells rang, they lifted their heads and raised their game at the very thought of another Lord's final. At Old Trafford Lancashire proudly matched Middlesex's tall score of 270 for 9. With eight balls remaining, and three wickets standing, they passed that sum, Hayes (61) and Pilling (82) the leading contributors. It was Gloucestershire yet again in the quarter-final at Old Trafford, but this time their effort was a paltry one. Their overseas stars failed and Lancashire only needed 126 to win. Barry Wood batted through for 62 not out. The semi-final at Edgbaston was a grand encounter, with fine batting the day long. Two hundred and thirty-three runs were accumulated by Warwickshire, and Lancashire, 40 for 2, began poorly. Wood and Hayes then partnered one another in a sparkling stand, full of vivid drives, of 160, Wood (105) and Hayes (93). Lancashire won by six wickets.

Lord's was crowded and colourful for Lancashire's sixth appearance in seven years, but it was to be a disappointing one. With Engineer and Pilling out and Wood injured almost before the spectators had settled, Lancashire never recovered. David Lloyd and John Abrahams did some repair work, but it was left to David Hughes, in the last over of the game off Bedi, to restore a little self-esteem. Inspired perhaps by memory of his battering of John Mortimore in the dusk at Old Trafford, he struck the Indian spinner mighty blows to the tune of 26. It was glorious, but vain. Northamptonshire had a trouble-free start, adding a hundred and more for the first wicket, and, whilst one or two wickets fell, they won easily enough by four wickets.

It was a morose finale to eight years of heroic adventure during which time six trophies had been acquired. Eight years would pass before Lancashire were to be again in contention. It had been a shimmering spell, gone, suddenly, like gossamer blown away.

## An Analysis of the One-Day Champions

The strategy for win or-lose cricket is, self-evidently, less elaborate than that for a season-round campaign of 20-odd Championship games. Attack with the bat; defend with the ball: those are the trusty tenets. There are sophistications, like introducing the fifth bowler just prior to lunch when the batsmen are understandably cautious, and the restriction on bowlers calls for some algebraic calculation by the captain. Played with *élan*, it can be spellbinding, particularly the 60-over-a-side variation which Lancashire mastered so effortlessly. Over the seven years 1970 to 1976, Lancashire played 29 Gillette Cup ties, winning 26 and losing a mere three.

J. D. Bond, captain for the first three years of that spell, deserves much credit. He whipped a flagging team into shape, insisted that the players enjoy themselves, sustained an excellent level of efficiency and pointed the team always in exactly the right direction. He was born at Kearsley in 1932, and made his début in 1955. It was 1961 before he won his cap, and he understood the rigours of adversity. When thus settled in the side, reaching 1701 runs in 1961 and the pinnacle of 2125 in 1962, a wrist broken against the West Indies in 1963 left him unable to regain his true form. However, his sympathetic control of the second eleven, and his ability shown when standing in as first-eleven captain, gained him the post in his own right. It was fitting that his success in 1970 led to his selection as a *Wisden* cricketer of the year. He was neither long nor successful at Trent Bridge as player-manager, nor, on his return to Old Trafford in 1980, after coaching in the Isle of Man, did he know of unalloyed joy as the Lancashire manager. He was somewhat unceremoniously booted out, along with the coach, Peter Lever, at the end of the 1986 season.

He scored nearly 12,000 runs for Lancashire, spread over 17 seasons, at an average of only 26. His 14 centuries included a top score of 157 against Hampshire and a sentimental journey to Lord's for 103, not out, in his last season. In 1961, batting at three and four, he emerged as a prominent batsman, the last Lancashire player, indeed, to score 2000 runs for the county in a season, before the advent of the curtailed Championship. Perky in stature and a stalwart driver, during his reign as skipper he properly relegated himself to the further end of the batting order, and, in truth, his career hinged on his jubilant lead towards two Player titles and three Gillette Cups. In that role, this amiable, hymn-singing Wesleyan and Lancashire loyalist earned much respect.

Two or three factors were to his advantage. The importation of two international stars, Clive Lloyd and F. M. Engineer, in conjunction with the peaking of half-a-dozen indigenous crick-eters, was a major benefit. It is accepted that, indeed, an aspect of that brightening of native form was the stimulation of the immigrants, as, in turn, they were able to ply their arts in goodly company. It meant that these were settled times. After years in which names had nebulously floated into half-view, come into focus, and then drifted away, this was a stable era of regular team-sheets. In 1974 16 players appeared in the Gillette Cup run, but in 1970, 1972 and 1975 it was only 13, in 1973 and 1976 it was just 12, and, most uncommonly, in 1971 only eleven players were required to lift the Cup. Freed from the incubus of injury and the curse of stuttering form, both the mechanics and the ambience of teamwork were strengthened.

The towering inferno of C. H. Lloyd was central. By the end of 1976, his 22 innings in Gillette cricket had produced 1068 runs and an average over 53. Foreknowledge of his arrival at the crease gave the opening batsmen the confidence to construct a platform, and avoid undue early breathlessness. This task was often left to Wood and David Lloyd, and the former, too, although in 33 innings, had also reached a thousand by 1976. Sometimes, for extra flourish, the dash of Engineer would be deployed to open Lancashire's account, and it was a valued boon that, for such competitions, Lancashire had a genuine wicket-keeper-batsman, and one whose disposition favoured daring assault. Harry Pilling, tickling and nudging impishly and to significant effect, followed, and, after Clive Lloyd, came John Sullivan or, later, Frank Hayes, burning the turf with coruscating drives. John Sullivan, least well-fêted of the party, scored 506 runs and took 13 for 228 in 56 overs in Gillette cricket. A native of Ashton-under-Lyne, this hardworking cricketer, who was also an excellent field, retired in 1976, though only 31. His main contributions were in the limited-overs encounters, and he scored over 1500 runs in John Player fixtures. Barry Wood and he tended to share the job of the fifth bowler, the one to which opponents looked, in their case often forlornly, for the easier pickings.

Lancashire batted on, and this was an enormous help. Lancashire, in these years, seldom died completely. Hughes and Simmons became almost as famous as Hobbs and Sutcliffe, albeit as a closing pair, while the fast bowlers, a choice of Lever, Shuttleworth and, to a lesser extent, Lee, were brave smiters. The first two scored over 3000 and just under 2000 runs in first-class cricket.

The bowling began and ended, in the normal fashion of the one-day format, with the controlled speed of two of this trio, although, on occasion, Clive Lloyd would replace one of them with his economical medium-pace. Simmons would more or less bottle up an end for 12 overs, whilst Hughes would often act as fourth bowler. Bob Ratcliffe, of Accrington, who bowled his dependable medium-pace off a moderated kangaroo run, made appearances around this time, playing in 13 Gillette ties and taking 21 wickets. He played for Lancashire from 1972 to 1980, before moving on to Perthshire, and he took 205 first-class wickets. He was only 30 when he left.

That was the size of it. Long, aggressive batting, matched by competent to accomplished bowling, controlled rather than hostile, with fielding of undeniable skill and adventure. Engineer was the pivot for this, begetting greatness in the field around him from the graceful perfection of his own wicket-keeping. Serving in two roles, he was, of course, wellnigh as influential as Clive Lloyd in Lancashire's one-day success. That said, Clive Lloyd bowled moderately well, and fielded, chiefly in the covers, like greased lightning. His speed over the ground and fast throw either left batsmen stranded and run out or, equally useful in this type of cricket, terrified other batsmen into refusing the mildest of hazards. Of David Hughes, fielding centrally at mid-wicket across from Lloyd, it need only be said that, in Lloyd's absence, he was the fastest, safest fielder on the ground. Barry Wood and David Lloyd were outstanding; Frank Hayes as stylish in the field as when batting; while Harry Pilling was a midget wonder on the boundary. The Lancashire team set new heights in fielding criteria, diving and chasing, two at a time, one stopping, one throwing, catching like old boots, throwing as if computer-programmed, menacing as they preyed on rather than walked in as the bowler ran up. The threat of that swiftly moving, closing circle, as the batsman faced the bowler, was all but atavistic. The broader-strung field of one-day play meant that, apart from the aware wicket-keeper, the entire team was alert and on the move inward. It was a grand sight and a sharp weapon.

It is difficult to compare this, the fifth and latest of Lancashire's great elevens, with its predecessors, because of the inherent problem of relating limited-over to first-class play. Observing Major Green's team in the 1920s was like quaffing, slowly and regularly, deep draughts of satisfying home-brewed beer. In the 1970s it was more the ping and pop-pop of the sparkling champagne cork, exhilarating for a moment, then the bubbles flat.

They probably batted longer than some of the previous elevens.

They probably needed to do so as well, for MacLaren's and Green's sides began with four or five prodigious run-scorers. Overall, however, with Clive Lloyd in full swing, the batting was excellent. The bowling, while defensively sound, was not as strong as in past teams. Basically, there was no destroyer. There was no McDonald, no Statham, no Briggs nor Mold, no Tattersall, on favouring pitches, to fillet an opposing team with the sudden, clean cut of a Fleetwood fish-gutter.

Where Bond's team had a definitive edge was in fielding. Engineer, third in the trio of Lancashire's world-class keepers, superintended a fielding machine without fault. One-day cricket may have caused bowlers to aim passively, but the fielding exploded with a gusto that was not and would not have been possible to maintain over the three-day campaign. Nevertheless, on their days out for the Gillette Cup, this must be judged Lancashire's finest fielding hour.

They were an extremely gifted group of cricketers. Of those who have played regularly for Lancashire, Lloyd and Engineer stand first and third by way of Test appearances, with Statham separating them. They were, of course, extraordinarily seasoned international cricketers. Beyond that, Barry Wood, David Lloyd, Frank Hayes, Peter Lever and Ken Shuttleworth were England cricketers, with 52 caps shared between them. Some felt Bond, before his enervating injury off Wes Hall's bowling, might have had such hopes; others that Pilling was unlucky, and that Simmons, for one-day matches, merited England selection. No one would deny the talents of the other remaining regulars, such as David Hughes and Peter Lee.

So they should have done well, and that puts Jack Bond's part in some perspective. Of course, his encouragement must have aided the younger players toward ambition's fulfilment, but it was A. N. Hornby's task to mould uncertain material into dominant shape. Jack Bond, then, was the very good captain of an excellent team. One or two of his predecessors, Hornby certainly, perhaps MacLaren, when the mood took him, were excellent captains of very good teams. Judiciously to complete the triangle, Leonard Green was the good captain of a mighty team.

Before moving from this scrutiny of a most entertaining team, it is right to examine some of their careers more personally, but not without trepidation. On the one hand, their deeds are recent and well known; on the other hand, their deeds are still the stuff of news, and not history, and it is, as yet, untimely to locate them in the referential frame of Lancashire's lengthy saga.

## Clive Lloyd

Clive Hubert Lloyd, born in 1944 in Georgetown, Guyana, bestrode Lancashire cricket from 1968 to 1986 like the Colossus he was. His adventures have been well rehearsed at international level, and his deeds for Lancashire are well known and require little further exegesis. Indeed, his domination of cricket's scene renders him still too close and too huge in merit to do more than marvel goggle-eyed, and the calmer mode of objective assessment is difficult.

Even the bare figures are indigestible, and, although it makes examination simpler by treating him purely as a county cricketer, shelving the great weight of his West Indian statistics, one is still faced with a gluttonous banquet.

Clive Lloyd scored over 5000 runs for Lancashire in Sunday league cricket; over 1300 in Benson and Hedges Cup ties; and nearly 2000 in Gillette and Nat West Trophy matches. His Gillette average is nearly 55, and his overall one-day average is 41. His limited-overs total of 8456 is, of course, a Lancashire record. Andrew Kennedy's 131 in 1978 is the county's highest score in Gillette/Nat West play, with Lloyd's 126 at Lord's in 1972 second, but the West Indian holds both other Lancashire records: 124 against Warwicks in the Benson's and 134 against Somerset in the John Player League. In these 268 games in the three competitions he took 60 wickets, accepted, often with baffling alacrity, 94 catches, and ran out countless scores of pitifully marooned opponents.

There is no doubt that Lloyd was, like many sportsmen, inspired by the importance of the occasion, and these occur more frequently in instant cricket. It is sometimes, conversely, believed that his contribution was less influential on the mundane county scene, but his figures belie this opinion. To be just, these are relative figures. Lloyd never carried Lancashire to a Championship on the powerful shoulders of his batting, but his record places him high in the county rankings.

He played 219 games for Lancashire, spread over 17 seasons, although a sundry mix of injury, international calls and restrictions on overseas players meant that he played in ten or more first-class games in only eleven of those summers. He scored 12,764 runs, one of 27 Lancashire batsmen to reach 10,000 runs, and his average – 44.94 – is second only to Ernest Tyldesley's 45.2. Thus Lloyd proved a more consistent scorer then Eddie Paynter or Cyril Washbrook. In spite of the reduced first-class list, he reached a thousand runs for the county in 1970, 1971, 1974, 1975, 1978, 1981 and 1982. He scored 30 centuries and 71 fifties for Lancashire, with a highest innings of 217, not out, in 1971, versus Warwickshire. He took 55 wickets and 161 catches.

He captained Lancashire in 1981, 1982, 1983 and 1986, resuming the post after John Abrahams, born in Cape Town but reared in his cricketing family in Lancashire, had had that responsibility in 1984 and 1985. He was never able to achieve the success the club and Lloyd himself devoutly wished for: his political acumen in the coalescence of the separatist factions of a West Indies eleven was less required than professional nous, day in, day out, on the county circuit. This he had in lesser measure, for his West Indians had been gifted enough, once cajoled into a co-operative mind, to conquer the world.

In the county game, then, he will be remembered for his right-handed fielding and left-handed batting. He came first to note playing with Haslingden and with the International Cavaliers Sunday team. The transformation of gangling giraffe into snarling tiger in the field forms one's earliest recollection. In his early twenties the switch from the gauche, almost awkwardly slouching posture to the athlete, running, picking up, turning and throwing with balletic perfection, was less familiar, naturally, than it became. Once more Lancashire found themselves, as so frequently in their past, with a world-class cover point. Later when the wear on his damaged knees pressed him toward the slips, he was to exhibit equal flair for unearthly catching.

The same slightly bemused discomposure attended his hesitant arrival at the batting crease, and it offered early hope to sanguine bowlers for a few balls as Lloyd stumbled and waved his bat anxiously, gazing with troubled eyes through lenses that might have seen service at Jodrell Bank. Then, suddenly, all fell into place. His Excalibur of a bat, hardly liftable by mortal hands, whirred through a perfect arc, reach and feet were aligned, and the ball discovered itself, shaken and bruised, in cosmic flight and circulation. That degree of co-ordination, allied to indecent force, gave Clive Lloyd generous scope on the drive from something fine of cover to a point between mid-on and mid-wicket. Add a frenzied hook that might have made Cyril Washbrook gulp, and one had, in essence, not only one of cricket's finest-ever batsmen, but, as significantly, one of its most attractive entertainers.

There was an unpredictability about his potency. Like Jessop, like, on occasion, Botham, he could distort the placid logic of a cricket match by a few minutes' flurry of shattering blows, undermining at once the physical resource and mental resolve of a rival. That Clive Lloyd did this peering through thick spectacles from under a white sun hat, for all the world as if he had ambled on to the sands at Morecambe and shyly accepted an invitation to join a few boys playing beach cricket, merely made it more difficult for opponents to accept.

There was something of John Tyldesley about him: gentle and courteous and reticent of demeanour, and yet, of a sudden, cruelly savage. On another wavelength, it perhaps reflected the mood of the times. Where Reggie Spooner gained mastery with the suave ingenuity of John Buchan's Richard Hannay, an agent of immaculate Edwardian manner, there was more in Lloyd's well calculated violence a flavour of a modern hero, such as Ian Fleming's James Bond. When Clive Lloyd hit you for six or ran you out by a couple of yards, there was neither compunction nor compassion in the style of it. To watch him smash down stumps with a right-angle throw from 30 yards and the batsmen scarcely crossed was like watching Sean Connery's instinctive decision to chuck an electric fire as accurately into a bath to dispose of the unprepossessing villain – and it was, if anything, more enjoyable. Lancashire spectators smacked their lips and crowed in hoarse and amazed ecstasy.

He joins the Tyldesleys and Washbrook as Lancashire's only bats with over 30,000 in all first-class cricket, and he approaches those talented brothers, and Washbrook and MacLaren, in the noble exposition of the batting art, and then perhaps passes them. Clive Lloyd is Lancashire's premier batsman.

## Farokh Engineer

Farokh Engineer proved to be Lancashire's most successful, some would say, only, wicket-keeper-batsman, and, in disporting himself with insouciance and chivalry, he ensured for himself a popular place in the Lancashire story. Originally from Bombay, he was 30 and an experienced Test cricketer, when, in 1968, he joined Lancashire, where he played for nine seasons. After Bond, he was the oldest of the Lancashire team, and, in the limited-overs games most especially, a necessary component. He scored nearly 3000 runs in 152 one-day outings, to which he added 183 dismissals as wicket-keeper, refusing, like some, to adopt the ultra-defensive posture of a half-baked long-stop.

He also contributed with nearly 6000 runs in first-class play, at an average of 26, with four centuries and a top score of 141 at Buxton in 1971. As wicket-keeper in his 175 matches, he stands third behind his only peers, Pilling and Duckworth, with 35 stumpings and 429 catches, in sum, 464 dismissals. Pilling had 465 victims in 173 matches: apart from an imbalance of stumpings and catches (Pilling had 149 of one and 316 of the other), their data is pleasingly similar. Only Clayton (183) and, needless to recall, Duckworth have kept wicket more often for Lancashire than F. M. Engineer. He twice had six dismissals in an innings (Northamptonshire and Surrey, both in 1970) and he four times had eight in a match, a Lancashire record. These were against Somerset in 1969, Northamptonshire and Middlesex in 1970, and Nottinghamshire in 1973. In 1970 he enjoyed a cull of four stumped and 78 caught, a total of 82, with another nine in other first-class matches. The consequent total of 91 is the fourth-highest in a season for a Lancashire keeper. In 1975 he had 72 victims, another good haul.

In 1976, aged 39, he left cricket to concentrate on his textile business, to the regret of his many admirers. His full, black mane and merry smile had made him something of a talisman. He was, like other coloured players, subject to some racial abuse from rival spectators and, private sources sadly reveal, occasionally players, but this he bore, on the whole, with an urbane tolerance shaming to his detractors.

Farokh Engineer was tall and squarely built compared to many wicket-keepers, but, armed with his vast gauntlets, his deftness and dancer's gracefulness enabled him to maintain immaculate standards. So personable and poised a wicket-keeper was a tonic for those around him, and, like his predecessors, he lifted great fielders to ever greater heights. It is no coincidence that three of Lancashire's five successful teams have had a world-class wicket-keeper, and there is a moral there for selectors who pick a lesser specialist who can bat more substantially. Alan Wilson, the keeper in Howard's team, was sensible and stalwart, as his 346 dismissals in 171 matches testify. In MacLaren's early days C. Smith, 427 victims in 167 matches, was highly regarded for his tidy effectiveness. Clayton, with the satisfying account of 422 dismissals in 183 games, is the only one of Lancashire's top six keepers not to have been part of some team triumph. He played from 1959 to 1964.

It cuts both ways. Whereas goalkeepers sometimes blossom in poor sides because of the pressure upon them (Manchester City, with Frank Swift and Bert Trautmann their formidable custodians, have been analysed after this fashion, normally by friends from the other Old Trafford), wicket-keepers do need to feed off predatory bowling. That said, Engineer did not keep wicket, like Pilling, Smith, Duckworth and Wilson, to bowlers of legendary destructiveness.

His superior batting entitles him to push Richard Pilling and George Duckworth hard for the specialised post of wicket-keeper when, on winter nights, with winds gusting through narrow Pennine valleys, rational men and women sit at home, picking Lancashire's all-time eleven.

Engineer's batting was forceful and cavalier. He invariably moved forward, even when determined to glide the ball legwards. He appeared to play the ball, both in driving and hooking, more on the full toss than most cricketers. Once feeling the fluency of which he was patently capable, in the middle order or opening the batting in a limited-overs spree, his venturesomeness was dramatic. One of the first hints that the Player League would have unusual dimensions was during its first season, when, almost before the Glamorgan field was set, Engineer had driven their fast bowling back past the bowler's wicket for a plethora of fours. He had 78, not out, from a winning total of 115 for 1, with 16 overs left.

Yet his optimism, so sunnily useful as he kept wicket gloriously, betrayed him into carefree, even careless shots, like his attempted leg glance in his last major game for Lancashire at Lord's against Northamptonshire, when J. C. J. Dye bowled him neck and crop for nought at start of play. On those occasions, Engineer's usually cheerful face would cloud over, not so much with annoyance for his own failure, but with guilt that he had let down others, his team-mates and his many fans.

He seemed not often to be stale or, like some cricketers, world-weary. His minute anticipations, suggesting some mystique of oriental clairvoyance, delighted him as they did the crowd. He enjoyed one or two pranks. A batsman who played forward and swayed or stumbled might find that Engineer would gently push him over, prelude to a mock-stumping. Like the artist he was, it was a joke practised sparingly, for, unlike the repetitious mannerisms affected by some sports personalities, he sensed, perhaps innately, that he should not let it become boring. And he was, of course, an international star of some magnitude, with 46 caps for India, for whom he scored 2611 runs, at an average of 32, and caught or stumped 82 opponents.

Bright as a new morning, Engineer possessed delightful characteristics as a cricketer and as a civilised man. As Peter Lever was explaining to Neville Cardus that his birthplace had, in reality, been just on the Yorkshire side of Todmorden, Farokh Engineer was heard to mutter satirically, 'bloody foreigner'.

### Frank Hayes

Through the dim mists and across the plains from Marple, a knight came a-riding. Fair of hair and countenance, open-visaged, fresh of eye and harmoniously built, this replica of the Arthurian legend was destined to save Lancashire and even resuscitate England cricket. Frank Hayes was Sir Galahad.

He was born a few miles, geographically and culturally, north of Camelot at Preston, on 6 December 1946. He decided to take a university degree at Sheffield, and, in the ancient regime, may have been taken on as an assistant secretary by some county and played as a shamateur. He was thus 23 when, in 1970, he made his début at Old Trafford against Middlesex and made 94 and 47 in dazzling style. In his second game at Southampton he scored 2 and 99 against Hants. He scored six fifties in 24 innings that season, ending with 780 runs and an average of 39. The next two seasons were less productive, and it was 1973 before he reached a thousand runs and his first hundreds, indeed five of them.

In the same year he made a glittering début for England against West Indies at the Oval, and, in his second innings, scored 106 not out, the last Englishman to make a century in his first Test.

In the modern Mazdaist equivalent of the struggle of light

and darkness, Frank Hayes appeared as Luke Skywalker, inheritor of the Force from the Ben-Kenobi of either Cyril Washbrook or Tom Graveney, according to whether your fancy was regional or national. Malcolm Nash, the Glamorgan bowler, perhaps surmised the Force was with Hayes when, his light-sabre flailing, he struck 34 off a Nash over at Swansea in 1977. That has only been improved upon for a six-ball over by, as every schoolboy knows, another knight-errant, Sir Gary Sobers, who hit six sixes off the same misused bowler on the same ground.

In keeping with the model of goodness, Francis Charles Hayes played straight as a die. The memory of his faultless extra-cover drive scudding across the turf evokes the kind of excitement some find in the thudding rush of pedigree racehorses on the flat. Only marginally less evocative is the recollection of his fielding, his swiftness in the chase and flatness and precision in the return. Sometimes, playing for England, whose athleticism was less general than in the then-current Lancashire side, he would be observed giving his fellow-internationals 15 and 20 yards start and beating them in a race to the fence.

From 1970 to 1984 he played 272 matches for Lancashire, and his run tally was 10,899 (13,018 in all first-class games). Thus he joined the coterie of Lancashire bats to cross the great divide in scoring 10,000 runs for the county, while his average – 37.45 – bettered that of Harry Makepeace and Archie MacLaren. He stands a highly commended eighth in the all-time Lancashire averages. Of his 23 centuries, his 187 against India in 1974 at Manchester was his highest, whilst his best score in the Championship was in 1977, 157 not out, at Nottingham. Six times he reached a thousand runs in a season.

He scored 4312 runs for Lancashire in limited-over cricket, and played in exactly 200 such games. His desire to carry the tourney to the enemy was ideal for the one-day game. Within the context of its team setting, cricket is adversarial, and Frank Hayes, handsome in style and daring of shot, looked born to the tournament. He had charisma; eyes were drawn continually to him. The same shapeliness of motion and action attended his fielding, and, in all cricket, he took, usually in effortless fashion, 210 catches.

Mortal man would have rested content. Ten thousand runs for your county; a century for your country: for most men, weekend cricketing after mundane hours in a Manchester office or driving a company car round the Fylde as a sales representative, it would have seemed an eminently acceptable fate. But Frank Hayes was not allowed the comfort of mortality. He had sipped of the poisoned chalice of promise. Promise can haunt sportsmen, and it hung like a miasma over the blond head of Frank Hayes. Nor was it one of those cases where some slight and early testimony had misled experts into believing potential existed where it did not. Frank Hayes's promise was unmistakable for all to adore.

By stringent criteria, then, F. C. Hayes did not achieve what was anticipated and did not enter the gallery of the exalted. He played only nine times for England, each one against the West Indies, and he scored only 244 runs, 106 of them, as we have noted, in one innings. He may have been unlucky always to have played against fiercesome West Indians, without a chance to consolidate his place by wreaking havoc on lesser breeds, but class, if class there be, will out.

The ratio of fifties to centuries in his first-class career is intriguing. It is one century to every three fifties. Take someone like Ernest Tyldesley. With him, similarly a middle-order batsman, the ratio is less than two to one. There was, for Hayes, the distraction of one-day cricket and the frequent curtailment of an innings after 100 overs under the bonus-points system. Even so, there seemed to be a lack of profound application. Frank Hayes never made a double century, and only three 150s. He took part in only three stands of 200, the highest 215. He was not, eventually, a player of the tall innings.

He captained Lancashire for three seasons, 1978, 1979 and 1980. He acted worthily throughout this time, but his assertiveness never appeared to be as noticeable as in his great innings. They were difficult years. Like Lord Jim, he found himself almost fortuitously the captain of a leaky tub, and undecided quite what to do. He played only 12 matches in 1981 and two in 1982, when nagging injury drove him from the first-class game, leaving a faintly acrid whiff of disappointment in the air. He was 35. He had never been the juvenile lead. After all, he had been seven years older than Johnny Briggs and Peter Marner at début time. Now 12 years later it was all over. The Empire strikes back.

It was as though that 99 at Southampton in 1970 in Hayes's first game had been some sort of malign omen. It was as if not getting that hundred was to set the pattern. There are, in cricket

as in all walks of life, has-beens. Most definitely Frank Hayes was
never that. But he was a not-quite.

## Harry Pilling

In 'Root's Boots', perhaps the pick of Peter Tinniswood's tall
tales from the long room, the pygmy opening pair are likened to
'a dusky Wee Georgie Wood and an extremely sunburned Mr
Harry Pilling'. The choice of Georgie Wood is intriguing, for the
Pilling generation was more familiar with Jimmy Clitheroe as the
manikin comedian of the age. However, Jimmy Clitheroe was the
mischievous Northern lad, a stagey version of Just William, while
Georgie Wood was precise, Eton-collared and choirboy-like. It
does not press literary analysis too far to remark that, in this
dualism, Jimmy Clitheroe would have been too close to the Pilling
mould, thus allowing the urbane Georgie Wood to serve, so to
speak, as his upright amateur partner. For Clitheroe and Wood,
read Paynter and Jardine.

What is significant is that Harry Pilling had become this kind of
folklore figure during his playing days, and thus it remained. He
became the short standard by which small-statured cricketers were
judged. In 1987, seven or eight years after the end of his first-class
career, the *Guardian* called the West Indian player, Gus Logie,
'Trinidad's answer to Harry Pilling'. He has become a human
simile, like Captain Bligh for cruelty or Mata Hari for vamping
espionage.

Harry Pilling, born in February 1943, packed an enormous
amount of professional expertise into his compact five feet and
barely more. He made his début at 19 against Sussex and played
his last first-class match 18 years later in 1980. He thereafter
proved a useful second-eleven captain and cajoler. He also
captained the first eleven in one match of monstrous topsy-
turveydom in 1977, when, having suffered the dearth of 33 all out
at Northampton in the first innings, the county rallied to the
affluence of 501 in the second, and an easy draw.

A native of Ashton-under-Lyne, at a time when its trolley-buses
and its fried fish and its tripe shops made it a prototype for South
Lancashire, he was capped in 1965, and, for a dozen years
thereafter, he remained perhaps the county's most reliable batsman. With 25 centuries, nearly 15,000 runs, an average of over 30,

and a highest score of 149, not out, versus Glamorgan, he presented a sturdy and valiant front, not least in years when Lancashire played but poorly. He reached a thousand runs in eight seasons, six of them concurrently, and was rewarded with a benefit of £11,500 in 1974, then Lancashire's third-highest individual testimonial.

His impact must also be measured by his success in the one-day game. He played in 34 Gillette Cup matches and 33 Benson and Hedges Cup matches, scoring close to 1500 runs in those two competitions. He was a consistent performer in Lancashire's grand run of cup wins, and, in the first of those against Sussex in 1970, his 70 not out, in a total of 185, won him the man-of-the-match award. The cover drive, off Tony Greig, which brought him to his 50 was described by one ecstatic reporter as the sweetest shot played at Lord's that summer. He also played a major part in Lancashire's early triumphs in the John Player League, and he scored well over 2000 runs in that competition. He was one of the first generation of cricketers to be tested by limited-over as well as conventional trial, and he conducted himself with the utmost tenacity.

Most cricket-lovers have a couple of lists knocking around in the rear of their heads: the one of cricketers who should have played for England; and the other of those who shouldn't have bothered. Harry Pilling finds a place on several people's former list. Some judges thought him unlucky to be excluded from Ray Illingworth's tour of Australia in 1970–71, and his best claim to representative honour was his 81, not out, for the MCC against India in his benefit season. He was a batsman of a resource at once tactical and tactful. He played with immense purity, his style rooted in orthodoxy. Almost always he batted first-wicket down. That position tends to be obliterated by your third-best opener or your most dependable middle-order bat, but Harry Pilling was nature's number three. To staunch the wound of an early breakthrough, to consolidate on a decent position, to capitalise with speed on a strong vantage: his mix of shrewdness and skill permitted him to adjust tempo and design accordingly.

Above all else, he was a busy batter, succinct in timing and placement, utilising the angle of his bat with a geometric grasp a snooker player might have admired. He was one of the first to learn the trailed shot through the empty slip-country of the one-day world, and he was not ashamed to add prolifically to the sum of leg-byes. Time and again, watching Pilling, spectators would enjoy his deflections and nudges, scarcely noting any huge hits or undue violence. Time and again, spectators, after only a few minutes, would gasp in surprise when they glanced at the scoreboard, for Harry Pilling would already have a dozen or a score to his name. Perhaps the most remarkable feat of his career was his becoming the first person to reach a thousand runs amidst the alarums and excursions of the John Player 40-over heave-ho. While others smote and biffed, Harry wheedled and coaxed, a lesson to those who believed that flinging the bat was the only way.

It was in the Player League that Clive Lloyd and Harry Pilling enjoyed the most celebrated of their several splendid stands. Somerset were the victims of a record cavalcade of 182 runs in 1970. It was a thunderous and rapid exhibition, with umpires and scorers bemused by the possibility that, on occasion, Harry Pilling only ran one to the lofty West Indian's three. Pilling himself agreed that his major fear during such stands was the menace of being trampled underfoot during performances by cricket's equivalent of music hall's Revnell and West, 'The long and short of it'.

That brand of pawky humour endeared him to a broad cricket audience, and the winter task he cheerfully undertook – this involved the sale of coffins – only added to that reputation. As the Lancashire team entered Lord's one morning, they were loudly abused by an antagonist of repulsive visage. 'Couldn't you get a job,' asked Pilling solicitously, 'haunting houses?' He was ever a bubbling and supportive team-mate.

It is a pity that the warmth of affection felt for him did not have a chance to burgeon in Australia. He may well have won many new friends, not least for his quick, neat outfielding. If one sat at the opposite end of a great arena from where his diminutive figure perched, usually with county cap square-on, it was like watching a clip from a cartoon. He would field the ball tidily, and draw back his tiny arm. Then, incredibly, unerringly, the ball would zoom through a startling parabola into the wicket-keeper's gloves, as if propelled by Mighty Mouse or by Popeye in post-spinach condition.

From Ulysses and Polyphemus, via David and Goliath and Jack the Giant-killer, to Tom and Jerry, legend abounds with the little man putting it over the titan with the help of a little cunning and nous. Assessed by the severest criteria, Harry Pilling was never a world-class player, but, when many such are forgotten, his place in cricket's folklore will remain firm.

His final accolade might be to guess that, had Sir Neville Cardus been allowed just one post-sixties Lancastrian to beatify in his faultless prose, he would have selected Harry Pilling. Harry Pilling really needed, not Kerry Packer, but Phineas T. Barnum, sponsor of Tom Thumb, to market him. He would have found a rotund Victorian billing for Pilling, such as 'The Minuscule Accumulator'.

## Jack Simmons

In 1985 Jack Simmons, to some surprise but much pleasure, was included in *Wisden*'s five cricketers of the year, in tribute to his lengthy and sterling service in county cricket. If one recalls another famous five – Harry Wharton and Co. at Frank Richards's Greyfriars – it was a little as if Billy Bunter had successfully incorporated himself within that clean-limbed quintet. This was, in part, because Jack Simmons never presumed to world stardom, although, of course, he led Tasmania to rare and unprecedented heights over seven seasons in the 1970s. This was also, in part, because Jack Simmons enjoyed an enviable reputation as a Bunter-like trencherman, in a sport whose adherents are not noted for their abstemiousness and where anorexia nervosa has significantly failed to make an impact.

During the early 1980s, the fish and chip shop near to the Simmons's residence at Great Harwood hailed this fame with the inclusion of a 'Simmo Special' on the menu. This dish drew together carbohydrates and cholesterol on to one plate with the keenness of college students making an attempt on the record for crowding people into a telephone kiosk. The calorific value of the 'Simmo Special' was astronomic, comparable, perhaps, with Sunil Gavaskar's runs total in Test cricket. When Jack Simmons dieted in 1987, the nation was alerted to this frightening fact, and bulletins were issued. When the Yorkshire number eleven refused to walk after being, in Simmons's usually dependable view, caught off his bowling, Simmons accused him in public of cheating. His diet and his mother's death were argued in apology for his quite uncharacteristic outburst, for which he was disciplined. Had that wicket fallen, Lancashire would have won the Championship in 1987.

Jack Simmons's bowling hardly tallied with his well-rounded and generous girth. There was nothing expansive about his off-spin attack to remind one of the groaning board. It was niggardly in the extreme, as if the spirit of Ebenezer Scrooge was struggling to free itself from the carcase of the Fat Boy in *The Pickwick Papers*. More competitive than possibly his friendly features and figure suggested, very hardworking, and, over by over and ball by ball, immensely thoughtful, he begrudged every run. Bred as a northern league professional and introduced to the county scene as one-day cricket came on stream, his forte was defence. He concentrated on a line edging toward middle-and-leg and on a length dipping toward the yorker, varying flight somewhat more than his sobriquet of 'Flat-Jack' inferred, and he frequently tucked up the finest of strikers by this careful approach.

He was born at Clayton-le-Moors on 28 March 1941 and he was a late entrant to the game. He made his début, aged 27, in 1968 at Stanley Park, Blackpool, where he was the local professional. He took three wickets against Northamptonshire in his only match that year, but soon became a permanent fixture and was awarded his cap in 1971. He was still going strong in 1987 and was a most important member of that suddenly successful team, although, at 46, of prime years indeed. Over some score of years on the first-class circuit, he had scored close on 10,000 runs, with 112 against Sussex in 1970 being the best of his six centuries. He has taken a thousand wickets all told, with 7 for 76 against Hampshire being his best performance for Lancashire. In 1982 he actually headed the Lancashire batting averages, and he has topped the bowling averages on six occasions. In 1980 his benefit total of £128,000 doubled the existing record, and remains an all-time high.

With over 3000 runs and well over 400 wickets in one-day competitions for Lancashire, his repute in that type of cricket is affirmed; indeed, in the 18 seasons of the John Player League, it was recorded that, with 261, he made more appearances than anyone in that entire competition. He has also appeared in over 50 Gillette and Nat West Cup games, and is an everpresent in all Lancashire's finalist elevens. Cautious judges, including fellow off-spinners, have thought him unlucky not to have won higher honours. Pat Pocock has said that Simmons, during the central years of his career, should have been an automatic choice for England's one-day internationals, purely for the tactical contribution of his ten or 11 cunning and, for the batsmen, unrewarding overs. For instance, in Gillette and Nat West play, 1963 to 1986, he bowled 555.5 overs, with 103 maidens for 70 wickets and no more than 1626 runs, an inexpensive matter of 2.9 runs an over.

His batting has also proved faithful and useful, either propping up the dwindling returns of the late order in the first-class game or walloping with fury, especially over square leg, in the one-day game. He has fielded sensibly at slip, and, until bulkiness and the toll of years inhibited him, he was not disgraced when his peers comprised one of the finest fielding sides ever admired. Off and on, he captained the county and often acted as vice-captain. Given his inspirational reign over Tasmania, it has surprised many that he was never invited to skipper the side formally. It appeared that, now and again, he was passed over, when it seemed the time was ripe. Jack Simmons, in this regard, became something of the R. A. Butler of Lancashire politics.

It is, however, as a defensive bowler he will be recalled with respect and affection. A portly, tallish man, he would, when called upon, fold up his Lancashire cap tightly for safe keeping, if not with the umpire, then in his rear pocket. The preliminaries were brief: Jack Simmons set a field briskly and shrewdly, without the apparent long-drawn anxiety of some of his colleagues; and, unlike some of them, he did not overindulge in practice balls and exercises. After all, with so much experience, there was little left to learn about how to adjust a fieldsman's location or turn one's arm over efficiently. Then, with a stuttering start and a shortish pace or two to the wicket, the over would commence. The batsman would find the ball gently swaying in towards his feet, and he might hastily scramble it to short mid-wicket through a puff of dust. A second later, while still pondering thankful deliverance from the first, the second ball of the over would be on its way, slightly different in point of delivery, in aerial route and pace, and in estimated time and place of arrival.

Once, in 1985, Lancashire played Suffolk at Bury St Edmunds, in the preliminary round of the Nat West Trophy. Admittedly it was a minor county and the pitch was not immaculate, but, even so, Jack Simmons produced a quietly astute performance that characterised a career during which each ball bowled was regarded as possessively as Silas Marner watched over each gold coin. He only took one wicket, but he bowled maiden after maiden, until, with swishes of panic and despair, the Suffolk batsmen managed three singles.

It is likely that 1 for 3 in 12 overs is something of a negative record. It must seem wellnigh impossible, in a competition devoted to fast and bountiful run-making, that someone might bowl 69 virginal deliveries out of 72. That someone was Jack Simmons in cameo.

## *David Lloyd and Barry Wood*

Lloyd and Wood do not felicitously trip off the lips like Hornby and Barlow or Laurel and Hardy, like Makepeace and Hallows or Murray and Mooney. They are not Morecambe and Wise. Double-acts are out on stage and field. Either at national or county level the reassurance of such dual permanence has disappeared.

Nonetheless, Barry Wood, from Osset, a Yorkshireman like Makepeace, and David Lloyd, from Accrington, a Lancastrian like Hallows, did open the batting a lot. Wood, recommended to Lancashire by Brian Sellers, the former Yorkshire captain, played 260 games for Lancashire, before receiving a then-record benefit of £63,000, and, after a contractual squabble, moving, not too productively, to Derbyshire. Lloyd played 378 matches. He also had – £40,000 – a most satisfactory benefit; he captained Lancashire from 1973 to 1977 and enjoyed the jubilation of lifting the Gillette Cup, if little else, and retired in 1983.

Their careers did have similarities. They were of an age: Wood born in 1942, Lloyd in 1947, and their span with Lancashire was not dissimilar: Wood 14 seasons, 1966–79; Lloyd 18 seasons, 1965–83. Both were bowlers, Wood more so. With his wobbly medium in-swing he took 251 first-class and 219 limited-over wickets. Lloyd bowled slow, left-handed and to a fullish length, and perhaps he did not bowl enough: he had 217 wickets for the county, plus 37 in one-day cricket. Both were, like almost all their colleagues, uncannily expert as fielders, unabashed at the thought that Clive Lloyd, Frank Hayes and David Hughes were also numbered among those present.

Eventually, however, their careers rested on their opening batsmanship. In this they maintained possibly the securest of all Lancashire traditions; that is, the production, recruitment or development of high-class openers. That they were not always wedded together was due to several factors. The exigencies of one-day cricket meant Engineer often opened, whilst, for a time, others assumed the role, notably Andrew Kennedy. Sturdy and bespectacled, this Blackburn left-hander, born in 1949, came, saw and appeared to conquer. Chosen as the young cricketer of the year in 1975, he seemed to be a stable and valued asset, scoring 6232 runs, at an average of 28 and including six centuries (together with another 3771 runs in instant cricket) before, as inexplicably as several white hopes around that time, he retreated to the minor counties.

David Lloyd and Barry Wood were both good enough to be Test openers, but, somehow, not good enough to consolidate the position. Lloyd played in nine Tests, and, in scoring 214, not out, against India in 1974 at Birmingham, he not only reached his own highest score, but became at that point the only Lancashire bat, other than Eddie Paynter and Clive Lloyd, to get a double century in a Test match. Then, in Australia during the 1974–75 winter, he was not alone in being reduced to ineffectiveness by Lillee and Thomson, a fate from which he never recovered or, more pertinently, was never proffered the chance of convalescence. He scored 552 runs for England. Barry Wood scored 454 runs in 12 Test matches – his highest score was 90 against Australia in 1972 – and he dealt solidly with pace attacks. His undoing was more the magic of spin, especially the Indian variety.

In county cricket Barry Wood totalled 12,969, average 35, with 23 centuries and a top score of 198 against Glamorgan in 1976. His partner emerged even more fruitfully. David Lloyd is eleventh in the list of Lancashire run-getters, in spite of the depredations of instant cricket on his first-class opportunities. His total stands at 17,877, with an average of 33 and 37 centuries for the county. In limited-overs play Wood scored 4331 and Lloyd 7254. In all matches Wood took nearly 400 catches, and Lloyd well over 300. They really were genuinely important county cricketers whatever the measure, ancient or modern.

Three times they combined in opening stands of over 200; against Sussex in 1970, 265; against Leicester in 1972, 299; and against Somerset in 1974, 265. In 1975, against Warwickshire at Birmingham, Barry Wood and Andrew Kennedy, with a partnership of 249, created the Lancashire fifth-wicket record.

Both feared and loathed dismissal as one might shudder at and detest the risk of plague. It was not that there was any dissent or recrimination – far from it: both were understanding of the code. It was more that they stumbled away from the scene sandbagged, as if the victims of a criminal affront. It did not mean either that they were unduly defensive and overcareful: both were prepared to play grand shots. Simply, they were concerned to bat well and build an innings.

Wood, blond-haired, often capless, always watchful, was dexter in style. He was correct in choice and orthodox in execution of shots, and, rolling his wrists cleverly, was at his most challenging when pulling short, quick balls hard and low to the fence. Lloyd was sinister of hand, a little taller, a little slimmer than Wood, but alike in determined application. Once set, he could harry an attack mercilessly, throwing his bat splendidly and forcefully through the arc from fine of square of the off-stump to mid-off.

Both left, Wood, aged 37, Lloyd, aged 36, on whatever grounds, prematurely. It was a loss. They represented a deep grain of common-sense and craftmanship. They were replete with wheezes and tips and knowhow. They were like experienced plumbers, who, after laymen have stared uncomprehendingly at a labyrinth of piping, know exactly where the trouble is, or the expert mechanic, who when car-owners have footled about for oil-stained hours, pick out the offending knock immediately.

One anecdote will suffice by way of example. David Lloyd was a practitioner of what he termed the 'concrete' shot. It was, in his confirmed opinion, the God-given obligation of an opening batsman from the County Palatine to assemble a mental dossier of where, on all first-class grounds, there were concrete walls and other hard surfaces against which the new ball should be steered, in order that the polish be dulled and the hardness reduced as early as possible. Were, for instance, Clive Lloyd to banjo a new ball two bounces across a tarmac car park and smack up against a brick wall, his namesake's effusive felicitations would be, not because of the effect on the scoreboard, but the effect on the bruised cherry.

In a frenetic era of Sunday thrashes and exotic foreign stars, David Lloyd and Barry Wood, along with Harry Pilling and Jack Simmons, were the urban tradesmen, recapturing the older tradition of artisan sanity.

## Three Quick Bowlers

The pace component of this sparkling team was provided variously by Peter Lever, Ken Shuttleworth and Peter Lee. Though in their most extravagant dreams Lever and Shuttleworth would not have perceived of themselves in the same category, they edged toward the models of Statham and Trueman, rather as excellent jumpers endeavoured to overtake Red Rum. Lever, fair-haired, placidly tempered, was more the Statham figure, rather withdrawn and dispassionate. Shuttleworth, heavy dark locks, large-booted, louring, was the more fiercesome and threatening one, after the manner of Fred Trueman. Neither, of course, attained the high pace and unnerving control of the maestros, but they were quick and wholehearted. Both worked hard, if, from the ring, they occasionally appeared to lack a trifle in confidence. However, in county matches and limited-over contests, they provided a hostile opening assault, and, along with Peter Lee, they were not often collared.

Peter Lever was born in Todmorden in 1940; Ken Shuttleworth in St Helens in 1944; and Peter Lee in Arthingworth, Northamptonshire, in 1945. Lever played many years for Lancashire from 1960 to 1976, and later returned as coach until 1986. Ken Shuttleworth played from 1964 to 1975, before shifting to Leicestershire. Peter Lee played for Northamptonshire from 1967, moving to Lancashire in 1972 and departing, sadly without a testimonial, in 1982.

Possibly the most clearcut method would be to tabulate their chief achievements:

|  | P. G. Lee | P. Lever | K. Shuttleworth |
|---|---|---|---|
| Matches: | 152 | 268 | 177 |
| Wickets: | 496 | 716 | 484 |
| Average: | 23 | 24 | 23 |
| Best performance: | 8–34 | 7–70 | 7–41 |
|  | (Oxford, | (Glamorgan, | (Essex, |
|  | 1980) | 1972) | 1968) |
| Limited-overs |  |  |  |
| wickets: | 198 | 256 | 147 |

This shows the product of substantial hard work. In 1973 Peter Lee took 101 wickets (average 18) and in 1975 he took 112 wickets (18). These were the first times a Lancashire bowler had taken a hundred wickets since Ken Higgs in 1968, and it has not been achieved since. He took eight wickets in an innings three times, and, against Warwickshire in 1975 at Edgbaston, he took 7 for 8. Shorter in stature than the other two, less well known, and with a moustache borrowed from some Lancashire bowler a hundred years before, he just raced straight up to the wicket and bowled persistently.

Ken Shuttleworth played five times for England. He had 12 wickets, including 5 for 54 against Australia during Ray Illingworth's tour, 1970–71. Peter Lever played 17 Test matches, and he took 41 wickets. His best bowling for England was 6 for 38 against Australia at Melbourne on the 1974–75 tour. At the Oval for England versus the Rest of the World in 1970, he took 7 for 83. He once scored 88, not out, for England against India at Old Trafford in 1971: another 12 runs and he would have joined Geoff Pullar as the only Lancashire players to score Test centuries at Old Trafford. Peter Lever performed the hat-trick against Nottinghamshire for Lancashire in 1969, while his 716 wickets for Lancashire almost match, by way of relativity, Richard Barlow's 736. Apart from Jack Simmons, Lever is the leading Lancashire wicket-taker of the post-Statham era.

The three were decent fielders: Shuttleworth and Lever were passable lower-order batsmen, although Peter Lee was a genuine number 11; all in all, they rendered yeoman service to the county.

## The Championship, 1969 to 1976

Why did this team of apparent wondermen never win the County Championship? They were talented and well equipped, and, as for most first-class cricketers, the Championship was the holy grail. The knock-out cup was exciting, but it had never reached the parity of the FA Cup and the Football League First Division Championship. The traditional county game was still regarded as the acid test, and, in truth, Bond's team did make two strong challenges for the title.

Lancashire were fifteenth in 1969, losing only once, to Yorkshire, but winning only twice, against Middlesex and Somerset. Only two batsmen – Pilling and David Lloyd – passed a thousand runs, while Higgs, with 65 wickets, was easily the chief wicket-taker. David Bailey, a bespectacled youth, took the eye, in part for his 136 (Lancashire's top score of the year) against Kent, in part for his fielding, reminiscent more of Bertram Mills than Old Trafford, such was its acrobatic zeal. Like so many Lancashire apprentices, he faded away almost immediately.

1970 and 1971 were much happier seasons, with Lancashire third each summer. With the Gillette Cup and the Player Trophy won, it might have been a triple celebration, and, even so, 1970 must stand as one of the greatest years in the county's history. This time Lancashire lost twice, but won six, with 16 drawn. They compensated for the over-many draws with more batting bonus points than anyone else, but insufficient wins left them 21 points adrift of Kent. Weather interfered toward the end of the season, but, after a magnificent victory over Sussex at Blackpool by an innings and 125 runs, Lancashire could not get a result in the last six matches. The batting was in fine fettle, with the three totals of over 400 being the first of that size since 1961. The two Lloyds, Pilling and Wood were the leading protagonists, with Shuttleworth and Lever bearing the brunt of the bowling.

It was rather the reverse in 1971, with Lancashire making a strong, late run, winning the last three games against Hampshire, Derbyshire and Worcester, the last by an innings and 32 runs. In all, nine games were won, against four lost and 11 drawn. Lancashire ended 14 points behind Surrey. The batting was once more prominent, with the same quartet – Clive Lloyd, David Lloyd, Harry Pilling, Barry Wood – dominant. David Hughes's 73 wickets left him the main bowler. Jack Simmons took 66 wickets. Failure to force victories home was the problem.

The next two years were unimpressive. In 1972 Lancashire were third from bottom, a result only partially explained by the cold and rain of the late spring. Only two matches were won – those with Kent and Yorkshire – and there were eight defeats. Ironically, the victory over Yorkshire was quite devastating, a leeway of an innings and 34 runs, the consequence of 181, not out, by Clive Lloyd, with good support from Pilling and Hayes, followed by competent spin-bowling by Simmons and Hughes. Lancashire also beat the touring Australians by nine wickets, with Pilling, 61 not out, starring amid a sound all-round performance. It was the county's first win against Australia since 1912. In 1973 Lancashire won four, lost six and drew ten, and finished in twelfth position. Despite Lee's productive bowling it was disappointing, especially as the batting, Barry Wood and Frank Hayes apart, did not seem so telling.

1974 and 1975 showed a distinct improvement. Eighth in 1974,

Lancashire lost not one match, the first time for many, many years that had happened. Yet they won only five, once more finding it difficult to remove opponents twice. Simmons, with 55 wickets, was the chief bowler, and that, of course, is a low haul for one's leading attacker. The batting was brisk enough. Four hundred and eighty for 6 against Leicestershire, with centuries from Pilling and Clive Lloyd, was the highest score in the 1974 Championship. Lancashire improved on that with 511 against India, with Hayes and David Lloyd scoring centuries on this occasion. During the kindly weather of 1975, Lancashire's batting was again in fine trim. Clive Lloyd and Frank Hayes had excellent seasons, and Andrew Kennedy had perhaps his most fruitful summer. Lancashire finished fourth, with nine wins against three defeats and eight draws. Peter Lee bowled staunchly, but with little key support, and there were at least three irksome occasions when Lancashire seemed to need only to puff to complete a victory, and failed to do so. With maximum points from such encounters, they would, needless to say, have pushed the champions, Leicestershire, harder. The most persuasive trouncing handed out by Lancashire was over Derbyshire at Buxton. Hayes and Clive Lloyd contributed hundreds to an excellent total of 477 for 5, whereupon Derbyshire collapsed unaccountably for 42 and 87, leaving Lancashire winners by an innings and 348 runs.

That year of drought, 1976, portentously marked the end of a small but colourful era. It completed the eight seasons during which Lancashire had won half-a-dozen trophies in one-day cricket, and also had appeared twice as losing finalists. Defeat by Northamptonshire in the Gillette Cup terminated this run of achievement, just as it drew to a close a season in which Lancashire crashed to sixteenth place. Only three matches were won – Glamorgan, Nottinghamshire, Sussex – while six were lost and ten drawn. Only Pilling reached a thousand runs in Championship cricket, and Peter Lee, with 65, was the only bowler with more than 50 dismissals to his credit. It was also to be the first of eleven seasons in which Lancashire never reached a single-figured position in the table.

There were operational reasons why Lancashire, in spite of its ministry of all the talents, could not secure a Championship success. Senior players, especially Clive Lloyd, had international calls: in 1973, for instance, Lloyd was constantly involved with the

West Indian tourists. We have already noted Lancashire's lack of a bowler capable of undermining all and sundry, and there is little doubt that, during this phase, the conversion of winning positions into genuine victories eluded Lancashire too frequently. Sometimes, strangely for so proud an instant cricket team, the batting was slow: Old Trafford wags used to suggest changing the pavilion calendar to delude the players into the belief that they only had 40 or 60 overs when it was a three-day event. It did seem that, and even allowing for the restrictive practices of limited-overs cricket, Lancashire sometimes achieved larger totals than when they were trying to be three-day batsmen.

Discussion ranged over the contrast of technique. Certainly the bowlers had the control to defend, if not attack, and there may have been an insufficiency of mental stamina for the long-drawn out campaign of the Championship. The adrenalin pumped for a few hours and all was heady, whereas the concentration lapsed, perhaps, as week followed week of travel and attrition. Many of these cricketers gave the impression of having 'big' match but not 'little' match temperaments. The huge, baying crowds, red rose favours and hats in abundance, created the atmosphere to which they responded with gallant authority and imaginative verve. Instant cricket was a popular form of theatre, and Lancashire had the most gifted actors for the new stage.

The comparison was often drawn with football, and with football supporters, and the overt presence of Manchester United nearby offered a principal instance. Although the cricket fans on the whole remained more good-humoured and temperate, there was the same air of buoyed emotion in limted-overs spectatorship. There is no more fatiguing experience than the draining fatigue of watching your favourites over 120 hours of swaying advantage.

To some degree, lifestyles in modern conurbations like Manchester were less solid and continuous than in generations past. They were glamorous and ephemeral. They were not worse: this is not a question of ethical assessment: they were different. It was a faster-moving world of discos and wine-bars. It was the George Best era. Where once cricketers had stolidly journeyed in third-class railway carriages, they now sped down motorways in fast cars with their names loudly painted on the side. Assessed by cruel yardsticks, Frank Hayes's lack of fulfilment, Farokh Engineer's occasional intrepid and foolhardy essays, Barry Wood's and David Lloyd's inability to consolidate England places, and, in general, a frothiness and transience about the careers of many players, all this bore witness to a pervasive mood of self-conscious novelty and fever.

Limited-overs cricket was a product of the swinging sixties, something like cricket's sacrifice to the permissive society. It is not, therefore, surprising that a great city like Manchester, struggling to be part of the modern era, struggling to keep up with the cultural Jones's, should have housed perhaps the finest regional exponents of one-day cricket there have been, and, in Clive Lloyd, found the Laurence Olivier of that cast.

# 8. David Hughes's Year

## *The Disintegration of Lancashire*

The rocket rose, flared and died. As the team that had monopolised the Gillette Cup left or aged, everything seemed to go wrong. In retrospect, one may observe that the decline, started in the early 1950s, had only been temporarily, if vividly, abated. Perhaps the less admirable record of the County Championship was a sager guide to what was happening to the county than the high jinks of one-day play.

The county's results over the next ten years from 1976 were lamentable and best quickly sketched without painful underlining. Lancashire's positions in the Championship over that decade were as follows:

|      |      |              |
|------|------|--------------|
| 1977 | 16th | (two wins)   |
| 1978 | 12th | (four wins)  |
| 1979 | 13th | (four wins)  |
| 1980 | 15th | (four wins)  |
| 1981 | 16th | (four wins)  |
| 1982 | 12th | (four wins)  |
| 1983 | 12th | (three wins) |
| 1984 | 16th | (one win)    |
| 1985 | 14th | (three wins) |
| 1986 | 15th | (four wins)  |

Par was fourteenth for this period, which meant that, alongside Glamorgan, Lancashire had the feeblest record of all 17 counties, with only 33 victories over that time. In 1985 only one batsman, Neil Fairbrother, managed a thousand runs, while the bowler taking most wickets descended from Paul Allott's 75 in 1981 to B. P. Patterson's 48 in 1986.

As for Sunday cricket, Lancashire barely ever crept into the top half of the John Player Special. Fourth in 1984 was by far their best result. Their penchant for knock-out competitions did not disappear quite so totally, although defeat by Scotland in the 1986 Benson and Hedges' preliminary rounds was an uncomfortable low in that field. Lancashire reached the semi-final of the Gillette Cup in 1978, only to fall rather dismally to Sussex, the eventual winners, and, in the introductory year of the National Westminster Bank Trophy in 1981, they again reached the semi-final. Northamptonshire won on the penultimate ball, with one wicket left, after a match that seesawed thrillingly. In 1982, in a game of modest totals, Lancashire were narrowly beaten in the Benson's semi-final by Nottinghamshire, while the following year Middlesex thrashed Lancashire on a speckled Lord's pitch at the same stage of the competition.

By far the peak spot during these lean summers was the Benson and Hedges' Cup win of 1984. It was the first year of John Abrahams' captaincy, and a most deserved reward for a most courteous and affable cricketer. Originally from Cape Town, he joined the club from Radcliffe, and, apart from his competence as a bat and his utility as an off-spinner, Abrahams, lithe and smiling always, was a princely fielder. Lancashire had won through without too many alarms to the quarter-final, where they defeated Essex by four wickets. Hughes and Abrahams added 107 for the fourth wicket after Essex had subsided to 157. Nottinghamshire set a more imposing problem in the semi-final, but Graeme Fowler and Mark Chadwick opened with a hundred-stand, and Lancashire won by six wickets.

On 21 July the Lancashire support rediscovered the route to Lord's after an eight-year absence, and they greeted the downfall of Warwickshire with fervent joy. Only Kallicharran stood defiantly, as Allott took 3 for 15, with strong support from his fellows. The fielding was again a joy for the spectators. Hughes and Fairbrother ensured that the 140 required was obtained with six wickets and seven overs outstanding. It was a tiny sign of plenty amidst dearth.

In 1986 Lancashire were back at Lord's for the Nat West Final, and were roundly beaten by Sussex. Cumberland having been despatched in the first round, Lancashire beat a strong Somerset team by just three runs, and with Somerset nine wickets down. That exciting win was followed by a more relaxed affair at Leicester, where a beautiful 93, not out, by Neil Fairbrother was the base of a six-wicket victory. The semi-final at the Oval was a momentous occasion. Clive Lloyd and Steven O'Shaughnessy guaranteed Lancashire a reasonable score after an indifferent start, and then superb catching – seven were taken – resisted a forceful Surrey riposte masterminded by Trevor Jesty. Lancashire won by four runs with seven balls to go.

Gehan Mendis and Fowler gave Lancashire a secure start to the final, and Fairbrother and Andrew Hayhurst batted briskly later on. Clive Lloyd appeared to a most sporting and hearty ovation, but precognition among those who recalled Bradman's duck in his final Test in 1948 was endorsed. D. A. Reeve had him lbw for nothing. Nonetheless, 242 meant that Sussex were faced with a score unsurpassed by a side batting second in a county final. Curiously, that fact never impinged. So commonplace was Lancashire's bowling, and, alas, so patchy the fielding, that A. M. Green, P. W. G. Parker and Imran Khan advanced in orderly calm to their victorious destination.

As so often happens, perhaps unjustly, it was this failure of Lancashire on a prestigious occasion which proved to be the final straw, the ultimate humiliation which caused many changes at Old Trafford.

Of course, there had been other meaty tastes to savour over the last ten years. In 1979 the wicket-keeper, John Lyon, and R. M. Ratcliffe, in scoring 158 against Warwickshire at Old Trafford, created a new eighth-wicket record for the county, the previous one having remained intact since 1900. There was a phenomenal game at Southport in 1982, when Warwickshire scored 523 for 4, Humpage and Kallicharran both passing the double-century mark in a stand of 470, the highest fourth-wicket stand in England and the highest either for Warwickshire or against Lancashire. Fowler scored 126 and Ian Cockbain 98 in Lancashire's declared innings of 414 for 6. L. L. McFarlane now took 6 for 59 and Warwicks were shot out for 111. Fowler scored his second century of the match, and, in company with David Lloyd, 226 were put on and an amazing ten-wicket victory recorded. Not since a similar instance in 1904, when Essex lost to Derbyshire, had there been such a reversal of fortune in the County Championship.

A third extraordinary, if somewhat sterile, achievement occurred in 1983. Steven O'Shaughnessy, an all-rounder from Bury, scored a century in 35 minutes, thereby equalling Percy Fender's fastest century, notched in 1920. The previous fastest century for Lancashire was Hornby's 106 in 43 minutes in 1905. Some of the gilt is rubbed off the gingerbread in that Leicestershire were eager to expedite a declaration and served up tempting long-hops and full tosses. O'Shaughnessy, who was out for 105, reached his hundred in 54 balls faced and with 25 scoring shots, 17 fours, five sixes, three singles. He added 201 with Graeme Fowler in 119 balls and 43 minutes, the fastest recorded partnership in first-class cricket by balls and time. Fowler hit ten sixes off consecutive scoring shots. A number of other mathematical records were broken, and, despite the artificiality of the occasion, it was no mean feat to sustain that tempo.

Attractive players did emerge from the sombre shadows into which Lancashire had been cast. P. J. W. Allott, a tall and beefy fast-medium bowler from Altrincham, made his debut in 1978 and took 349 wickets in his first eight seasons. Latterly, he developed his batting somewhat, and became a willing and aggressive asset. He played 13 games for England in the early 1980s and his hostile persistence gained him 26 wickets.

Graeme Fowler, a dashing left-hander, was born in Accrington, and, like Paul Allott, had a university background. His winsome strokeplay also earned him England caps, 21 in all, and he was England's regular opener for four years or so. He scored 1307 runs, average 35, and became only the seventh Lancastrian to reach a thousand Test runs. One of his three Test centuries was 201 against India in Madras, 1984–85, whereby he became only the fourth Lancashire Test bat to score a double century. Unluckily, his somewhat wayward, if enchanting, method played him false in the following summer of 1985, when he struggled to scarcely 400 first-class runs. A wholehearted cricketer, he fought his way back to form and, by 1986, had scored 6589 runs for the county, averaging 37, with a highest score of 226 versus Kent at Maidstone in 1984. Fowler thus maintains Lancashire's lengthy production of England opening batsmen, and he also adorns the covers after the grand manner of the County Palatine. He is probably the most splendid outfielder of his generation, fleet of foot, sure of hand and throw, and constructing new prototypes of excitement with the fearless abandonment of his diving.

Fairbrother, inspired, perhaps sometimes burdened, with Neil

Harvey as his forenames, has caused older watchers to recall Eddie Paynter. This young man from Warrington certainly had the same slight stature, cheery, toothy grin and rather gauche gait of the maestro. He bats left-handed with the same sweet assurance and exquisite timing, and, like Paynter, he is a supremely adept outfield. Batting in a faltering side, he scored 4572, average 38, in his opening seasons. His highest score was 164 not out, against Hants at Liverpool in 1985. His early forays for England proved unhappy, and maybe the transparent class he exhibited had been tested prematurely in the international arena.

## The Background to Decline

Curios and celebrities notwithstanding, the mainstream of Lancashire cricket was dull and stagnant. Rumour whispered of rifts between committee and playing staff, of a disjointed captaincy and of a dejected atmosphere in the dressing-room. Rumour was probably right. The cycle of practical failure and psychological frustration is evident enough. History books tell of both demoralised armies being easily vanquished and of battered armies growing demoralised. It would have been asking too much of a club to withstand such humiliations and not also be fraught with dissension and argument.

The most sorrowful aspect was the dribbling away of players whose names had been spoken in hushed tones and whose gifts had been complacently hailed and lauded. Bob Arrowsmith, a slow left-hand spin-bowler from Denton was marked down as another Malcolm Hilton; Mark Chadwick, a Rochdale opening bat, seemed likely to consolidate his place; Ian Cockbain, a good-looking right-hand batsman from the Liverpool area, whom many thought had a bright future; Kevin Hayes, a Yorkshireman, educated at Blackburn and Oxford, where he captained the university, was another likely prospect; Willie Hogg, from Ulverston, was a hardworking bowler who transferred to Warwickshire; Stephen Jefferies, another bowler, who became snared by the regulations about overseas players; Andrew Kennedy, whose loss has already been mentioned; Les McFarlane, a Jamaican fast bowler with an England qualification who came and went rapidly; Steven O'Shaughnessy, spoken of in glowing terms as a possible England all-rounder; Neal Radford, a Zambian with English eligibility, who played with Bacup, and who, wryly, moved to Worcester with startling success; Bob Ratcliffe, another fine bowler whose passing has already been mourned; Bernard Reidy, a hefty Whalley all-rounder of whom good things had been anticipated; Ken Snellgrove, a Merseysider from a slightly earlier vintage, who scored nearly 4000 runs for Lancashire, but somehow faded; David Varey, a Cambridge University player, born in Darlington, who appeared to be a solid opening bat; and Nasir Zaidi, that rarity, a beguiling leg-spin bowler, who failed to make the grade . . .

Arrowsmith to Zaidi: like inscriptions on a war memorial they represented a lost generation. Of course, managements make errors or youngsters do not live up to expectation, but this was a haemorrhage like the earlier one of the 1960s. Either those responsible should have been knowledgeable enough to assess promise more adequately, or sufficiently expert to have mobilised cricketing energy were it present. The Lancashire establishment cannot have it both ways: some at least of these signings were either badly chosen or badly directed.

All this was in spite of the Lancashire region enjoying perhaps the most sophisticated network of league and federation activity of anywhere in the country. Some 30 leagues, often with commercial sponsorship, possibly 600 teams, frequently with a number of elevens down to colt and junior level, and with, in the leading competitions, the use of highly paid professionals: it is a mesh of a most elaborate organisation. As throughout its history, Lancashire seemed unable to establish the most fruitful liaison with this burgeoning source of players.

The incantation about fateful meteorology and debilitating injuries was chanted every year when the blame had to be apportioned for Lancashire's decline. One grants that weather and injury affected matters, just as, conversely, in the cupwinning days, regular appearances and freedom from damage had been a bonus. However, once these short-term factors, alongside the possibility of ineffectual administration, have been entertained, there are still two perspectives to be scrutinised, about which Lancashire, as a club, could do little.

In the first place, a number of aspects conspired to create an evenness, almost an anonymity, about the county scene. At base, this was financial. From an era of wealthy and impoverished clubs, reliant, for richer or for poorer, on membership, spectators and the charitable subventions of local magnates, we have moved to one in which fiscal viability is not dependent on such domestic manifestations. Especially in the wake of post-Packer revisionism, international receipts, television dues, sponsorship and advertising, real estate investment and countless variations of lottery have given a similar standing to most counties. This has reached the point, absurdly, where it scarcely matters whether spectators attend or not. Observe Lancashire's typical accounts for 1986. Of close on a million pounds' income, 16 per cent came from subscriptions (with over 10,000 members Lancashire is one of the largest clubs in the country) 25 per cent from receipts from Test, tours and broadcasting, and 42 per cent from sponsorship, executive suites, ground advertising and year-round catering. Catering pulled in more than match income, which was worth only 9 per cent.

Of course, members do attend, sometimes in healthy numbers, but it is salutary to glance over the Old Trafford attendances for Britannic Assurance Championship matches in 1986, to wit: 449, 65, 146, 168, 617, 384, 942, 391, 779. Crowds at alternative grounds (Liverpool, Southport and Lytham a fixture each) and for one-day matches were larger. Nonetheless, fewer than 4000 people paid at the gate to watch county cricket. Lancashire had, profitably and wisely, improved the ground to palatial standards, but, on many match days, it was akin to Sleeping Beauty's palace.

A half of the income was spent on salaries and wages, a reminder that some degree of financial stability allows all counties to compete with like bravura in the labour mart. The scope for employing a famous international star is utilised by almost all, and that has, in one step, leavened the lump considerably. With the exception of Yorkshire's rather truculent insularity, the counties have, throughout their histories, acted something like repertory theatres, attempting to deploy, within their means, the most attractive ensemble possible for the delectation of the fans, always in the knowledge that the supporters have a mild, but by no means exclusive, prejudice for local heroes. Now that those means are more equitably divided, the county competition is no longer composed of a strong octet and a weak nonet, as in pre-war years. Lancashire has had to come to terms with defeat at the hands of Leicestershire or Glamorgan. It is no longer a superpower. It is a Switzerland or Austria like everyone else, and respect and rewards have to be earned by dedicated application. Had Northamptonshire beaten Lancashire, as they soundly did in the 1976 cup final, in an equivalent contest in the 1920s, it would have been conceived of as Belgium overrunning Germany, or Halifax Town winning the FA Cup.

Until about 1960, for almost the first hundred years of the County Championship, it was dominated by the big six, with Kent, three times winners, and Sussex, never, making up the original octarchy. Only Warwickshire, in 1911 and 1951, Derbyshire, 1936, and Glamorgan, 1949, shook that stately oligarchy. Now the title swaps about in much more egalitarian fashion, and Northamptonshire, Somerset and Sussex are the only counties never to have won it. As for the two cup competitions, only Glamorgan and Worcestershire have, thus far (1988), mourned an empty sideboard, while ten counties have already won the Sunday 40-over league. Lancashire is just one of the pack.

In 1972, as Clive Lloyd scored his century against Warwickshire in the Gillette Final at Lord's, with Lance Gibbs, D. L. Murray, Kanhai and Kallicharran among the opponents, an intelligent Lancashire wit cried, 'Our West Indian's better than your West Indians.' It was a sally as much appreciated by the West Midland as the North Midland support, all recognising that county cricket had been, in part, invaded by mercenaries.

In the second place, and as a counterpoint to this democracy, there is the question of the North–South divide, and how that is reflected in sport. It would be odd were sport – so significant a factor in the country's social and cultural life – to remain unaffected. Lancashire began its life as Manchester and its surrounds led the world industrially, and Manchester bid fair to be one of the world's senior cities. Now Manchester is set at the weakening centre of industrial wastelands, and, along with Liverpool, has actually lost population over the last decades. The once teeming Trafford Park stands desolate, and, although the city itself contrives to keep its economic pecker up, the townships that had fed energy into both the commercial and cultural activity of Manchester lie static, broken and empty. Like the rest of the North, from Liverpool across to Burnley and up to Barrow, what had once been the workshop of the world is a ragged and despairing ruin. The history of Britain has chiefly been the story of its south-east province south of a line from Norwich to Bristol, in close communion, as in medieval times, with north-west

Europe. The natural resources and accompanying circumstances of the North-West and other non-Southern areas created what, in historical time, was a brief spell of bristling industrial growth. Against a thousand ages, it was, as the hymnist sang, 'like an evening gone', a tiny respite, all but illusory, before the national forces regrouped in the South-East and the bridges to north-west Europe again vibrated with commercial traffic.

There is no escaping the becalming imbalance of the Northern doldrums, and, not least because money and people are sucked out of these regions, sport, as well as other socio-cultural phenomena, suffers. Take the parallel of football. The systematic mechanics of Liverpool have too long disguised the collapse of senior football in Lancashire, indeed, in the North. Manchester United, after the most glorious adventures in its history, became tarnished and struggling. Ironically, United, like Lancashire, won the Cup a time or two, but has not seriously challenged for the League Championship for 20 years. The bizarre Harlequinade of Manchester City continues, while Everton enjoy years of light and shade. In the First Division, 1987/88, only three of these conurbation-based teams are members, and there are no other North-Western representatives. There are only three sides north of Stoke in the division, while, these days, there are no less than nine teams from the London region. The other Lancashire football teams languish now in the lower depths, with once proud sides like Preston North End and Blackpool in the Third and Bolton Wanderers and Burnley in the Fourth Division.

Similarly with cricket: as well as a more democratic spread of quality, there was a southward swing. Between 1972, when, for the first time there were four competitions, until 1987, the 17 counties had 68 chances of titles. The Northern quartet of Lancashire, Yorkshire, Derbyshire and Nottingham won just nine of these. Even on the law of averages it should have been 16. Middlesex, Essex, Sussex: they were the names that kept popping into the frame. In short, to employ educational jargon, there was now more equality of opportunity, tempered by positive discrimination in favour of the South.

*1987*

For Lancashire supporters the summer of 1987 was like the

flickering rush-light espied by fatigued medieval travellers in the casement of the monastery where they sought shelter from the sombre wintry evening.

With John Bond and Peter Lever dismissed in the aftermath of defeat in the 1986 Cup Final and amid acid internal controversy, Lancashire turned to Alan Ormrod and David Hughes. Under the command of these two experienced cricketers, Lancashire had won the second-eleven championship of 1986, with nine wins, nine draws and no losses, and it was decided to make them coach and captain of the first eleven. It was a brave step, some said a foolish one. J. A. Ormrod, born in Ramsbottom in 1942, had played almost all his cricket for Worcestershire as a placid, orthodox opening bat. He joined Lancashire in 1984, and, after a couple of seasons, gravitated to share control of the reserve side with Hughes. D. P. Hughes, aged 40 as the 1987 season began, seemed at the end of a long and meritorious career. The choice seemed to lie between retirement and captaincy, rather like an elder states-man faced either with the premiership or the obscurity of the backbenches of the Lords.

That was not the end of the politics. Did Cedric Rhoades see the moody 1952 film *Viva Zapata*? Marlon Brando, the young Zapata, is one of the deputation visiting the Mexican president, who, remarking Zapata's thrust, circles his name on the list in front of him. Years later, with Zapata the incumbent, another deputation waits upon the president, and Zapata circles the name of its most outspoken and threatening member. Yesterday's rebels are today's establishment. Cedric Rhoades, it was generally agreed, had righted Lancashire's finances, facilities and relations with cricket throughout the county during his long and autocratic reign, but, beyond the clutch of one-day triumphs, he had not restored their cricketing fortune. His place was taken during the year by Bob Bennett, who had played 49 matches for Lancashire in the early 1960s and who promised to introduce a less rigorous and less paternalistic regime.

Now, cricket is like hymns, ancient and modern; and, in the modern sector in 1987, Lancashire were feeble. They lost their first Nat West Cup match to Gloucestershire and could only beat Scotland in the Benson and Hedges' tournament, while, with only five wins, they were ninth in the Refuge Assurance League, as the Sunday competition had been retitled. Indeed, twice, against Kent and Northamptonshire, they had 290, the most monstrously high total ever, taken off their bowling in the 40 overs. Yet, in the ancient tourney of conventional county play, where long they had languished, they were second, winning more matches (ten) than anyone and finishing a mere four points behind Nottinghamshire.

The season began at Taunton with Lancashire, 150 behind on the first innings, sportingly set 240 to win, and doing so by dint of a Fairbrother century. At Old Trafford Gehan Mendis carried his bat in the grand manner for 203 out of 453, but Middlesex, despite following on, survived. Swansea witnessed Lancashire's only genuine débâcle of the season in an innings defeat, but, composed and willing, two fine victories were recorded over Leicestershire – the Jamaican, Ken McLeod took 5 for 8 in startling fashion – and Worcestershire – 12 for 123 for Jack Simmons, his best-ever match figures. It was a reassuring beginning, but then there were mid-term setbacks, starting with six draws, in most of which Lancashire tended to have the advantage. They included the match where the Yorkshire last pair survived for 18 overs, bar one ball, and where Simmons felt aggrieved at a Yorkshireman not walking.

Worse was to follow in the shape of three defeats, the first at the hands of Derbyshire a mix of absurdity and sorrow. At 271 for 7, only five runs were required for victory, when hysteria struck, and Derby won by three runs with three balls remaining. Essex and Northamptonshire were the other victors, but Southport introduced a change of mood, with Ian Folley, the left-hand spin-bowler, taking 12 for 57 (7 for 15, 5 for 42) in the convincing defeat of Warwickshire. Four draws followed, days of rain and stalemate and tough cricket, and then the eccentricity of the fixtures granted Lancashire an uncommonly long mid-season break. David Hughes claimed this was a time for thought and practice, not, as others might have believed, a fearful gap with the hazard of losing form.

His optimism was justified. Lancashire now progressed to victory in their last six matches. Michael Watkinson took 7 for 25 as Sussex fell at Lytham, and Patrick Patterson, Lancashire's overseas signing from the West Indies, took 6 for 40 to undermine Kent at Maidstone, with a swift Fowler hundred enabling a target of 200 to be reached with eventual ease. A similar goal – 208 – was set by Gloucestershire at Old Trafford, and, in spite of occasional shocks, that, too, was reached. John Abrahams, 140, not out, and 92, was the leading light in a narrow win over Surrey at Old Trafford. Mike Watkinson, 57 not out, ensured that, ultimately, the 276 runs needed were obtained. And so to a disappointingly unhelpful wicket and outfield at Chelmsford, requiring maximum points to level with Nottinghamshire and win the title on the basis of more wins. The match was well won, but only four of a possible eight bonus points were acquired, and Lancashire ended second, their best performance since the days of Washbrook and Ikin and Tattersall and the shared Championship of 1950, 37 years before, although they had come second in 1956 and 1960.

Given the morbid prognostications and gloomy mutterings at the start of the summer, this measure of achievement must be reckoned one of Lancashire's most surprising and one of their most creditable performances ever. That final wicket against Yorkshire, a little steadiness against Derbyshire, and Lancashire would have been winners. Unluckily, being second does not quite make for a fairy-tale ending. It is like 'Cinderella' finishing with Prince Charming seriously considering a permanent relationship, rather than joining in dazzling nuptials, with Princess Crystal.

Had a Yorkshire tail-ender or a Derbyshire bowler had romance in his soul, he might have weakened, realising that, for the pitiful narrator, a Lancashire Championship might have enabled this long story to have ended in crescendo. Nevertheless, it was a remarkable and it was an emotive attainment.

Suddenly, from a bunch of has-beens, no-hopers and gangling youths, a coherent team emerged. Gehan Mendis, of Colombo, eschewed by Sussex, and Graeme Fowler, his England days behind him at 30, developed into one of the surest opening pairs in the country. Both scored over a thousand runs, and Fowler, with irrepressible verve, topped the averages, 47 from 1689 runs. His total of 1800 in all first-class games was only 79 behind G. A. Hick's total, the highest of the year, thus making Fowler the leading English-born scorer. Right-hand defensive, left-hand aggressive, they constructed a decent base in most games. Neil Fairbrother missed five games, but his 963 runs, average 44, were touched with the intangibility of class, and Hughes himself, grittily, the only everpresent, scored over 400 runs. Toward the end of the season, two other batsmen won satisfying notice. The hideous nightmare of John Abrahams' early season gradually melted into the sweeter dream of its later weeks, when he scored some 500 runs, and passed 10,000 runs in first-class cricket. The precocious talent of Michael Atherton, with 600 runs in the second half of the season, was another factor. Only 19, living in Failsworth and already a force for Cambridge University, his excellent progress was as pleasing as the recovery of form for Abrahams, that most genial and honest of cricketers. Perhaps Michael Atherton, a hundred years on exactly, may yet emulate the grandiose feats of Archie MacLaren. He was – like Neil Fairbrother in 1983 – chosen as the most promising young cricketer of the year by the Cricket Society.

The batting was sound throughout. Mike Watkinson, yet another son of Westhoughton, proved to be a resourceful and genuine all-rounder, scoring 776 runs and taking 42 wickets. Paul Allott, with over 600 runs, also pushed up the order, and he also had 56 wickets and headed the bowling averages. Patrick Patterson took 52 wickets, and, paired together, they formed a bellicose start to the Lancashire assault. Colin Croft had previously been Lancashire's overseas fast bowler, and this had not been a success. An empty Old Trafford, on an early May morning, with the rain-clouds convening over the Derbyshire hills, was too far removed from the glaring heat of Barbados or Jamaica. Patterson, who first played in 1984, appeared to settle down more persuasively to what the hymn-book called the common round, the daily task. More-over, the purists were also overjoyed to note that, after this fierce opening, Lancashire increasingly turned to orthodox left-hand and off-spin in the May and December shapes of Ian Folley and Jack Simmons. Simmons, aged 46, took 63 wickets, while Ian Folley, of Burnley and at 24 almost half his partner's age, took most wickets, 68 in all, having transposed himself from medium to slow pace.

With David Hughes the exemplar, the fielding was youthful and zestful, although one or two ordinary fieldsmen meant the side was not as steely a combine as that of the early 1970s. The wicket-keeping was a little problematic, as it had been since Engineer's disappearance, with no one quite consolidating the position. However, Warren Hegg, affectionately if predictably nicknamed Chucky, played the last half of the season with merit. This diminutive 19-year-old from Stand had 35 victims and a maiden century against Northamptonshire. Only two batsmen with a thousand runs and no bowler with even 70 wickets: ten county wins despite that lack of individual brilliance testifies to a cohesive and hearty team effort. Seven scored over 500 runs, and five took 40 wickets or more, and, from the shreds and patches of previous years, there was the balance and symmetry of an opening pair of batsmen, a tailor-made number three, fine talent at four or five, a forceful all-rounder, two fast bowlers and two complementary spin-blowlers. It was a radical transformation, and the stage-manager was David Hughes.

## David Hughes

Many moons ago at Southport a boyish David Hughes was fielding at the boundary's edge as the ice-cream seller made his round. David Hughes made, in exaggerated mime, as if to find small change in his flannels and mock-purchase a cornet. It brought simple amusement to the knot of deckchairs behind him and enlivened a dullish passage of cricketing arms. It was not the profound stuff of Molière's humour, but it served to demonstrate a cricketer aware of his prior responsibility. Back through a nostalgic lineage of Pilling, Washbrook, Paynter, Duckworth, Parkin and Barlow, there have been Lancashire cricketers with an innate grasp of the need to discover rapport with the audience. D. P. Hughes knew this intimately, and, in his agreeable book on how to watch cricket, John Arlott recognised this. When watching Lancashire, he advises, observe the patent and infectious enjoyment of David Hughes.

Partnered by the knowledgeable and pragmatic Alan Ormrod, David Hughes shamed the critics and ill-wishers by ensuring that this spirit prevailed. After several seasons of tedium and sourness, an anonymous player informed the press, one looked forward with pleasure to arriving at Old Trafford. In any walk of life, the difference between waking up with a shudder or a beam at the prospect of the day ahead is very significant. In sport, it is crucial. The idea of playing cricket without enjoyment is alien and miserable.

David Hughes was born in Newton-le-Willows in 1947, and was aged three when Lancashire last won the Championship. He was on the ground staff at 17, made his debut in 1967 and was capped in 1970. By 1987 he had played 369 matches for Lancashire, placing him in the top 20 of the Lancashire roster of first-class appearances. Mention must also be made of 362 appearances by Hughes in the major one-day tournaments by the end of the 1987 season. In first-class cricket he had at that point scored nearly

9000 runs for Lancashire, and, with 596 wickets, he makes what golfers call the cut *vis-à-vis* the 25 bowlers with more than 500 victims in the Lancastrian cause. His highest score is 153 against Glamorgan, his best bowling in 1970 at Oxford when he took 7 for 24. His 6 for 29 against Somerset in 1977 is the best performance by a Lancashire bowler in Sunday league cricket. His 242 catches in first-class cricket, plus 85 one-day catches, is but one piece of evidence as to his dextrous and clean-cut fielding. And, like the band in the song about the strawberry blonde, he 'plays on'.

Strongly built, with a somewhat hooked nose above the warm grin and below the tousled hair, his open-faced, bright-eyed demeanour is that of the young and enthusiastic physical education teacher. Straightness is the watchword. He bats right-handed and straight as a guardsman, and his firm driving has saved several lost causes, although it was, perhaps wrongly, only later in his career that he moved sufficiently up the order to develop this skill. What is sure is that, in the darkness against Gloucestershire or facing Bedi in the last over at Lord's, only the most puristic of driving could have reaped that just benefit. He bowls straight, perhaps too straight, as one-day cricket flattened the arc of his flight and cunning deviation materialised too rarely. He runs and throws straight in the field. Above all, he plays straight, as a man and as a colleague, treating his players with the respect and firmness that he would expect and look for in a captain, were he an other-ranker. As a captain, he worked tremendously hard to create and maintain an ethos in which everyone strove to the maximum, for himself and for each other. Every day saw a search for advantage and an attempt to gain points. It was refreshing, positive and audacious.

It was a time for legitimate sentiment. Great Lancashire captains had had reasonable teams, just as great Lancashire teams had had reasonable captains. But no Lancashire side, consigned by the commentators as this one was to the back-alleys of mediocrity, has ever risen to such heights. A Falstaff's army became the Brigade of Guards. Of course, one swallow does not make a summer, and one summer rarely makes a success-story. Nevertheless, and with whatever trepidation, one must fairly turn back through many ledgers to reveal as pronounced an act of captaincy. The dusty pages of over a hundred years ago fall open at seasons 1881 and 1882, when Albert Hornby drilled a wayward if gifted bunch of individualists into a team of champions. David Hughes's achievement was not so telling, but it was second only to that feat of command, and, come what may in other years, it must be judged in context as remarkable. He was rightly showered with awards and plaudits, including a proud listing among *Wisden*'s famous five. 1987 was David Hughes's year.

## 1988

All defeated cup final captains vow they will be back next year, but the only ones remembered are the rarities who make good the pledge. Rising again to the occasion is immensely difficult, and what, in 1987, had seemed a well-drilled fighting force looked, in 1988, rather more bedraggled. Lancashire were dispatched summarily from both the cup competitions, but they did make something of a fist of the championship. There were useful wins, but there were also frustrating games where Lancashire found it impossible to topple wobbling opponents, and there were cruel defeats, notably at the hands of Middlesex, Yorkshire and Surrey. Having kept up a cheerful end for much of the season, Lancashire tumbled and subsided to the mid-table obscurity of ninth. Fowler and Mendis, while providing occasional individual nuggets, did not offer the solidity of 1987, and neither Trevor Jesty, a veteran import from Surrey, nor Fairbrother enjoyed much success. Watkinson, Hayhurst and Atherton performed pleasantly, but Folley disappointed, and Wasim Akram, the young Pakistani all-rounder, was beset with injury. He spluttered and sparked in turn like a Roman candle, leaving the valorous Allott to maintain the quick bowling. Jack Simmons contrived to take his thousandth first-class wicket and edged a couple of rungs up the ladder of Lancashire wicket-takers.

The county saved its most consistent forays for the Refuge Assurance Sunday League, where, sabbath after sabbath, they discovered novel devices for escaping from tight corners. They finished third – their highest for years – in that watery summer, and qualified for the Refuge Assurance Cup. In addition to the league title, a cup was played for by the top four clubs, and, in a low-scoring semi-final at Bristol, Lancashire defeated Gloucestershire. On 17 September they met the Refuge League and Championship winners, Worcestershire, at Birmingham – and it was a melancholy commencement: Lancashire were 4 for 2 in the third over. Fowler and Fairbrother rallied well, and Jesty and Watkinson struck out finely, so that Lancashire reached a creditable 201 for 5. Watkinson soon bowled Hick, a prodigious run-scorer that summer, and Worcestershire never recovered heart or resolve. Simmons had 1 for 22 to show for his piece of characteristic economy, and Allott also bowled aggressively early on. Hayhurst and Austin, a burly young all-rounder, captured wickets as Worcestershire collapsed, and wicket-keeper Hegg took five catches. Worcestershire were dismissed for 149, leaving Lancashire the first winners of the new cup by 52 runs.

Thus on the very last day of the 1988 season, David Hughes raised a trophy aloft before an exultant throng . . . and this log of Lancashire cricket can end on the happy note of a well-merited success for the county and for its resolute and honest captain.


*Envoi*


It is 1989. Lancashire had played 125 seasons and approaching 3000 first-class matches since the county's cricketing gentry strode disdainfully past the starving, ill-kempt, sickly destitute of the Cotton Famine, and started a famous cricket club in the Queen's Hotel.

The textiles have mostly vanished, but the cricket has endured. The Queen's Hotel has changed its name, other edifices from the first flush of Mancunian power have gone. And, in spite of some characteristic buildings and façades, Manchester, like most modern cities, has been reduced to a transatlantic sameness of urban motorways, retail arcades and litter-strewn shabbiness. Manchester has, wryly, been throttled by the very ideology of self-centred economics it espoused in the period of Lancashire's formation, albeit without the moderation of those schemes of public works the city also proudly mounted.

From famine to depression, from times when Manchester rested smugly on its commercial laurels, to the present era of wretched deterioration and the apparent death-knell of Northern influence, the cricket persists. The story of a county cricket club is not like that of a war or a reign or a ministry, with a finite termination and the opportunity to make a last judgement. Seamlessly, without remorse, the seasons pass, leaving us nostalgically sad, and also a little anxious that they come and go so rapidly, each September's final drawing of stumps a reminder of mortality.

Eleanor Farjeon knew that the night will never stay:

> The night will never stay,
> The night will still go by
> Though with a million stars
> You pin it to the sky;
> Though you bind it with the blowing wind
> And buckle it with the moon,
> The night will slip away
> Like sorrow or a tune.

Cricket seasons are as inexorably transient, and Lancashire's, like sorrow or a tune, continue to slip away. Washbrook and Place are now as 'long ago' to Lancashire cognoscenti as Hornby and Barlow were to Francis Thompson when he penned the most exquisite of cricket's poetry in 1907. It is indeed mournful to observe the swift passage of summers, to know that Clive Lloyd, Washbrook, John Tyldesley and MacLaren, or bowlers back from Statham to Briggs, are finished and done with. Yet it is good to recall these entertainers in personal memory or by proxy narrative, and it is good to sense the fresh hope of seasons to come, for ourselves and for the next generations of Lancashire *aficionados*, who, all to quickly, will only know dimly of Graeme Fowler and Neil Fairbrother as the ancient heroes of 'long ago'.

# Notable Lancashire Data

## A. *Playing Results*

**i.** *First-class matches*, 1865–1988:
played: 2801, won: 1030; lost: 580, drawn/tied: 1191.

**ii.** *Major one-day matches*, 1963–88:
played: 478; won: 248; lost: 183; tied/no result: 47.

**iii.** *Championship honours (\* shared title):*
1879\*; 1881; 1882\*; 1889\*; 1897; 1904; 1926; 1927; 1928;
1930; 1934; 1950\*.

**iv.** *One-day competitions:*
Gillette Cup winners: 1970; 1971; 1972; 1975.
(Runners-up: 1974; 1976; Nat West Bank Trophy: 1986)
Benson and Hedges Cup winners: 1984
John Player League champions: 1969; 1970.
Refuge Assurance Cup winners: 1988

## B. *Team Records*

**i.** *Highest innings:* in 1895 v. Somerset at Taunton: 801.
*Lowest innings:* in 1871 v. Derbyshire at Old Trafford: 25.
*Highest innings against:* in 1898 v. Surrey at the Oval: 634.
*Lowest innings against:* in 1924 v. Glamorgan at Aigburth: 22
*Best victory:* in 1911 v. Hampshire at Old Trafford:
an innings and 455 runs.

*Worst defeat:* in 1950 v. West Indies at Old Trafford:
an innings and 220 runs.

ii. *Largest attendance* (Lancashire matches only) *at Old Trafford:*
on one day: 46,000, August Bank Holiday Monday, 1926;
for three days: 78,617, same match, v. Yorkshire, 1926.

iii. *Record wicket-stands:*

| | | |
|---|---|---|
| 1st | 368 | A. C. MacLaren and R. H. Spooner 1903 |
| | | Aigburth (Gloucestershire) |
| 2nd | 371 | F. B. Watson and G. E. Tyldesley 1928 |
| | | Old Trafford (Surrey) |
| 3rd | 306 | E. Paynter and N. Oldfield 1938 |
| | | Southampton (Hampshire) |
| 4th | 324 | A. C. MacLaren and J. T. Tyldesley 1904 |
| | | Trent Bridge (Nottinghamshire) |
| 5th | 249 | B. Wood and A. Kennedy 1975 |
| | | Edgbaston (Warwickshire) |
| 6th | 278 | J. Iddon and H. R. W. Butterworth 1932 |
| | | Old Trafford (Sussex) |
| 7th | 245 | A. H. Hornby and J. Sharp 1912 |
| | | Old Trafford (Leicestershire) |
| 8th | 158 | J. Lyon and R. M. Ratcliffe 1979 |
| | | Old Trafford (Warwickshire) |
| 9th | 142 | L. O. S. Poidevin and A. Kermode 1907 |
| | | Eastbourne (Sussex) |
| 10th | 173 | J. Briggs and R. Pilling 1885 |
| | | Aigburth (Surrey) |

## C. *Individual Achievements*

i. *Batsmen who have scored 20,000 runs for Lancashire:*

| | runs | average | (all first-class) |
|---|---|---|---|
| 1. G. E. Tyldesley | 34,222 | 45.20 (1st) | (38,874) |
| 2. J. T. Tyldesley | 31,949 | 41.38 (3rd) | (37,897) |
| 3. C. Washbrook | 27,863 | 42.15 (2nd) | (34,101) |
| 4. J. W. H. Makepeace | 25,207 | 36.37 (7th) | (25,799) |
| 5. F. B. Watson | 22,833 | 37.07 (5th) | (23,596) |
| 6. J. Sharp | 22,015 | 31.18 (9th) | (22,715) |

| | | | |
|---|---|---|---|
| 7. J. Iddon | 21,975 | 37.05 (6th) | (22,681) |
| 8. K. J. Grieves | 20,802 | 33.39 (8th) | (22,454) |
| 9. C. Hallows | 20,142 | 39.72 (4th) | (20,926) |

ii. *Bowlers who have taken 1,000 wickets for Lancashire:*

| | wickets | average | (all first-class) |
|---|---|---|---|
| 1. J. B. Statham | 1816 | 15.12 (2nd) | (2260) |
| 2. J. Briggs | 1696 | 15.60 (4th) | (2221) |
| 3. A. W. Mold | 1543 | 15.15 (3rd) | (1673) |
| 4. R. K. Tyldesley | 1449 | 16.65 (5th) | (1509) |
| 5. A. Watson | 1308 | 13.39 (1st) | (1383) |
| 6. H. Dean | 1267 | 18.01 (7th) | (1301) |
| 7. R. H. Tattersall | 1168 | 17.39 (6th) | (1369) |
| 8. E. A. McDonald | 1053 | 20.96 (8th) | (1395) |
| 9. K. Higgs | 1033 | 22.90 (10th) | (1531) |
| 10. R. Pollard | 1015 | 22.15 (9th) | (1122) |

iii. *Wicket-keepers who have 400 dismissals for Lancashire:*

1. G. Duckworth    922
2. R. Pilling    465
3. F. M. Engineer    464
4. C. Smith    431
5. G. Clayton    422

iv. *Cricketer's doubles: 1000 runs and 100 wickets for Lancashire:*
J. Hallows: 1071 runs and 108 wickets in 1904;
J. L. Hopwood: 1660 runs and 111 wickets in 1934;
J. L. Hopwood: 1538 runs and 103 wickets in 1935.

NB J. Briggs is the only Lancashire player to score 10,000 runs and take 1000 wickets for the county: viz. 10,707 runs (14,092 in all cricket) and 1696 wickets (2221 in all cricket). He is the only cricketer to have performed the hat-trick and scored a century in England and Australia matches.

**v.** *Highest totals for Lancashire:*

| | |
|---|---|
| Most runs in a season: | 2633 (3041 all games) J. T. Tyldesley 1901 |
| Most wickets in a season: | 198 (205 all games) E. A. McDonald 1925 |
| Most catches in a season: | 63 K. J. Grieves 1950 |
| Most runs in an innings: | 424 A. C. MacLaren v. Somerset 1895 |
| | 322 E. Paynter v. Sussex (Hove) 1937 |
| | 300* F. B. Watson v. Surrey (Old Trafford) 1928 |
| Most wickets in an innings: | 10 for 46 W. Hickton v. Hampshire (Old Trafford) 1870 |
| | 10 for 55 J. Briggs v. Worcestershire (Old Trafford) 1900 |
| | 10 for 102 R. Berry v. Worcestershire (Blackpool) 1953 |
| Most catches in an innings: | 6 R. K. Tyldesley v. Hampshire (Aigburth) 1921 |
| | 6 K. J. Grieves v. Sussex (Old Trafford) 1951 |
| Most catches in a match: | 8 K. J. Grieves – same match. |
| Most wickets in a match: | 17 for 137 W. Brearley v. Somerset (Old Trafford) 1905 |
| | 17 for 91 H. Dean v. Yorkshire (Aigburth) 1913 |

*Wicket keeping:* Most dismissals in an innings: 7 W. Farrimond v. Kent (Old Trafford) 1930
Most dismissals in a match: 9 G. Clayton v. Gloucester (Gloucester) 1959
Most dismissals in a season: 107 G. Duckworth 1928
Most centuries for Lancashire: 90 (102 all matches) G. E. Tyldesley
Highest benefit for Lancashire player: £128,300 J. Simmons (Yorkshire) 1980

D. *Test Appearances by Lancashire Players*

54 Lancashite players have played for England while playing for the county, the leading numbers of caps being:

     J. B. Statham: 70 (765 runs and 252 wickets)
     C. Washbrook: 37 (2569 runs and six centuries)
     A. C. MacLaren: 35 (1931 runs and five centuries)
     J. Briggs: 33 (815 runs, one century and 118 wickets)
     J. T. Tyldesley: 31 (1661 runs and four centuries)

Among regular overseas players, C. H. Lloyd (110 matches for West Indies) and F. M. Engineer (46 matches for India should be noted.

E. *Appearances for Lancashire*

Eleven players have played 400 or more first-class matches for Lancashire:

| | | |
|---|---|---|
| 1. | G. E. Tyldesley: | 573 |
| 2. | J. Sharp: | 518 |
| 3. | J. T. Tyldesley: | 507 |
| 4. | C. Washbrook: | 500 |
| 5. | J. W. H. Makepeace: | 487 |
| 6. | J. Iddon: | 483 |
| 7. | F. B. Watson: | 456 |
| 8. | K. J. Grieves: | 452 |
| 9. | J. B. Statham: | 430 |
| 10. | G. Duckworth: | 424 |
| 11. | J. Simmons: | 422 (as of 1988) |

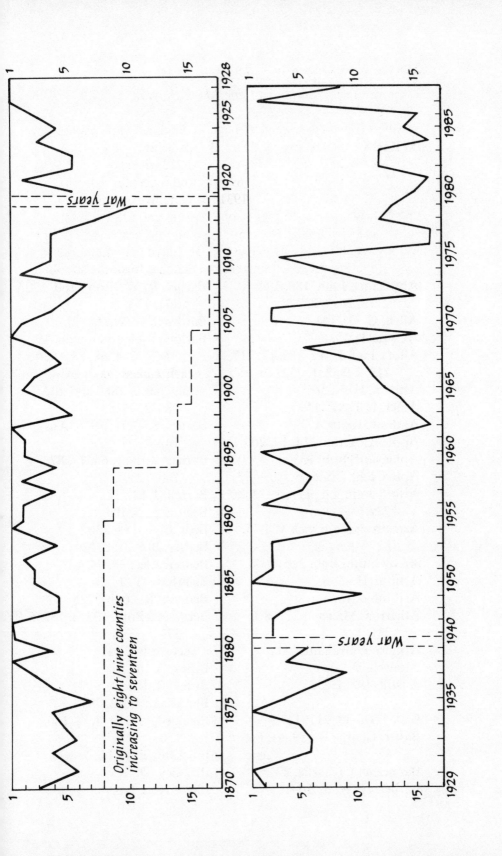

Originally eight/nine counties
increasing to seventeen

War years

War years

# Index